Working at the Margins

SUNY Series, Power, Social Identity, and Education

Lois Weis, Editor

Working at the Margins

Moving off Welfare in America

Frances Julia Riemer

STATE UNIVERSITY OF NEW YORK PRESS

Published by
State University of New York Press

© 2001 State University of New York

For information, address the State University of New York Press,
90 State Street, Suite 700, Albany, NY 12207

Marketing by Patrick Durocher • Production by Bernadine Dawes

Library of Congress Cataloging-in-Publication Data

Riemer, Frances J.
Working at the margins : moving off welfare in America / Frances Julia Riemer.
p. cm. — (SUNY series, power, social identity, and education)
Includes bibliographical references.
ISBN 0-7914-4925-4 (alk. paper) — ISBN 0-7914-4926-2 (pbk. : alk. paper)
1. Welfare recipients—Employment—United States. 2. Single mothers—
Employment—United States. 3. Public welfare—Government policy—United
States.   I. Title. II. Series.

HV95 .R54 2000
331.5'4—dc21

00-064086

1   2   3   4   5   6   7   8   9   10

Contents

Foreword   ix

Preface   xix

Introduction: Myths and Realities   1

PART I: THE STORIES

Chapter 1:   Development and the Hardest to Serve   21

     Naming the Hardest to Serve   21
     An Institutional History   22
     The Reality of the Hardest to Serve   25
     Conceptualizing the Hardest to Serve   27
     Socialization for Work   28
     Computers in the Learning Lab   29
     Life Skills   31
     Supported Work   36
     The Social Organization of Work   38
     Justification   41
     Exceptions to the Rule   44
     Perceiving Inequities   48
     Negotiating the Naming   51
     An Imperfect Fit   52
     Resistance   57
     Against Each Other   61
     Cooling Out   62
     Staying   63
     Full Circle   67

Chapter 2: Church Hall and Single Mothers on Welfare   69

Getting There   69
Single Mothers and Welfare   72
Training to Compensate   75
Blending In   79
Certification Training   81
The Work   86
Local Knowledge   92
A Professional Hierarchy   94
Different, Strange, and Even Dangerous   97
A Lack of Respect   98
Carving Spaces   100
Few Options   101
Protests of Denial   105
Viewing Practice in Piecemeal   109

Chapter 3: Concordance Steps and Southeast Asian Refugees 112

Refugee as Identity   112
A Political History   114
Adult Learners   116
The Labor Market   118
Skills Training and Hands-On Learning   120
Job Placement   121
The Social Organization of Work   124
Cambodians Are a Little Better   128
The Language Barrier   130
Errors on the Floor   131
You Have to Know People   133
Appreciating Kindness   135
Accommodation in the Workplace   137
Learning to Juggle   141

Chapter 4: Jackson Hospital's Pharmacies and the Cream of the
            Unemployed   143

Getting There   143
The Collaboration   147
The Best Five   148
Broad-Based Funding   153
Learning Specific Knowledge   155
Getting Hired   157
An Occupation in Transition   159
A Good Salary   164
Active Members   166

Becoming Supervisors   168
Embracing the Role   170
Something's Keeping Us Here   175

PART II: WHAT THE STORIES MEAN

Chapter 5:   Analyzing the Circle   181

The Pieces of Choosing   182
Training Programs   185
Sorting the Poor   188
The Underclass   190
Refugees   193
Assessment and the Cream of the Unemployed   196
Ranking Individuals   198
JTPA and Job Training   200
Downscaling Training   202
Defining Work   204
Making Sense   206
Distancing from an Imperfect Fit   207
A Better Fit   210

Chapter 6:   Other Possibilities   212

Prioritizing Work   213
Cooling Out at Work   216
A Foot in the Door   218
Imaginings   222
Flexible Training Models   223
Educational Networks and Supports   226
Good Jobs, Good Pay, Good Benefits   231
Bucking the Natural Trend   235

Appendix A: Ethnographic Methodology and Methods   237
Appendix B: The People   257
Appendix C: State Mandated Content of Nurse Aide Training 262
Appendix D: Church Hall's Clinical Performance Summary   265
Appendix E: Pharmacy Committees at Jackson's Hospital   266

Notes   267
Glossary   273
References   277
Index   287

Foreword

"THE FOREMAN WAS PREJUDICE' "

Thirty-five years ago I was teaching a basic education class in an on-the-job training program for high school dropouts at a steel fabricating plant in a major American city. In the three years before the establishment of this program the company had hired about two hundred young men from the inner city neighborhoods surrounding the plant. Most of the new workers were African American. None had lasted on the job more than three months. One of the senior vice presidents was very concerned about this. He and some of the personnel staff had concluded that the problem had to do with lack of knowledge of language and math—the new employees did not possess the basic skills in reading, writing, and arithmetic that were necessary to read work orders and set up the machines that cut various kinds of steel stock into specified lengths. Accordingly, a five-month "work experience and training program" for a small cohort of high school dropouts was established by the company. After all the plans for the program had been made I was offered the position of principal instructor for a group of twelve trainees. Since I needed money right then, I took the job.

For two hours a day the trainees attended a class that I led in a foreman's meeting room in the plant. For the next six hours the young men worked on the floor of the plant each day. Groups of four or five workers operated large cutting machines at work stations throughout the plant. The workforce was predominately Eastern European and many of the workers lived in neighborhoods near the

plant, just beyond the borders of the African American and Latino
neighborhoods nearest to it. At many of the work stations only one
person in the work group spoke English. The foreman would communicate instructions to that worker, who would translate to the others in the group. There were Czech-speaking work groups at some
machines and Polish-speaking groups at other machines. Yet "language" was not a problem for these workers, from the point of view
of management, as it had seemed to them to be for the high school
dropouts. One of the job interviewers, who had had an orienting
stint as an apprentice foreman in the plant, told me that in order to
maintain rapport with the workers, "You have to be able to swear in
Polish and Czech."

After two days of basic skills classes it became clear to me that ten
of the twelve trainees could read work orders readily and measure
steel and set gauges accurately. So a "basic skills" curriculum didn't
make sense for most of the trainees. With one week less than five
months to go in the program, in order to fill the time I developed sets
of "reading and social studies lessons" based on African American literature and history. Included in the social studies component were
units on basic consumer rights, personal finances, and tenants' rights.
We took a field trip, using a company van, to see firsthand how Dr.
Martin Luther King was organizing a rent strike at a building in a
neighborhood near the plant where some of the trainees lived. I per-
suaded some of the trainees to enroll in night school so that they
could resume work toward their high school diplomas.

As the weeks went by the trainees would talk with me before
class as they came into the foreman's meeting room first thing in the
morning. It was not long before one of the trainees entered looking
dejected. "What's the matter, Roger? Did you get hassled by the
Vice Lords on the way to night school?" I asked, knowing that Roger
was a member of a rival gang, the Roman Saints. He shook his head
slightly. "Yesterday the foreman was prejudice'," he said, deleting
the final "d" of the word *prejudiced*. I knew that such deletion of final
consonants was characteristic in what was then called black dialect,
or "Non-standard Negro English." (This may have been part of
what management was considering "a language problem" contributing to low scores on employment screening tests.)

A number of similar complaints began to come from other
trainees—complaints that foremen and other workers were "racist."
Accordingly, I went back to walking around the plant after class was
over. I had done that initially to see particulars of the ways in which
work was done and what reading and math skills were involved in
doing it. Now I paid attention to the relationships between the trainees

and their fellow employees. One day I walked past one of the work stations where a trainee was standing next to a machine, lifting boxes of cut steel rods onto a stack on a pallet. The young man—my student—moved very efficiently and smoothly in lifting the boxes. Near him at the next machine an older Middle European worker lifted boxes much more jerkily and swung them more rapidly to his stack. Yet each worker's stack was the same height—the team-operated machines were producing output at the same rate and so were the workers who were stacking the boxes. The foreman came by and barked at the young man, "Move it, you black son of a bitch! We're not paying you to stand around here with your finger up your ass!"

In that moment the foreman *was* prejudice. For Roger and the other trainees "prejudice" was embodied in the actions of many of the white workers—many, not all. I mused on the way in which the formal feature of black dialect—final "d" deletion—symbolized that. It was if we were living on the shop floor in a medieval mystery play, with Pride, Envy, and Anger personified. And Prejudice, a modern-day deadly sin.

It seemed that the turnover of racial minority workers in the plant was not so much a matter of their lack of basic skill but of the character of their work environment and its influence on the existential character of work life for dominators and dominated. I held gripe and consciousness-raising sessions with the young men—who will have the power, you or they? Will you give them the power to fire you? I recommended to the vice president that for the next cohort of trainees the company spend its money mostly on antiracism training for supervising foremen, establish closer regulation of their supervisory activity, and make consciousness and coping sessions available to the trainees rather than providing instruction in basic skills that most high school dropouts already possessed.

At the end of the training program all but one of the trainees were still in attendance and those eleven were hired as regular employees. I kept in touch with some of them for a while. I don't know how long they lasted on the job as a cohort. Some changes were made in the next iteration of the "(Company Name) Work Experience and Training program."

FRAMING POVERTY AND THE POOR IN THE WORKPLACE

This book, so resonant in its descriptive reporting, is most fundamentally about how workers are "framed" where they work. As in the title of Michelle Fine's *Framing Dropouts* we can read that verb both literally—the semiotic consequences of the boundary-setting of a picture frame—and ironically—the attribution process that produces false accusation of a subject as criminally suspect. Riemer shows us that in the work setting it is not simply the workers who are framing themselves by the ways in which they act, but that the ontologically defining interpretations of them by management are also "framing" them, in both of the usual senses of that term.

This framing and being framed, as Riemer cites Michael Katz in arguing, is not simply a matter of local cultural production by ill-intended managers. It is a matter of historically influenced cultural reproduction by which we continue today the Anglo-American late-eighteenth- and nineteenth-century distinction of social worth (and cultural capital), which draws a boundary line between the "deserving" and "undeserving" poor.

That distinction, as Weber and Tawney noted, has cultural roots even deeper in time, from the theological/ontological distinction made in the sixteenth century by John Calvin between the "elect" and the "damned." The elect could be identified by their asceticism and by their prosperity here on earth, which presaged their reward in heaven. The damned could be identified by their licentiousness and poverty here on earth. Destined as they were to perdition, their sufferings here were one part of a total penalty they were condemned to pay eternally. No one should presume to interfere with God's will by attempting to mitigate the material suffering of the poor of this world. That, in this life, was their just deserts. Both Marx and Weber observed that this view of the poor was more merciless than that of the medieval era preceding the rise of capitalism in Europe, and Dickens put a mid-nineteenth-century secularized version of it (in a parody of the harsh forms of utilitarian social philosophy) in the mouth of Ebenezer Scrooge in the beginning chapter of *A Christmas Carol.*

This "de-theologized" social Calvinism appears to be alive and well in late-twentieth-century Philadelphia, especially at two of the sites where work life is described by Riemer, Development and Church Hall, and even at Concordance Steps and Jackson Hospital Pharmacy. What makes the poor "deserving," in the contemporary American cultural system, is that they are morally admirable. First of all, their manner of life fulfills the Protestant project of secular asceticism—impulse control for the laity as well as for the clergy. The deserving poor today are those who try hard and stay sober, on multiple dimensions of sobriety or recovery. They may also have acquired a threshold level of cultural capital through having tried hard in the public or parochial schools, thus having learned the "three

R's" combined with a fourth—Reading, 'Riting, 'Rithmetic, and Responsibility.

Today's deserving poor do not look like the street gang members I taught at the steel plant. Rather, the deserving poor as adults appear as the kind of people who when they were children at school finished their dittoed work sheets and got awards for good attendance. For them the high school diploma functioned as a certificate of docility. They are people who, as Michael Katz observes in *Improving Poor People*, responded positively to the well-intended attempts at their uplift that were provided by private charity and public expenditure. (Or they are immigrants, and thus exempt from this process of moral double-entry bookkeeping. They couldn't reject society's attempts at their improvement since they weren't here in their childhood to be improved.)

IMPLICATIONS OF THE BOOK FOR UNDERSTANDING AND ACTION

One line of implication runs to social theory. In Riemer's analysis the "culture of poverty" explanations for the plight of the poor (held in differing ways by Oscar Lewis, John Ogbu, Daniel Patrick Moynihan, Pierre Bourdieu, and the American Right) are demonstrated to be even at their best only half correct. Those explanations show one side of what is a whole coin. Early socialization before one enters the work force may indeed explain some tendencies toward self-destructive behavior and lack of skills by the "undeserving" kind of poor person who is trying to get off welfare. But the side of the coin on which management inscribes its "framing" of workers' worth and potential goes unreported and untheorized in empirical work on the "culture of poverty" and in the derivation from it of maxims for social policy. In this book there is a powerful corrective to this oversight, both empirically in the rich narrative documentation that Riemer provides, and in midrange theorizing as she reviews the implications of her findings for policy.

In addition, I think we can see a further implication for general social theory. Although Riemer makes judiciously limited explanatory use of Bourdieu's notions of cultural and social capital (and the reader should note that Bourdieu's sense of social capital differs a bit from that of Hilary Putnam), she stops just short of articulating what to my mind can be a subtle corrective to Bourdieu's conception of social reproduction. This involves his treatment of the relations that obtain between what he calls *habitus* and *field*.

By *habitus* Bourdieu means a pattern of learned and intuitively held dispositions toward strategic action, which he characterizes as a "sense of the game." (In a nutshell, the culture of poverty argument is that the habitus of the underclass, transmitted from generation to generation, produces self-defeating behavior among those at or below the bottom of the labor market.) By *field* he means the occupational arena in which individuals vie for advantage in relative position. Bourdieu's own work has focused on prestigeful occupational fields in France, such as medicine, academia, and the church's episcopate, but by extension "field" in Riemer's study can be applied to entry-level positions requiring few or no formal educational credentials at all, such as the job of providing physical health care services to the elderly or the job of doing woodworking.

The various local workplaces that Riemer describes, in their differential framing of the comparative worth of workers, can be seen to be constructing (together with what the workers do themselves within that local institutional framing) qualitatively differing "fields" within which the habitus of workers can be employed as constrained agency. In other words, the "field" as materially and subjectively experienced by the local worker differs somewhat in its local manifestation from one workplace to the next and so does the habitus of the worker. Thus, "field" and its accompanying habitus should not be considered as unitary or uniform in their relations within a society at a given historical moment, as Bourdieu seems to maintain in his study of elite fields such as academic scholarship, and as his theory of reproduction appears to require. His claim is that habitus will remain the same so long as the field does as well. By showing us ways in which both the nonelite "field" of entry-level occupations and the habitus of the entry-level workers differs from one workplace to the next, Riemer forces us to conclude that habitus/field relations are not necessarily constant across differing local settings of work practice. They are more labile, more situational than Bourdieu's model allows them to be. In its still externally constrained but not *totally* constrained lability, habitus appears to us in Riemer's work as not simply a matter of prior socialization to class position but seems also to involve a situated response by the worker to the micropolitics of the local work environment. (Since Bourdieu claims that his critics are mistaken in seeing him as overly determinist, I expect he would argue with my contention that his model of the reproduction process does not take proper account of the lability of habitus/field relations as they are locally constructed within the workplace, although admittedly only in part locally constructed.)

In other words, what we face, if Riemer's descriptions of local work settings are accurate, is the prospect of something like a locally situated habitus/field relation that can vary considerably from place to place. Thus, we can conceive of a kind of interpositon, constituted by the cultural framing that takes place at the level of the workplace as a formal organization, between, on the one hand, the workings of class and cultural production at the macrosocial level and, on the other hand, what is happening in the lived everyday experience of particular workers on the job—a lifeworld of work practices that is both prestructured and situatedly innovated. All the more reason why the theme of "framing the worker" is so important in this book.

A second theme is a portrayal of the workplace as a community of practice, and of on-the-job learning as a process of moving from legitimate peripheral participation to more and more central participation in the conduct of work practice. Riemer's analytic description of the differences in kinds of life and learning on the job across four different sites highlights one of the implications of the "community of practice" notion of learning environments, as articulated by Jean Lave and Etienne Wenger. That implication is that one is often able to learn full participation in the practices of a local community, but that what one learns is also limited to the set of practices to which that community affords access. When there is a social hierarchy of practices within a community of practice, such as was especially evident at Development and Church Hall, then that local division of labor structures "glass ceilings" for the opportunities to learn on the job for those who join that particular community of practice in an entry-level position. Different local settings provide differing affordances for workers' learning.

There is a hopeful side to this analysis of ceiling effects on learning in the workplace. Riemer's analysis presents an argument for some aspects of what home-grown American socialism at the turn of the twentieth century used to call "industrial democracy," a vision to which each new generation of reformers in America seems to return.

A third theme, perhaps a bit hopeful as well, is that entry-level workers construct an analysis and critique of what is happening—in incisive statements they show that they can and do understand issues as matters of justice that management might more likely call "morale." The glass ceilings present in the workplace are not transparent to them. Riemer cites James Scott, and her description and analysis supports his proposal for a "paper thin theory of hegemony" (in *Domination and the Arts of Resistance,* New Haven and London: Yale University Press, 1990). This kind of awareness among the working poor, who trade at extreme disadvantage at the bottom of the labor market, may be reflected in recent trends in receptivity to union organizing. These trends may point to new possibilities for success in "bottom up" efforts to effect social change.

On a more pessimistic note, the two sites where worker morale and productivity were high, Concordance Steps and Jackson Hospital Pharmacy, show features in keeping with our more usual understanding of hegemony. At Concordance Steps the entry-level workers are immigrants from Southeast Asia. They are "framed" positively by management, but their exemption from the moral accounting processes by which domestic minority members of the underclass are usually defined as "undeserving" can be seen as the kind of exception that proves the general hegemonic rule. The case of Jackson Hospital suggests that women on welfare can be combined with trainees from other demographic backgrounds in ways that are not invidious, and that is hopeful. But the women on welfare who were allowed to become trainees were very carefully screened for cultural capital in the interview process. This "gatekeeping" was done deliberately to select a cohort of trainees from the welfare rolls who were a "creamed" set, in terms of conventionally defined academic skills and motivation, treated as individual traits. They could readily "pass" as being like everybody else, thus preserving the existing hegemonic cultural structure of distinction making.

The "undeserving" American poor, as defined by the hegemonic culture of American common sense, were not present among the entry-level employees at either Concordance Steps or the Jackson Hospital Pharmacy. The message of this book would be even clearer had some of the successful new employees at Concordance Steps been of domestic minority underclass background rather than being immigrants, and had some of the successful new pharmacy technicians at Jackson Hospital, who were of domestic minority background, not been "creamed" for social and academic skills. If you know of a site similar to Concordance Steps or Jackson Hospital Pharmacy at which domestic minority entry-level employees are treated noninvidiously and are successful in work performance, Frances Riemer wants to hear from you. Contact her and tell her about it.

Which brings me to my final point, a note on the nature of generalization from case studies. This book is unusual as an ethnography in that it compares four settings at once. Riemer does not report on a hundred sites, randomly sampled, only four sites that were opportunistically sampled. Even if she had a hundred instances in a sample, each local community of work practice would be unique. How then are we to learn anything in general from the set of particular examples that Riemer presents?

If her analysis is correct she has identified some basic social processes at work in each setting, as Howard Becker observes in his essay "Generalizing from Case Studies" (In Elliot W. Eisner and Alan Peshkin, eds., *Qualitative Inquiry in Education*, pp. 233–241 [New York: Teachers College Press, 1990]). One such process is the "framing" of new workers as "deserving" or "undeserving" and the organization of daily work life as a learning environment on the basis of that framing. Another is the presence or absence of "glass ceilings" for learning and for the demonstration of competence in work practices that is a consequence of certain patterns in the division of labor in the workplace. It is the social process that generalizes, not the particular details of worklife and of individual biography in each of her four sites. The test for the generalization of a social process, and the responsibility for demonstrating it, lies in the reader's own knowledge. Do you know of other workplaces in which can be seen the social construction of framing and glass ceilings? Then Riemer's argument in this book generalizes. If where you are you can't find any places like Development, Church Hall, Concordance Steps, or Jackson Hospital Pharmacy, then her argument does not generalize, at least for you. Generalization of her claims, in other words, is an empirical matter, not one of formal demonstration through sampling and statistical analysis. The empirical judgment of generalization is yours to make as the reader. Later you and others may do more formal research on the issues Riemer has presented to us.

FREDERICK ERICKSON

Preface

Time comes into it.
Say it. Say it.
The universe is made of stories,
not of atoms.

—Muriel Rukeyser,
"The Speed of Darkness"

The stories that are told here are not mine; they belong to the thirty-seven men and women who so graciously allowed me to enter their worlds and see life from their vantage. I thank them for their openness and their kindness, and hope these pages accurately reflect their voices, trials, and triumphs.

Many other individuals also supported this project over the course of its long life. The staff at Development, Church Hall, Concordance Steps, and Jackson Hospital, and the trainers at Department of Public Welfare, Vocational Employment Services, and the health care local granted me access and allowed me to roam. They were welcoming, and their hospitality was more than I could have hoped for. The support of my friends at the Department of Public Welfare and the Employer Advisory Council was also invaluable to this work. Without their interest and cooperation, I would not have had questions to ask, nor places to ask them. I am especially grateful to Sally Lockner, who introduced me to welfare, work, and all the places in between. Colleagues at the University of Pennsylvania and Northern Arizona University provided much needed guidance. Fred Erickson took me under his wing long before I knew what it meant to be an ethnographer, and it was under his tutelage that I learned to look, ask, watch, and listen. Michelle Fine and Elaine Simon read the earliest version of this work, and gave me encouragement and direction. Karen Rappaport and Jean Zukowski-Faust helped me make this text more accessible, and I thank them for their keen eyes and kind words. And early financial support from the Spencer Foundation gave me the important gift of time—time to reflect, analyze, discuss, and write when I needed it most.

Above all, my greatest thanks go to Dennis, for his enduring support, understanding, patience, and love, and to Julian, for reminding me to laugh.

Introduction:
Myths and Realities

Over the past decade, we have been reminded again that public welfare in the United States is a problem. When the topic has been put to the floor, everyone, from senators to academicians, policy analysts to newspaper editorialists, the air conditioner repair man to my cousin at a family picnic, has voiced an opinion about welfare and welfare reform. In the debate playing out in these very public discussions, both the welfare system en masse and, in particular, single female heads of households, have been blamed for social problems that range from juvenile delinquency and high drop out rates to the breakdown of the traditional family and the annihilation of moral values. As we as a nation become increasingly frustrated by changes in postindustrial America, too few government dollars, the cost of being middle class, and the bewilderment of a blue collar labor force that has seen its jobs disappear overseas, welfare recipients become a more visible target for both politicians and their constituencies. Out of these economic incongruities, a search for answers has arisen. Out of the dissonance in our own lives, a discourse of blame has surfaced. Sociologist Ruth Sidel writes in her *Keeping Women and Children Last* (1996, 20):

> Blaming the poor and powerless for America's social and economic problems is far more comforting and acceptable than blaming the rich and powerful. Blaming the poor upholds a fundamental tenet of the American dream: that individuals can dramatically alter the course of their own lives, that they can rise in the class hierarchy on their own initiative. To maintain our own dreams of success we must blame the poor for their failure; if their failure is due to flaws in the structure of society, these same societal limitations could thwart our dreams of success. The notion that the failure of the poor is due to their character weaknesses enables others to blame the impoverished for their

1

own poverty while simultaneously preserving the faith of the non-poor in the possibility of success.

Myths ground our conversations, popular myths about welfare recipients who choose to be on welfare because they don't want to work, or who continue to have children out of wedlock in order to stay on the dole. At least since Reagan's "welfare queen" stories, we have been told that the welfare system encourages indolence, dependency, and illegitimacy, and that these flaws can only be addressed by reforming welfare itself (Zucchino 1997).

Catalyzed first by experiments on the state level, welfare has indeed been reformed, and work has been made paramount in our new policies regarding the poor. To quote President Clinton in one of countless interviews on reforming the welfare system, "Most Americans believe that working, even if it's in a subsidized job, is preferable to just drawing welfare and not working" (Gibbs 1994, 28). Oregon's Jobs Plus was an early manifestation of this trend from support to work. The state program converted food stamps and Aid to Families with Dependent Children (AFDC) benefits into cash that was used to subsidize temporary jobs for welfare recipients, most of whom were AFDC mothers who were required to work for their benefits. Given the array of state-level demonstrations with similar objectives, Oregon's Jobs Plus program was only one battle in what a June 1994 issue of *Time* magazine called "The War on Welfare Mothers." The state of Wisconsin pushed these changes even farther with its Wisconsin Works (W-2) legislation. Even though questions about the availability of full-time jobs, affordable child care, and health care remain unanswered, by 1997 the state, under Governor Tommy G. Thompson, ended all cash assistance to the poor and put in its place a network of contracted job placement services and supports (DeParle 1997).

While these two states may have been at the forefront of the movement to reform welfare, they have not been alone. By 1996, Wisconsin and Oregon numbered among forty-three states that had received waivers from the federal government to test new strategies for moving welfare recipients into work. Welfare reform was a sound bite in the political campaigns of the year, a symbol of all that was wrong with the United States. In a television ad for his race for a Senate seat, for instance, Democratic Representative Dave McCurdy stood in front of an American flag and a grain elevator to state, "When I was growing up here in the Yukon, my parents taught me to work hard, earn my own way, and stand my ground and fight. That's why today I'm fighting to change welfare" (Dixon 1994, 1). Accompanied by rhetoric that resembled nothing less than religious fervor, the Clinton Administration's 1996 Personal Responsibility and Work Opportunity Reconciliation Act (PRWORA) institutionalized these state-based reforms. Not finding work now translates to a five-year limit on benefits that has been hung over the heads of recalcitrant welfare recipients by representatives of both the right and the left. Transferring responsibility for the poor from federal to state governments, PRWORA has eliminated AFDC, created block grants to states for their own welfare programs, linked benefits to work requirements, and set time limits of two years to find work and a five-year lifetime limit on the receipt of welfare payments (Cammisa 1998, 66).[1] In the process, welfare has been transformed from an entitlement to a work-based assistance program, and the relationship of the federal government to the health and welfare of the country's citizens has been fundamentally altered. The focus on work is reflected in the dramatic changes that have been made to the welfare category Aid to Families with Dependent Children (AFDC). Growing out of a provision of the Social Security Act of 1935, AFDC's original intent was to "keep the children of poor mothers out of orphanages." Under the current wave of reforms, however, AFDC has been replaced with Temporary Assistance for Needy Families (TANF), its authorization has been shifted to the states, and cash assistance for single mothers has been terminated (Spears 1994). Mary Jo Bane, a former assistant secretary in the Clinton Administration's Department of Health and Human Services, wrote,

> The new law abolishes the AFDC program, which guaranteed cash assistance at levels set by states to needy children whose parents were unable to provide for them, and guaranteed federal matching money to the states in amounts sufficient to provide the stipulated benefits. The old law was nothing to be proud of; it badly needed reforms to require and provide opportunities for work and parental responsibility and to hasten families off the rolls rather than lock them into dependency. But the new law goes much further than these sensible reforms. It abdicates federal responsibility for needy children by abolishing any entitlement to benefits or services and providing very flexible block grants to the states, while mandating tough work requirements and a five year lifetime limit on the receipt of assistance. (Bane 1997, 48)

States, utilizing funds from federal block grants, have developed a range of strategies to comply with federal guidelines to move individuals off the welfare rolls, with work requirements and time limits often far more stringent than those set by the federal government.

The strategies cluster into two categories: those that require employment (that is, unsubsidized, subsidized, or community work experience) for continued receipt of cash assistance; and those that
also include job search, education, and training as permissible activities (Holcomb et al. 1998, 3). For welfare recipients who do not find
unsubsidized employment in Wisconsin, for example, the state's
Wisconsin Works (W-2) initiative offers three options—trial jobs,
community service jobs, or transitional placements—all generally
limited to a period of twenty-four months. In a somewhat similar
vein, New York State has developed a massive workfare program to
accommodate individuals who have not found unsubsidized employment. More than 30,000 former welfare recipients in New York
City alone can be seen each month in their bright orange work vests
cleaning the city's streets and parks (DeParle 1998). New Jersey's
"Work First" program, on the other hand, allows welfare recipients
the option of looking for work or participating in state work assignments while continuing to receive cash assistance. States have
adapted a carrot and stick approach with regard to these and other
aspects of their efforts. Some propose drug testing and fingerprint-
ing individuals on the welfare rolls (Meredith 1999). Others have
developed personalized educational accounts that individuals can
access after being on the job for a designated number of months
(Reichert and Tweedie 1999). Regardless of strategy, however, official praise for these efforts has been widespread; leaders across the
country tout the shrinking of their state's welfare rolls. In New
Jersey, Governor Christine Whitman stood next to three former welfare mothers to announce that her state's welfare caseload has dropped nearly 50 percent in the last two years (Siegel 1999). In New
York City, Mayor Rudolph Giuliani proudly proclaimed that 400,000
people, more than the entire population of Buffalo, have left the
city's welfare rolls (DeParle 1998). And in Wisconsin, where the
state's 90 percent decrease in welfare rolls makes it the frontrunner
in this national race to end welfare (Wiseman 1999), Governor
Tommy G. Thompson boasted to reporters that "[w]elfare reform in
America would not have happened without me" (DeParle 1997, 34).

A little less than one year after PROWRA took effect, President
Clinton marked July 4, 1997, in a weekly radio address by proclaim-
ing, "This Independence Day, all Americans should be very happy
that three million of our fellow citizens are now off welfare rolls. Let
us redouble our determination to give more and more of our fellow
citizens their own personal independence day" (No author 1997,
A10). Shrinking welfare rolls is unequivocally the country's primary
objective; the very act of leaving welfare in and of itself has been

framed as both restorative and liberating. Far less concern has been placed upon what happens to the people represented by these numbers. Thanks to state-sponsored surveys on former welfare recipients conducted in eighteen states during this past year, however, we now have a Pandora's box of particulars about what life postwelfare has been like. Across states, we now know that the welfare rolls are not only smaller, but that more people are working. According to researchers at the National Conference of State Legislators (NCSL), "Most recipients who leave welfare are finding jobs. In a majority of surveys and administrative data reports, between 50–70% are currently employed or have work earnings. This work rate is around 5–10% higher than the proportion of recipients who left welfare for jobs under the AFDC program"[2] (Tweedie et al. 1999, 2). The data also show that across states, wages have been above the minimum wage. Fifty-nine percent of the former welfare recipients in Pennsylvania who found work between March 1997 and January 1998 for instance, earned a wage of $6.50 an hour, while in Wisconsin the median hourly wage for former welfare recipients was $7.00.[3]

But despite a rhetoric of golden futures, the reality of postwelfare life has been less rosy. To quote from one of a series of articles on welfare reform researched and written by *New York Times* reporter Jason DeParle, the initial data also suggest that work in and of itself has not been enough to transform lives and neighborhoods:

> [A]fter three years of tracking the nation's boldest antiwelfare campaign, what seems most noteworthy about the lives of the poor is not the change at all. It is the long list of things that remain the same: violent neighborhoods, absent fathers, bare cupboards, epidemics of depression, the temptations of drugs. Those hardships endure, not just for families who are obvious failures, those left with neither welfare nor work. They endure for the seeming successes. They endure for those with jobs. (DeParle 1999a)

Although individuals are finding work, the jobs are primarily entry-level service or retail trade, with few connections to career ladders. In Pennsylvania, 18 percent of former welfare recipients who found work moved into minimum wage, temporary jobs in "business services," 13 percent moved into health services, 10 percent into bars and restaurants, and the remainder into the service sector, which includes retail stores, hotels, and security firms (Pennsylvania Department of Welfare 1999). All pay poorly; all are bottom-rung jobs. When this reality is translated back into numbers, the preliminary results of our efforts to reform welfare become even clearer. In Wisconsin, average earnings for former welfare recipients in 1998 were approximately $7,700, $400 less than they would have received from welfare, and considerably less than the $13,100 poverty threshold set by the government for a family of three (DeParle 1999a). Even when supplemented by the federal government's earned income tax credits,[4] wages of former welfare recipients have continued to hover around the poverty line, job mobility has been limited, and bills remain unpaid.

MOVING THE POOR INTO WORK

Based upon two years of ethnographic field work, this book is an effort to contribute to the dialogue on welfare reform by providing a closer look at why, to quote from the NCSL research report (Tweedie et al. 1999, 2), "So far, few families who leave welfare have been able to escape poverty." By opening the doors and stepping inside four workplaces in which former welfare recipients found employment, I attempted to go beyond public discourse about welfare reform to examine the opportunities our society affords the poor. The thirty-seven men and women who moved from welfare to work—at Development, an inner-city supported work program, Church Hall, a long-term health care facility, Concordance Steps, a woodshop building customized stairs, and the pharmacy department of Jackson Hospital, a large urban teaching hospital—were all considered to be successful in their move from welfare to work. Their experiences extend over ten years, and the supports that were first made available to them are far more extensive than those offered today. As welfare recipients, they were provided with case managers, World of Work classes, training in vocational skills, English as a Second Language classes, substance abuse counseling, internships, and supported-work positions that in our present economic climate are considered far too costly. Yet while their stories may not reflect the current supports offered by states' welfare reform initiatives, they are compelling manifestations of what it means to be an official victor in the war on welfare. Matched by counselors, trainers, and employers, and matching themselves to training programs and work roles, the thirty-seven men and women successfully navigated the welfare bureaucracy, bought into and actively participated in training programs, sold themselves as valuable employees to employers, were delighted to be offered employment, and stayed at their jobs longer than the six-month followup period then mandated by federal and state governments. Thirty-one of the thirty-seven had worked at the same job for more than six months, and ten had been at the same work site for more than five years. Considered successful by training program providers, they viewed their own training and employment experiences, at least initially, within that same light.

I had assumed that an examination of their successes would bring a greater understanding of how training programs and workplaces encourage and support a move from unemployment to unsubsidized work, but I soon learned that for many of these men and women, the official version of success was a farce. Some men and women found work as pharmacy technicians and craftsmen; others were employed as nurse assistants and assemblers. Some earned salaries of $15 an hour; others received a wage of $4.50 an hour. Some were offered generous tuition reimbursements along with their benefit packages; others received neither paid sick leave nor vacation days. Contrary to the conversations surrounding welfare reform, however, motivation and skill levels did not define these differences in salary, benefits, and opportunities. The men and women I came to know lacked neither the motivation to access training and obtain employment nor the skills required to function competently on the job. It was instead their access to particular training programs and their subsequent move into the four companies that determined the differences in wages and benefits and, in turn, shaped their productivity on the job, their engagement with work, their perceptions of themselves as workers, and their likelihood of returning to the welfare rolls. And as the following chapters illustrate, access to training programs was based upon the welfare category to which each individual had been assigned and the official identity that was attached to each category.

CATEGORIZING THE POOR

The experiences of Henry Thompson and Ruth Fallows[5] at Development, a nonprofit training organization in the inner city, provide a good example of the apportioning of the unemployed and underemployed. Both ethnic whites from the historically rooted working-class community that bordered one side of Development, they were referred to the organization's training program for single adults on welfare by their Department of Public Welfare (DPW) case managers. Pale-skinned, with light brown hair that was graying on the sides, Henry Thompson was forty-nine but looked older. The worn look that comes from a loss hope added ten years to his appearance. Still physically strong, Henry was a worker, and he was most comfortable in his daily uniform of T-shirt and jeans. Before coming to Development, Henry had been employed in the same neighborhood dye factory for twenty years. He had worked his way up to purchasing agent at the factory, and, when the company went bankrupt in 1980, he had been left with neither a pension nor job prospects. Henry spent the intervening years in a tailspin, living with his mother and working odd jobs. "I was in shock after the closing," he confessed. Ruth Fallows, younger at thirty-six, also had a background of factory work, but her work had been more varied. Ruth was of medium build and might best be described as ordinary looking. She was one of those women who can pass unnoticed on the street, with her mousy brown, shoulder-length hair, jeans, and plain T-shirt. Ruth had a long list of factory jobs, "Gaskets, chewing gum, Mack Truck . . . hell, it's all about the same. It put food on the table. Not much but . . ." Her paychecks had left her perennially short on cash, and during a particularly long dry spell between jobs she had registered for welfare and moved with her teenage son into her brother Lenny's house. Welfare put food on the table, at least for the short term, and staying with Lenny was the only way Ruth had been sure of a roof over their heads.

Although their proximity to Development was attractive to Ruth and Henry, the agency's inner-city location, compounded by its mission to serve the hard-core unemployed, resulted in complicated and often frustrating training and work experiences. Located just north of center city at the intersection of three distinct ethnic neighborhoods, Development sat in a grid of trash-strewn fields and streets of narrow, graffiti-splattered row houses reminiscent of many inner-city landscapes in the United States. The road from center city to Development meandered through a sprawling African American neighborhood, its blocks alternating between neatly kept owner-occupied homes and abandoned brick shells and empty lots. To the west was a burgeoning low-income Latino neighborhood, 51 percent of whose Puerto Rican residents lived below the poverty line. In the summer they scented the air with meat barbecuing in covered grills that decorated their pavements out front. To the east lay the aging neighborhood into which Ruth and Henry had been born, a community of white ethnic families who had provided the labor force for the area's once-thriving factories. "Long troubled by tension among whites, Hispanics, and blacks" (Sipress 1992, A-1), these three contiguous communities were the source of 25 percent of the hate crimes reported to police citywide in 1993. During my eighteen months at Development, area residents were still feeling the aftershocks of a series of driveby murders that had been committed across the invisible lines that separate these ethnically bounded communities. The outlines of dead bodies, enshrined in blue and green spray paint by local youth to commemorate their fallen peers, could still be seen on sidewalks. Equally important, over the last ten years these three intersecting communities had become known as the city's Badlands, a place where drug dealing had replaced factory work as the only available employment option.

Located at ground zero of the city's poverty and crime, Development was composed of three separate buildings walled in by concrete and razor wire from the chaos outside. A tan stuccoed, one-story building housed administrative offices, the Human Resource staff, and the Redistribution Center. A three-story cement-colored building contained a garage, furnace, and an indoor putting green. A five-story L-shaped, red brick factory building housed what the staff at Development called its economic development activities. Known throughout the area for its welfare-to-work and inner city renewal efforts, the agency trained the "hard-core" unemployed, and subsequently hired many of its graduates, including Henry and Ruth, to work as assemblers, weatherization technicians, archive assistants, trainee supervisors, and clerical workers in its small on-site businesses. While I got to know all of Development's employees and many of its training participants, I spent most of my time with Henry, Ruth, and their colleagues in the educational kits department, housed on the top floor of the old factory building that functioned as the organization's small-business incubator. The words INCLINE CARPET CO. INC., painted in large white letters down one outside wall, served as reminder of both the building's previous incarnation and the neighborhood's former manufacturing base. The department's eight employees, all former welfare recipients, arranged thermometers, cotton balls, rubber bands, and other miscellaneous ingredients of science experiments into cardboard boxes that were sent to area elementary schools for use in science classes. The following is from field notes taken during one of my first visits to the department.

> The wooden floor of the large warehouse room that served as the kits department was dirty, strewn with paper, rubber bands, bits of string, and other discarded packing supplies. Eight long tables ran the length of the room and boxes, labeled "Thermometers," "Plates," "Scissors," were stacked high on shelves against two walls.
>
> Ruth Fallows and Henry Thompson, the department's two white employees, were perched on stools at the end of one of the long tables. Both were busy. Henry cut box patterns from flat pieces of cardboard. Ruth taped the cut cardboard into boxes and put fifteen small

cans into each box. She taped the boxes shut and stacked them on a skid, three boxes to the front, three to the side, following the pattern Henry had begun earlier that day. When the skid was piled high with boxes, Henry counted seventeen boxes on each of eleven rows, and made note of the total on a pad of paper. Using a pulley, he moved the skid to a room on the other side of the elevator and returned with more flattened cardboard and cans on the otherwise empty skid. Ruth explained that pre-packing cans inside a box, later to be placed in an even larger kit box, was Henry's idea. Their previous practice of packing thirty cans separately into each kit took a great deal of time; pre-packing fifteen cans in smaller boxes now would save time later. Henry added that this modification required cardboard boxes wider than the pre-cut version, which was why he was re-cutting the cardboard. "This will save us a lot of time. After this we'll put ten jars in a[nother] box . . . Those boxes have to be cut in half." I asked how he learned to size the cardboard. Henry shrugged and said something about just measuring to size, to which Ruth added, "Men know that stuff."

I wondered aloud how much of Henry's ability to visualize these three-dimensional solutions to packing demands was learned in training. Henry shook his head as he explained, "You don't get trained for anything here. I'll probably get fired for saying this when Bill [the company director] reads your paper. They need to give people training. All you get is one hour of computer lab every other day, because there are too many people."

Referring to other members of his training cohort, Henry continued, "The men got jobs as security guards," and Ruth added, "The women got jobs in day care . . . [and in] cleaning." Henry chimed in, "Of the guys in my group, I'm the only one hired here. One guy worked real hard at Adam's House[6] in the hope of gettin' hired there. He didn't. They were up there mopping floors, cleaning windows. What kind of training was that?"

Henry hadn't planned on participating in Development's training program; he had wanted to attend training at a local university. "I heard they had more hands on electronics. [But] it didn't get funding." Ruth, reflecting on Henry's comments, offered, "I think they only pay for training when it leads to a poor paying job. Any training that leads to well paying jobs you have to pay for yourself." (June 1, 1992, field notes, Development)

Written in response to Ruth's and Henry's assertions, at its most basic, this book is a description of who got what from their investments in government-funded employment training. Ruth, Henry, and thirty-five other men and women moved off the welfare rolls and into work in four very different workplaces. Not all applicants accessed the same kind of training, nor did each training lead to jobs equitable in terms of salary, benefits, responsibilities, and status.

The twenty women and seventeen men, ranging in age from twenty to fifty-eight, came to training bearing an array of local identities. They were mothers, fathers, grandmothers, godmothers, sons, daughters, refugees, substance abusers, alcoholics, church goers, problem solvers, team builders, Puerto Ricans, Cambodians, Afghanis, African Americans, ethnic whites, college educated, high school dropouts, sports fans, dancers, and more. But based upon only a few of those characteristics, that they were single adults, female heads of households, refugees, or that they scored a particular number of points on reading and math tests, they were divided into four distinct relief categories. The categories then became the framework for case managers' diagnoses of their lack of work, prescriptions for their unemployment, and finally, their referrals to Development, Church Hall, Concordance Steps, or Jackson Hospital. As the following chapters illustrate, this organization of men and women into categories was neither accidental nor coincidental. Instead, it reflected choices made by well-intentioned policy makers, donors, and trainers, choices based upon beliefs about ability, need, and potential, choices that resulted in discretely bounded work paths and grossly inequitable work lives. The four companies represent a continuum of work tracks that afforded employees unequal responsibilities and opportunities and offered discrepant salary and benefit packages. As the following chapters illustrate, some welfare recipients moved into well-paid, and others, like Henry and Ruth, into poor-paying jobs. Stratified in the labor force, these differentiated work tracks mirrored what historian Michael Katz (1989) calls "deserving and undeserving poor."

STORIES OF WELFARE, TRAINING, AND WORK

As researchers, we research our own lives, and the stories of these thirty-seven men and women stem in large part from my own stories. The first person in my family to graduate from college, I have long realized the benefit of education on a very personal level. From elementary school through graduate studies, teachers have opened doors to other worlds and led me down paths of exploration, discovery, and transformation. My professional life, however, often contradicted these more personal experiences. Involved in issues surrounding education, mobility, and social reproduction for the past twenty-five years, I taught in, wrote curriculum for, and directed programs for single adults and Spanish-speaking mothers on welfare in the United States, in community-based development initiatives in East Africa, and in orientation programs for Southeast Asian refugees in Indonesia. These efforts, as well as my research on in and out of school programs for youth and adults, helped me understand how training and development activities are implemented in the field, and how they affect and are affected by the individuals they are designed to support. But they have also suggested that education in and of itself is not an ameliorative for poverty or economic inequities.

The defining moment for this investigation came during my work as director of an employment-training project for single, unemployed adults on welfare in the late 1980s and early 1990s. The project, one of twenty-six throughout the state to provide transitional educational support to welfare recipients who had been unsuccessful in other government-funded training programs, had a clientele largely composed of African American men. Many had been incarcerated, many were substance abusers. All the clients, regardless of skill levels, had been unable to enter and stay in the mainstream workforce and so had supported themselves in the underground economy. Our project was statistically successful, measured both by criteria set externally by a state-level task force and by nearly 90 percent participant retention in project activities. Yet we on the staff saw very little upward mobility. In fact, despite their investments in training, most men found work in low-paying service jobs within the same employment sector in which they had spent most, if not all, of their lives. Their experience was similar to that of individuals throughout the state who participated in welfare-funded training grounded more in theories about a culture of poverty than in investments in human capital (Becker 1975).

Propelled by my own questions about why our best efforts weren't more successful in moving men and women from welfare to jobs with livable wages, I focused my dissertation research on workplaces in which welfare recipients had made a successful transition to stable work. In the dissertation, I examined the ways success in moving from poverty to the economic mainstream was officially constructed, and how that success was reconciled by those deemed most successful, the men and women, former members of the welfare rolls and working poor, whose lives had been abbreviated and encoded into government statistics. That research was the basis of this project, begun as a personal search for answers to my own questions about poverty, education, empowerment, and government policies. The outcome is a collection of stories about welfare, training, and work, and about sorting and stratification that was negotiated on multiple levels of personal, local, and political. Starting with and revolving around our shared beliefs about the poor and our myths about education and poverty, the stories illustrate how government policies and welfare-funded training programs, ostensibly designed to create opportunities, more often reified existing inequalities. These forces of social reproduction, however, were not faceless bureaucratic structures, nor were they conspiracies of a powerful elite. Instead, they were embodied in the best intentions of welfare case managers, trainers, and employers, who acted within a web of beliefs about being poor in America, and in the local practices of men and women who contested and negotiated these collective ideologies.

Unlike the classic ethnographies by anthropologists written between the great wars, this book is not a portrait of a society, freeze-framed into a timeless present. Neither is it part of a more recent genre of anthropological-driven political economies, in which questions of culture and class are answered with historiographies, charts of caloric intake, and economic distribution. It is instead a narrative of the everyday struggles of men, back at work after neighborhood factories closed or moved overseas, of drug addicts focusing on their recovery, of mothers entering or re-entering the job market after the birth of a child, of young women who left high school, maybe graduating, maybe not, with neither plans nor certain futures. It is a collection of stories of Puerto Rican citizens and Cambodian and Afghani refugees, of African Americans and poor and lower-class whites, all searching for a better life, all striving to upgrade minimum-wage jobs. Some of their stories have happy endings. They highlight the agency of men and women, and their attempts to carve out spaces where their voices are heard and their knowledge and skills are respected. But all too often they are stories of working at the margins, of raising families on insufficient incomes, amidst dangerous streets, and in jobs that minimized skills and offered few opportunities for continued learning and growth. It is my hope that through the unfolding of their stories, the impact, both positive and negative, of moving off welfare will become as real to the reader as it did to me. For only when we stop seeing men and women as the stuff of welfare myths, but instead, as rational individuals attempting to make life better for themselves and their families, will we be able to begin a real conversation about poverty, education, and welfare reform.

ETHNOGRAPHY AS RESEARCH METHODOLOGY

In February 1992 when I began talking with people about getting off welfare, I wasn't an ethnographer. I was a teacher and a student, living in the city, pondering questions about education and social mobility, poverty and work. As I describe in Appendix A, I wasn't aware that even the initial step of finding sites for the research would be so daunting, or so costly in terms of time and energy. I knew I wanted to gather information on the role government-funded initiatives played in the lives of the men and women who had moved from the welfare rolls and into the labor force. But no one warned me that local workplaces responsive to government-subsidized employment-training efforts were limited, and that those whose directors would agree to host an ethnographer's continued presence, enigmatic function, evident eavesdropping, and probing questions were even more rare. After ten months of searching for workplaces in which graduates of means-tested employment-training programs (that is, training in which participants were required to show proof of economic need) were successfully employed, and after telephoning, talking to answering machines, and visiting government offices, banks, restaurants, and other workplaces, I finally found four companies whose managers welcomed me into their halls, workspaces, and meeting rooms.

I spent the next two years in these four companies, where I learned how to ask my questions, and to watch, listen, and document the moments of everyday practice that would help me find answers. I constantly felt as though I were groping in the dark, making research-based decisions with the tentativeness of most first-time ethnographers. Uncertainty was my own repetitive refrain. Over and over I asked myself, is this an appropriate site? Should I be spending more time there instead of here? Should I be observing more, or observing less? How can I make myself more visible? How can I make myself invisible? Months passed before I felt comfortable groping in the dark. Even more time passed before I understood that my uncertainty was a fundamental part of the ethnographic method and its dependence on real life settings, people, and practices. I became an ethnographer by doing all the things that ethnographers do. I spent time with and slowly came to know the former welfare recipients, their colleagues, and supervisors in each workplace. I talked with them, and I observed their engagement in and negotiation with their work. I watched them interact with one another, celebrated with them, and counseled them on career moves. I studied any and all available documents that might help me understand the workplaces, took endless notes, and returned home each night to write up my scratches and make sense of the myriad of details that made up each day. I also retraced the steps of the thirty-seven former welfare recipients, visiting them at home and returning to the training programs that had linked them with work. I observed training sessions, reviewed training materials, and interviewed instructors of skills and work readiness classes, counselors, job developers, and directors to better understand the goals, activities, funding histories, philosophies, and beliefs about moving from welfare that were reflected in each training initiative.

Alternating between companies to allow time to follow up on events, activities, and developments as they unfolded, I spent two to four days each week in the field, and observed, interviewed, and reviewed employment-related documents in each company. But while my data collection strategies remained constant, the nature of work dictated the particulars of my activities. At Church Hall I wheeled and talked with elderly residents, at Development I counted and bagged articles for educational kits and interviewed applicants for upcoming training programs. Assisting even in small ways in these workplaces allowed me to become acquainted with (and earn the gratitude of) staff members and gain a better grasp of the demands of the workplace. Positioning myself next to men and women in the midst of work, I listened to and engaged in conversations held over work, between work, or instead of work, utilizing what Roger Sanjek (1990a, 244) called "situated listening . . . [when] ethnographers purposefully put themselves in events where they will hear, and later write what they hear in their field notes." From information gained during these conversations and from following individuals around the workplace as they worked, I was able to ask direct questions; confirm or disconfirm hypotheses about experiences, training preparation, and workplace responsibilities; and formulate plans for future investigation. Assisting on Concordance's shop floor or in Jackson's pharmacy satellites, however, was far more complicated. The work required specific skills, and the risks and liability to the companies were far greater. In those two workplaces I spent very little time doing. Instead, I watched and talked. I engaged men and women in informal conversations that ranged from a series of brief ten to fifteen minute encounters conducted in passing to conversations that stretched over hours while they worked. In consultation with company or division managers, I also scheduled more formal interviews that lasted from thirty to ninety minutes and were held in a variety of deserted places, including waiting rooms, reception areas, empty dining rooms, offices, TV lounges, a cafeteria, a stairwell, a window sill bordering an elevator bank, and even a concrete outdoor walkway at Jackson Hospital, thirteen floors above busy city streets.

Over the two years I came to know 162 employees in the four

companies, fifty-two training and workplace supervisors, twelve trainees, and eighteen city- and state-level administrators. My discussions with these men and women, my observations, and the other data collection strategies described in this section produced piles of field notes that I transcribed, coded according to inductively derived categories, and sorted by these codes to detect emerging themes. Using a process described as analytic induction, I constituted and reconstituted the categories to accommodate new sources of data and divergent experiences and meanings. The process was like making a jigsaw puzzle, adding pieces and rearranging patterns to accommodate the additions. I spent an entire winter arranging and rearranging the pieces of interaction that I had recorded. Then I read everything I could find about poverty and welfare, human capital, stratification and reproduction, the construction of identity, and structure, agency, and resistance, in order to know how to talk about the images that began to form.

Slowly, stories emerged from the data, stories of individuals making their present within, as anthropologist Sherry Ortner (1984, 159) wrote, "the very powerful constraints of the system within which they are operating." The following chapters illustrate that the stories are a collection of empirically based examples of interactional patterns, roles, and statuses mapping over dynamic webs of race, gender, ethnicity, and class. Together, they provide insight into the workplace practices of individuals previously marginalized from the labor force, their efforts to move from welfare to work and our shared cultural beliefs about education, work, and the poor.[7]

ORGANIZATION OF THE BOOK

This book is organized into two main sections. Part One consists of the stories of thirty-seven men and women who moved from welfare and unemployment rolls to steady employment, as well as those of their co-workers, trainers, and supervisors in four different workplaces. Written with their urging, the stories describe the everyday work lives of real people who moved off welfare. This first section builds around two main problems: first, how educational systems in and outside schools prepare adults who are marginalized from the mainstream by race, ethnicity, first language, and economic status, for the workplace, and how the private sector accommodates these workers and their differences; and secondly, how adults who are labeled economically "disadvantaged" negotiate the contradictions of race, class, and ethnicity as students and as workers.

In the second half of the book the experiences of these men and women are analyzed across training and workplaces. In this section questions are posed concerning our most commonly held beliefs about and prescriptions for poverty, about who deserves what and who gets what. Both the positive and negative consequences of those prescriptions on the formerly unemployed are examined. The last chapter in this second section is an examination of these welfare-to-work experiences in light of our current political climate. It addresses the assertion of William Julius Wilson (1996, 234) about "the need to re-train low-skilled workers," by imagining other images for linking welfare recipients to job-specific roles. The welfare-to-work initiatives exemplified by Development, Church Hall, Concordance Steps, and Jackson Hospital are not the only possibilities. These stories might have been very different had more men and women been given opportunities to participate in challenging training programs and work roles, or had they been encouraged and rewarded with a work upgrade for a continued investment in accessible training. By reframing the debate about welfare reform from a discussion about moving welfare recipients from the welfare rolls to a conversation about a responsive, inclusive adult education system, I imagine stories with different endings, where work provides family and community, and affords all individuals the opportunity to be productive, appreciated, and rewarded.

Part I
THE STORIES

Chapter 1
Development and the Hardest to Serve

People who stay at Development are too insecure about their
own capabilities to look for another job. People here have low
self-confidence. They don't think they can do anything else.
—Joan Chance, homeless project manager, Development

This is a job work, job readiness program. In other words, you
learn how to work, you learn how to behave. You learn how to accept authority, all those things that people who are disenfranchised have for some reason not learned. We teach them and
they go out and look for a job.
—Joe Jenkins, human resource director, Development

I think they only pay for training when it leads to a poor-paying
job. Any training that leads to well paying jobs you have to pay
for yourself.
—Ruth Fallows, educational kits department, Development

NAMING THE HARDEST TO SERVE

When Henry Thompson and Ruth Fallows asked their case managers at the Department of Public Welfare (DPW) about skills training, they were referred to Development, one of nine training
programs in the city that specifically targeted the Transitionally
Needy (TN). Like similar General Assistance (GA) welfare categories in other states, the TN category had a short yet tumultuous
history. A state-funded welfare category for economically disadvantaged, single adults between the ages of eighteen and forty-five, it
was created in 1984 to provide food stamps, medical insurance, and
ninety days of cash assistance each year to economically needy individuals who did not fall under the purview of Aid to Families with
Dependent Children (AFDC). The category was amended in a 1994

attack on welfare; it was collapsed with the Chronically Needy, the state's other GA category, and receipt of TN cash benefits for all GA recipients was scaled back from ninety days a year to two months every two years (County Assistance Office 1992). In 1995, only eleven years after its conception, the category was completely abolished by state legislators caught up in the nationwide frenzy to reform welfare.

But back in 1992 when Henry and Ruth requested assistance, state money was still being funneled into supports and job training programs for TNs. According to state mandates, programs were to focus on the "hardest to serve," an identity defined by one or more of the following characteristics:

- recovering substance abuser
- no recent work history
- ex-offender
- homeless
- score below seventh grade on literacy assessments
- limited knowledge of English

Like Henry and Ruth, participants of TN training programs statewide reflected these criteria. According to records complied in the state capital, from 1987 to 1993, 35 percent of TN program clients throughout the state were recovering substance abusers, 32 percent had no recent work history, 27 percent were ex-offenders, 21 percent were homeless, 20 percent scored below seventh grade level on literacy assessments, and 4 percent were limited in their knowledge of English (Bureau of Employment Training Programs 1993).

AN INSTITUTIONAL HISTORY

Over the past twenty years, the Transitionally Needy category had sustained Development. Consequently, the identity of TN was closely interwoven with Henry and Ruth's move from the welfare rolls to work in the old factory building that housed Development's educational kits department. At Development, being a TN implied that Henry and Ruth were among the hardest to serve of the welfare population. At its most basic, it meant they lacked both stable work experiences and knowledge about the workplace. These implications had precedent at Development. Originally incorporated in

1974 as one of fifteen sites nationwide designed to test the effects of a strategy called supported work, Development was described by its founders as "a demonstration program which provided subsidized-work opportunities for former criminals, ex-drug addicts, young school dropouts, and women who had been receiving welfare for long periods of time" (Grinker 1979, 12). Like other 1970s-era subsidized-work programs throughout the country, Development's supported work borrowed on ideas from public-service employment and sheltered workshops to provide the most economically marginalized individuals with opportunities to learn the expectations of work, gain work experience, and overcome fears of entering the labor force. During the program's initial stage, those objectives translated to the assignment of the agency's yearly allotment of 120 ex-addicts, recovering alcoholics, ex-offenders, AFDC mothers, and youth to work crews that were responsible for sealing abandoned buildings in the neighborhood, renovating the houses of low-income home owners, maintaining Development's grounds, operating the company's furniture shop, installing carpets, and painting the building. Each work crew, closely supervised by staff supervisors, stayed at Development for a maximum period of eighteen months (Ball 1984; MacDonald 1980). As Kenneth Auletta wrote in *The Underclass* (1983, 22), an investigation of supported work programs across the country, Development's model incorporated "three programmatic techniques designed to make participants initially comfortable with the world of work and to gradually increase their ability to succeed in that world: peer-group support, graduated stress, and close supervision."

This national version of supported work was heavily researched. Evaluated by Manpower Demonstration Research Corporation (MDRC), the initial findings on Development's supported work were less than positive. The program's demonstration phase was marked by particularly low retention and high termination rates. In fact, the program's retention rate was the lowest of all fifteen national sites and its rate of firings was the highest. Interviewees described Development as "a particularly tough program with respect to discipline" (Skidmore 1984, 84). But despite the mixed evaluation and a 1982 funding cut that ended this large-scale demonstration phase, Development's managers remained committed to the concept of supported work. They continued the project by building a broad funding base from state, local, and private sources, in-kind donations and profit from its small businesses on site. These six for profit-businesses included:

- an educational kits department, where Henry Thompson, Ruth Fallows, and six other former welfare recipients assembled reusable educational kits for a science museum downtown
- a weatherization unit, where Andy Johnson and five other men, three of whom were from the welfare rolls, weatherized area residences under contracts with city housing agencies and the local gas company
- a redistribution center from which Juan Martinez sold new and used building materials to low-income home owners
- an archive storage facility for center-city businesses
- a copying and binding service for local businesses
- a recently renovated forty-six-unit transitional housing complex, providing care management and support services to its formerly homeless tenants

According to Bill Perkins, Development's founder and director, the businesses provided supplemental income to broaden the company's funding base, offered supported work slots for trainees, created jobs for graduates and community members, and contributed to the development of the local economy. The agency's comptroller, who had been with Development since its inception, added:

> We broke away in 1978. Now it's more business oriented; before it was just a funded agency. In '80 when Reagan got in, the funds were cut. We were originally to contribute one-third of the funds. Now we earn two thirds from fees for service and other businesses. It was planned, so we didn't have to rely on public funding. (Mike Small, Comptroller, Development)

Development's Corporate Model showed an integrated system in which the training and small businesses utilized and supported each other to accomplish the corporation's mission, "to empower people in need to attain the hope, motivation, and skills necessary to reach their fullest human potential and highest level of personal and family self-sufficiency" (Development fact sheet).

When I arrived at the agency in April 1992, both the TN program and corresponding beliefs about cultural deficiency were still much alive. They were embedded in this lofty mission and reflected in the agency's public relations materials. A brochure about Development's services described its target population as "at risk," and "having little to no work history and lacking for the most part employable skills." The state government also encouraged this continued emphasis on the "hardest to serve." State report forms, submitted each month by Development's staff members to a state level task force on employment training, instructed program operators to "list the number of participants with characteristics shown. Duplicate count if participant has multiple characteristics." These forms offered additional descriptors to characterize the "hardest to serve" that included:

- ex-offender
- homeless person
- person who reads below the seventh grade level
- person with limited or no fluency in the English language
- person with few or no marketable occupational skills
- person with emotional or mental health problems
- recovering drug or alcohol abusers
- victim of domestic violence
- high school dropout
- minority youth (aged 18–25) without full-time employment experience
- displaced homemaker

According to staff lore, more was better, and case managers made consistent efforts to fit program applicants and participants into as many of these categories as possible. In practice then, unlike other training programs that screened out individuals according to prescribed criteria, Development was encouraged to seek out participants with multiple barriers in order to maintain funding levels.

THE REALITY OF THE HARDEST TO SERVE

This "hardest to serve" nomenclature was broad, and the eighteen former welfare recipients who worked at Development reflected this expanse. Twelve had no recent work history, six were recovering drug abusers, three spoke little to no English, three scored lower than grade seven in reading and math, four were high school dropouts, two were ex-offenders, and one had been homeless. Both Ruth and Henry lacked high school diplomas. Henry dropped out of the tenth grade to work in a factory down the street. Ruth got pregnant in ninth grade and didn't return to school after the birth of her only son. Because they had been out of work during the previous year, Development's case managers had also counted them as part of the

"no recent work history" category. Most of their co-workers in the
kits department also fit into multiple categories. Noreen Diaz, a
short, compact woman with bleached blonde hair, worked beside
Ruth and Henry in the old warehouse. Noreen had attended school
in Puerto Rico until the seventh grade, and her last full-time job
had been a three-year stint in a toy factory twenty-three years ago.
At forty-one with three adult children, she qualified as a high school
dropout, as a displaced homemaker, and as a person scoring below
seventh grade on literacy assessments. The others also had a long
checklist of hardest to serve attributes. Josefina Burges, tiny as a
bird with a tongue that chirped Spanish like a loquacious sparrow,
was a newly hired member in the department. Josefina spoke virtually no English, and although she had worked in a cafeteria in
Puerto Rico, at twenty-one she fell under the limited English, minority youth without full-time employment who scored below seventh grade on literacy assessments. Maria Lopez was also Puerto
Rican, but unlike Josefina, she spoke nearly fluent English. Maria,
young and shapely with neatly curled shoulder-length brown hair,
was the "looker" of the group. Maria was a TN because at twenty-
two, she was a minority youth without full-time employment. Edith
Jenkins, now twenty-seven, was one of two African American
women in the department. Dressed in reds, yellows, and greens,
Edith often referred to herself as a "rasta man." She had used drugs
since she was a teenager, an addiction that caused her to drop out of
school in tenth grade, and later catalyzed the breakup of her family.
Edith's parents were willing to raise her fourteen-year-old son and
eleven-year-old daughter, but they couldn't cope with Edith's drug
abuse and wouldn't allow her to stay in their home. Edith, homeless
for two years before she found work at Development, could be
counted as homeless, a recovering drug addict, and a high school
dropout with few or no marketable skills. Barbara Wilson, also
African American, had had a more promising start. She had graduated from high school and spoke warmly of her retail work in local
department stores. But her jobs had been through temporary agencies, and now twenty-five years old, she voiced concern that her
dark skin and pockmarked face would decrease her marketability.
Barbara fit under minority youth without full-time employment experience. And the list of the multiple labels and multiple categories
went on and on.

But regardless of their histories, Development offered these people the same prescription for a perceived lack of work ethic and
work experience. Joe Jenkins, Development's new Human Resource Director explained:

This is a job work, a job readiness program. In other words, you learn how to work; you learn how to behave. You learn how to accept authority, all those things that people who are disenfranchised have for some reason not learned. We teach them, and they go out and look for a job. (Joe Jenkins, human resource director, Development)

At Development, Henry's twenty years in a textile factory, one of many that had been the economic mainstay of the neighborhood in his youth, weren't relevant. Neither was the fact that Ruth Fallows and Barbara Wilson had a combined twelve years of work experience, that Josefina Burges lacked English language skills, not work experience, or that Edith Jenkins was plagued by her drug addictions, not by an inability to follow directions or work in a team. The theme, that trainees at Development didn't know how to work, and as a correlate, didn't how to behave or to accept authority, had followed Henry, Ruth, and their co-workers from Development's demonstration phase to this more recent reincarnation. It was embodied in the beliefs and opinions of Development's case managers, the design of the agency's training sessions, and in the social organization of the workplace.

CONCEPTUALIZING THE HARDEST TO SERVE

I got my initial introduction to the imposed identity of TN recipients during my first visit to Development in April 1992 when James Taylor, the manager of the agency's small Human Resources department, gave me a tour of the facility. Walking through the halls of the agency's low-slung classroom building, we passed a crowd of men and women, ranging in skin tones from white to brown to black, hovering near the time clock. Taylor referred to them as trainees from the welfare office, adding in a lowered voice that they clock in, but "we don't see them all day. A friend clocks them out." I wasn't immediately sure what he meant, but I soon heard his suspicions about the trainees echoed in the comments of counselors, trainers, and job developers. Accusations of untrustworthiness and irresponsibility were common in interviews and informal conversations with these supervisors. Nava Gopalan, an Indian woman with a master's degree in social work, had been hired as a counselor to work with Development's younger clients. She talked about the program's trainees in terms of their gender.

I think the girls realize the need to graduate. Men drop out to work. I think they find hanging out on the street corner they make ten times

more money than [working at] McDonald's. One student has been in
and out of jail. It's very difficult to me; he may be driving a new car,
but he can't be out of the ghetto. (Nava Gopalan, counselor,
Development)

For John Harris, an employment counselor and part-time job developer who had just obtained his undergraduate degree in social work,
ethnicity was a concern. In Harris's opinion, it was his Puerto Rican
clients who lacked knowledge and skills. "Working with Hispanics
who haven't been in this country for too long . . . they really need a
lot of guidance and instruction," asserted Harris. "They don't come
with skills. The language skills, there's an educational barrier even
in their country."

For other staff members, welfare status alone provided rationale
for the deficiencies they perceived in their TN clients. Theresa
Randle had been hired as a counselor at Development one and a half
years before my arrival. Tall, thin, and in her late forties, Theresa
was African American herself. But she was from the Bahamas, a
member of the old guard who advocated a bootstraps philosophy of
personal improvement. According to Randle, her clients didn't live
up to her standards.

> You can always tell people on welfare. Did you ever notice, they
> never open the blinds? Their houses are dark; they're afraid someone
> will peer in. Welfare will pay; why pay the electricity if you know you
> can get help once your bill is more than five hundred dollars? Gas too.
> Most people have no experience beyond welfare. They live check to
> check. They don't realize they could do better. (Theresa Randle,
> counselor, Development)

Schooled in a social-work tradition grounded in theories of cultural
deprivation, Randle and her colleagues on Development's administrative staff, in the counseling department, and in management believed that the welfare recipients, both those in training and those
like Henry and Ruth who found employment at Development after
their six months of training, were devious, weak, and inexperienced;
they were also in dire need of the work experience and counseling
that the agency provided.

SOCIALIZATION FOR WORK

These preconceptions did not initially pose a problem for Henry,
Ruth, and their colleagues. Development had been a route back

into the labor force for them all. Henry had been out of work so long that he was beyond restless; he was desperate to fill his days. Development had been his second choice. Since his preference—an electronics course at the local community college—had not been funded, he took the training slot at Development and rationalized that anything was better than nothing. Ruth had been laid off from her last job two years ago, and as sole support for herself and her son Jake, she found herself relying too heavily on her brother's largesse. Development had been a second chance for their co-workers as well, and they each had their own stories about enrolling in Development's TN Program. For Noreen Diaz, Josefina Burges, Maria Lopez in the kits department, and even Maria's husband Tomas, who found work as a crew supervisor at Development after training, location had been a concern. Development was in the neighborhood, and as Spanish speakers in a city thick with ethnic animosity, the proximity made them feel safe. Sam Jessup, who worked as a crew supervisor in Development's redistribution center, was impressed that the agency saved him a training slot while he was in drug rehab. When he finished his forty-day treatment program, Development had been his first stop. Will Chandler, another crew supervisor, confided that he had been lured by Development's training stipends, the highest in the city he had been told.

Despite these differing motives, they all welcomed their case managers' referrals, and when the staff at Development prescribed an hour of job-readiness, an hour of computer-assisted learning, and four hours in a work crew each day for their unemployment ills, they didn't question the package. Each component, the emphasis on group counseling, the individualized, computer-based tutoring, and the supported work, was based upon the supposition that as welfare recipients, they lacked the middle-class norms, experiences, and coping mechanisms that employers required. According to the company's director, Development's broad-based reliance on the supported work model was based upon two premises. "We don't cream," he asserted. "Our basic philosophy is everybody deserves a chance." He continued, "For some people just being in the day-to-day job environment is important."

COMPUTERS IN THE LEARNING LAB

Henry and Ruth spent the sole hour of explicitly didactic training each day in Development's computer lab. The lab housed ten computers, all arranged in a row against the room's yellow and brown walls. According to Bill Perkins, the agency's director, the room was designed to counter welfare recipients' prior lack of success in formal educational settings.

> Our clients don't like school. They may have had bad experiences. Work doesn't seem like school. We can spoonfeed the school part. Even better with the advent of the computer, if you don't use them [computers] as games. Computers in the learning lab help people learn they're not stupid. We're not telling them, the box is. A real learning curve is around the idea of learning, [which brings a] change of respect of yourself. (Bill Perkins, Director, Development)

Karen Casey, Development's computer lab coordinator, added some insights.

> Any anxiety dwindles away pretty quickly. Some people tell me that they're anxious. I tell them I've had five-year-olds sit down and work on these computers. Lots of people come here and think that they can't learn; then they can't. A lot of people are breaking down barriers. This is a noncompetitive atmosphere. You're only competing with yourself. . . . I try to concentrate here on learning is fun. (Karen Casey, lab coordinator, Development)

Casey was right about the lab. People liked working there. It was crowded all hours of the day with men and women sitting mesmerized in front of computer monitors, reading text, typing words in blanks on the screen, and choosing from lists of possibilities. The problem was that the time there was always too short. "All you get is one hour of computer lab every day," Henry complained. "Because there are too many people." As Carla Whitaker, Henry's colleague in the kits department, spelled out, the computer lab closed promptly at 4:30, the same time Development's employees left work. "I can't go [to the computer lab] because we're working all day. They should keep it open two hours after work." But Development wasn't a place where people stayed late. Despite its rhetoric, Development wasn't a community center. It was a workplace in the inner city and its trainees, trainers, counselors, administrators, and assemblers alike punched out and left each afternoon at 4:30.

Even if staff members had been willing to stay, Carla's suggestion would not be easy to implement in a neighborhood where drug dealers took ownership of the sidewalks once the sun set. Field notes taken after a walk outside the compound reflect the strong feelings that the area engendered.

Ronnie James, the agency's fifty-eight-year-old maintenance man, told me that work crews were outside cutting the grass earlier in the morning, and so I walked around the building in the hope that I might watch them work. I peered across the street to an abandoned field that Development had twice tried, without success, to transform into a park. It was empty, littered with broken bottles and overgrown with weeds. I walked around the perimeter of the compound hoping I'd find the crews along my way. The building's walls were covered with blue, green, red, and yellow swirls of names tagged in spray paint, the medium of choice for these urban statements of identity. The first three floors of windows were boarded up, and razor wire hung from the compound walls.

I was alone in the back of the compound except for a refrigerator that lay on its side next to tires that had been dealt out like a hand of cards on the bare windswept field. The emptiness was silent and desolate. Two cars drove past while I walked; I was careful to keep my distance.

Coming back around to the front, I saw Ronnie cleaning broken glass from the pavement with a piece of cardboard. He joked saying, "Next time, Miss, don't break the beer bottle here," and added that broken glass on the sidewalks is a frequent problem in the summer. Inside the compound, Walt Smith, newly hired by the Archives Department, sat on a shaded step, eating a sandwich and drinking a soda. I joined him on the stoop, and we talked about the razor wire that decorated the old factory building. "But that won't stop them," Walt commented, referring to potential thieves. "They're like monkeys." (June 26, 1992, field notes, Development)

The neighborhood was indeed the source of much concern among Development's staff members. This was a place people avoided. Daytime in the neighborhood had an eerie feeling; nights were not a place for the living. As a journalist for the local newspaper wrote, "[T]he commercial center of the neighborhood was skid-row ratty and rundown, especially at night, though it wasn't as scary as a lot of the row house streets. It sat in eternal darkness and gloom under the El, and the tracks were supported by an archway of rusted iron crab legs, a symbol of the city's industrial death" (Lopez 1994, 9). Despite Carla's optimism, no one would be using Development's computer lab after sunset for some time to come.

LIFE SKILLS

The remainder of the five hours of Development's training day was dedicated to reforming Henry, Ruth, and their colleagues, purging them of bad habits and instilling new values and standards of behavior. Life Skills was the classroom venue to explore their marginalization from the economic mainstream. According to Life Skills instructors, the hour-long class was dedicated to helping poor men and women both become aware of their own deficiencies and learn new, more successful ways to approach work and life. As illustrated in the course outline (Chart 1.1), during the six weeks of Life Skills, sessions moved from an analysis of the psyche to an orientation to the workplace.

Chart 1.1.   Life Skills Course Outline

Week 1:   Life Skills

Day 1:   Orientation
Day 2:   Drawing of recent past/today
Day 3:   Who determines your future? What barriers hold you back?
Day 4:   Values, needs, and wants
Day 5:   Resources vs. constraints

Week 2:   Life Skills

Day 1:   Transitional analysis
Day 2:   Parental state
Day 3:   Adult/child state
Day 4:   Reviewing the tapes
Day 5:   Goal setting

Week 3:   World of Work

Day 1:   Defining work/working to live
Day 2:   Attendance/Punctuality
Day 3:   Accepting criticism
Day 4:   Getting promoted/fired

Week 4:   World of Work

Day 1:   Anger/Stress
Day 2:   Recreation and work
Day 3:   Budgeting/making the best of your lifetime
Day 4:   Discrimination at work
Day 5:   Review of the week

Week 5:   Job Development

Day 1:   Applications
Day 2:   Resumes

Day 3: Resumes
Day 4: Cover letters
Day 5: Review week

Week 6:   Job Development

Day 1: Job search, how to look for a job
Day 2: Job search, how to read ads
Day 3: Appointments
Day 4: Interview, speak, dress, act
Day 5: Interview practice

The following, from field notes taken during the third day of week one in Life Skills, provides a glimpse into the sessions. While particular to one group meeting, the interaction was characteristic of all the Life Skills classes I saw and all those attended by Henry and Ruth one year earlier.

1:00 P.M., Helena Gay, a stylish African American woman in her late twenties, facilitated a conversation about obstacles and goals with the six men who were attending her Life Skills class. The men, one white and five African American, sat scattered in poses that ranged from outwardly attentive to casual deference.

On the board, Helena, who had been employed as a case manager at Development for the past year, had written the following steps:

> Talking about excuses that get in your way
> 1. Discussing your goal
> 2. Achieving your goal
> 3. Identifying obstacles
> 4. Overcoming obstacles
> 5. Evaluating your progress

She read through the five steps aloud, and then asked the men to talk about their goals. Barely prompted, Charles Henderson, a large man with shaved head and dark spectacles, began talking about "obstacles in the way of puttin' money away." He spoke with ease, as though accustomed to this public soul searching. "I don't really want to do this. I'm scared to do this. I was throwin' a lot of obstacles in my way [of] building something. So I'm gonna' do it. I'm kind of tired of this place. I'm kind of tired of the people here. Everybody's ready to leave; they just don't know what they're gonna leave to. People get relaxed with the program."

Tyrone Brown, smaller in build, spoke as soon as Charles stopped. "You need two hundred no's for one yes. It just took me two no's [to stop my search for a job]. Annette got a job. That's what it shows, being persistent. People want to sit back and see how it goes for other people."

Ten seconds of silence passed until Helena paraphrased Tyrone's comment with, "There's the motivation, watchin' other people." Looking around the group, Charles queried, "Who else got a job?" Tom Clark, sitting in the back of the room, replied "Mohammed," and Charles responded with "That's not a job; it's a tradeoff." Someone added that Mohammed found a free apartment, for which he traded maintenance work.

Helena asked, "What about you, Robert?" Robert James, a tall, thin man, took a minute and then responded with, "I know what my obstacles is. I start somethin' and don't finish it. And somethin' else I learned at Development. Just because this guy say he's gonna get me a job, that doesn't mean I'm gonna stop." Helena paraphrased, commenting on the importance of persistence and followup. Charles spoke up again. "A lot of people say I can get a job, but can I keep it? I get that big paycheck. A lot of reports have been comin' back, a lot of people goin' out and gettin' a job, get that big paycheck. They go back to drugs. Talk about goal. A lot of people say the goal is gettin' a job. I think of that sign in the lunchroom, *Anyone can get a job. It's keepin' one that's important.*" Tyrone added, "I learned that I can never get too comfortable. I need resources, 'cause that kind of job can go away."

No one stepped in, and the ensuing silence seemed to stretch on for minutes. Helena finally asked, "What about you, Blake?" to the only white man in the group. Blake Danner, a large man who with his unruly brown hair and plaid flannel shirt more closely resembled a young woodcutter than a resident of the inner city, waited a few seconds before beginning. "Keeping a job. Nothin' will hold me back. The problem is getting a job in the first place." Helena asked pointedly, "Have you been looking?" Blake said he had submitted his resume "to my off-site," a Catholic relief center where he had been doing office work and computer inputting for the past three months. It was common knowledge among the Human Resource counselors that Blake was only targeting his off-site training site for possible employment, refusing to send resumes to other companies. Helena commented, "You have enough resumes to send them to other places. Well, Blake, I'll tell you, if they're not talkin'," referring to the center, "you have to let them know that you're valuable." "They did say they'd like me to stay through," Blake persisted. Helena asked if the center has any money to pay him. Blake shook his head no, saying, "They don't have funding."

Helena looked around, waited another minute for someone to begin speaking, and when no one volunteered, asked, "Anybody else? How will you evaluate progress? By keeping your job?" Tyrone took the floor again, saying, "Gettin' on my subject, I'm gonna get me a nice full-time job. I had a part-time job. I couldn't do the things I wanted to do. Not enough money. I had a nice stable job. Kids. I got divorced. I need a nice stable job." Helena asked Tyrone about ob-

stacles, and Tyrone, referring enigmatically to his history of substance abuse, responded, "I have a couple of bad habits, but I have
them under control." Helena continued, "Are you doing anything to
keep them under control? You know that that is an obstacle. What do
you think could help you overcome that?" Tyrone, reciting the litany
he had memorized from the Alcoholics Anonymous meetings that
many of the group members attended, stated, "changing my peoples,
people, places, and things."

After what seemed far longer than the minute or two of silence
that followed, Helena responded with, "Anybody can interject, can
share here." Charles took the floor. "A big thing is changes, people
you hang with. You may have one percent resistance left and meeting
a person may make it go. Gee, it'd be good to be straight. I got to stop
hangin' with you, you got to stop hanging with me." Helena paraphrased, "You have to change it," and Charles continued, "It's hard
being an addict. It's a lonely type thing. Straight people don't want to
be around you. They don't want to trust you." Helena asked, "What
are you going to do?" Tyrone interjected, "Another obstacle is not
giving up." Changing topics, Charles commented directly to Tyrone
now. "A personal observation, you get mad quick. You get mad at Will
[the men's work crew supervisor]. Sometimes I think you're gonna
kill him. You have to be like a willow tree. You got to learn how to
bend, not break. These ain't slavery days."

The conversation continued in the same vein for fifteen more
minutes. Each man articulated his goals and barriers, and Helena
closed with, "Well everybody's shared today." As the men stood up to
leave, they commented that the last several sessions had been like
twelve-step meetings. On his way out, Charles summed up their
thoughts. "For the last couple weeks, you've been really diggin' into
our cases," (May 6, 1992, field notes, Development)

In addition to "diggin' into [their] cases" in the therapy-like sessions, Life Skills also included videotapes of the motivational speaker
Les Brown and confessionals by former clients who returned to
share wisdom concerning life postwelfare. But regardless of the particular topic or format, the sessions were all designed as opportunities for men and women to reflect on their experiences and those of
other trainees, and for Development's trainers and case managers, as
representatives of middle-class norms, to advise them in their move
toward economic stability. Trainers outlined procedures for opening
a checking account, highlighted the benefits of property insurance,
and shared strategies for obtaining job leads. For Frank Young, a
young African American physical education major who taught Life
Skills classes at Development, the trainees' problems were "maybe
ninety percent the system, ten percent the individual." But while

barriers may be structural, at Development, it was the individual that was prodded and poked, pushed, and pulled. Like Helena Gay, in Frank Young's Life Skills classes, he stressed that "you have to do your ten percent."

SUPPORTED WORK

While Life Skills sessions attempted to teach Ruth and Henry how to negotiate the demands of life and of work, Development's work experience was the vehicle to teach them how to work. Assigned to work crews in various departments at Development, they were guided and monitored by crew leaders, many of whom had been hired by the company after completing training themselves. Some trainees, suited up in navy blue work coveralls and gloves, painted steel H-shaped bars with bright orange paint. Others, such as Mia Sanders and Joan Coltrane, were placed in the kit department, where they counted and bagged small scissors, springs, and Q-tips for future kit assembly. For their work support, Henry and Ruth had been placed in work crews not unlike that of the three-man work crew cleaning Development's boiler room one spring morning in 1992. Tomas Lopez, Maria's husband, was the crew's leader. A twenty-two-year-old Puerto Rican man, Tomas had been hired straight out of training and had worked as crew supervisor at Development for the past year.

> Tomas filled two buckets with water and brought them back toward the steps where I stood in the boiler room. His three-man crew waited quietly as he added liquid from plastic containers marked AMMONIA and DETERGENT to the water. The closed, dark space of the basement-like room was filled with the boiler itself, which stood low and wide in its center. Last week Will Chandler's crews had painted the room's floor. This week Tomas's crew removed the newspaper coverings from the boiler's pipes. During their work experience today, the men were washing down the floor for the third time.
> Despite his two years in the United States, Tomas's English ability was still negligible. His crew, all African-American, spoke no Spanish, and so they communicated through bits of Pidgin English and gestures, relying on their knowledge of the task at hand to get the job done. Like a flock of birds in flight, they moved silently, working in tacit synchrony and coordinating rhythm and tasks. First Tomas hosed, then two men soaped while the other squeegeed the floor. After about ten minutes Tomas was called out of the room, and while he was gone, the men's dance continued. One hosed the floor; the

other two squeegeed the water into the corner drain. (August 10, 1992, field notes, Development)

This scene was like other work assignments, variously described by crew supervisors and case managers as "working in the warehouse, mixing paint . . . receiving, shipping, and also dealing with customers." "Work on the first floor, cleaning, stack the cabinet[s], work in the fifth floor with the trash." "Doing general maintenance of the building, sweeping, cleaning." Like Blake Danner in Helena's Life Skills class, a few clients had been given work experience slots with Development's clerical and administration staff, and a few were able to access work experience off site with area nonprofits. Because of budget constraints however, these outside placements were drastically reduced in 1992 and 1993.

During my time at the agency, two contracted training programs, one to train security guards and the other to train individuals for jobs as radon inspectors, were the only deviations from Development's supported work. In each case, Development staff members obtained training manuals from a company or industry representative, trained a few participants who had tested into the cohort, and took responsibility for job placement, along with the clients themselves. While one security company gave the trainees priority when hiring (although it didn't assure employment), employment in the radon industry was far less certain. In fact by the end of the radon classes, the agency failed to place any of the trainees into jobs in the radon industry. Instead, nine of the original ten trainees found employment in telemarketing and housekeeping. Only one man, Richard Price, remained. Proud that he had taken the GED test during his tenure at Development, Richard was awaiting his scores and networking to find a job when we talked. He was relying on Catherine Peace, a consultant at Development, to help him find work, but had not yet received feedback from this contact or from a radon company.

By official definitions, Development's work experience had been successful in preparing welfare recipients for the workforce. Between 55 percent and 60 percent of its 1992 graduates found employment at wages averaging $6.44 an hour, a rate substantially higher than the state-mandated goal of 50 percent placement in jobs that pay at least $.75 more than minimum wage. More importantly, 75 percent of those men and women placed in jobs, or 30 percent of Development's total training participants, were still in their jobs after the ninety days required by the state. The project had been acclaimed by state monitors as one of the best TN projects statewide and was awarded a Governor's Achievement Award in 1991. In practice, Development's training mirrored the findings of a 1984 evaluation of the demonstration phase conducted by Manpower Demonstration Research Corporation (MDRC). During my research at the agency, its most vocal supporters were men and women with few options outside the project.[1] As the next section illustrates, they included ex-addicts who found work at the agency and women whose clerical training and subsequent employment at Development afforded them a long-sought-after sense of self in the workplace. But Henry, Ruth, and many of their colleagues were conflicted about their own successes. Despite their time at Development, they knew they still lacked the technical skills and certification needed to become competitive in the labor force, and over time, they became increasingly angry that they hadn't been able to acquire either at Development.

THE SOCIAL ORGANIZATION OF WORK

After every training cycle, Development hired a small percentage of the trainees to work permanently in one of its several on-site businesses. Men and women clamored for the opportunity to stay at Development; trainees talked with admiration about graduates who had been fortunate enough to be offered full-time jobs as office assistants, training supervisors, kit assemblers, or warehouse workers. By my arrival in 1992, eighteen, or 40 percent of Development's forty-five full-time employees, had first participated in the agency's training. Referred to as "roll-overs" by DPW case managers, these men and women had been at Development from a period of less than one year to longer than ten years, and their salaries ranged from $4.50 to $6.00 an hour.

In spite of the envy of their juniors, Henry Thompson and Ruth Fallows soon realized that no matter how long or how hard they worked in Development's Educational Kits Department, they would always be seen as less than. But it was not the work itself that defined their status positions at the company. According to a management consultant at Development, work in the kits department

> requires attention to detail. No box can be overlooked. Maybe they [the graduates] take those skills for granted. They aren't looking at what they do as skills. They are more responsible in pressure times and there is pressure. That's also something everyone can't do. And in kits they have several different kits and a lot of different materials in each one. It's not like assembly line work. (Catherine Peace, consultant, Development)

Ray Smith, the kits department supervisor, was responsible for developing work assignments. But Henry and Ruth organized and accomplished that work in collaboration with the other women in the department. They divided tasks, prioritized activities, and completed them as they saw fit. In fact, for the former welfare recipients, Development was a place where, as Ruth explained, "No one's looking over my shoulder." In fact, none of the work at Development, providing clerical support, weatherizing area houses, supervising work crews, or assembling educational kits, was more routine than most jobs. None was assembly line; none was separated into discrete activities in the fashion of classic Taylorism.[2]

It was not the work, but the social organization of that work that defined Henry's and Ruth's status at the company. Through a two-tiered system, Development divided its employees into salaried and hourly positions that were differentiated by pay and benefit packages. Salaried staff included the agency's managers, counselors, and support staff, who were hired either in response to a newspaper ad or through social contacts with the executive director. While race and ethnicity were often signs of this higher status, they were not the sole markers. Instead, difference was constructed through a melding of characteristics. For counselors, many of whom were African American or Puerto Rican with at least a bachelor's degree, education was high on the list. But not all salaried employees had these educational credentials. Other men and women, ethnic whites from the nearby neighborhood, were friends of Bill Perkins, Development's founder and director. They had what social scientists call *social capital*, and social capital (it) went a long way at Development. French anthropologist Pierre Bourdieu (1997, 51) defines *social capital* as "the aggregate of the actual or potential resources which are linked to possession of a durable network of more or less institutionalized relationships of mutual acquaintance and recognition—or in other words, to membership in a group—which provides each of its members with the backing of the collectively-owned capital, a 'credential' which entitles them to credit, in the various senses of the word." At Development, this "durable network" had been developed through informal sports contacts that webbed around the agency's director. Dick Jones, business manager in the company's Archives Department, coached Bill's son Andrew in football. Helen Anderson, Archives' office manager, explained that her son also "played football with Andrew. I met Dick that way, and Bill." Ron Duncan, the systems coordinator, "played golf" with Bill, who had been his golfing coach at college.

Like the counselors, the credit of these salaried staff members translated to:

Chart 1.2.   Development's Personnel Policies

SALARIED WORKERS
- 6.67 hours/month accrued paid vacation
- tuition reimbursement of up to $600/year
- three paid administrative leave days/year
- ten paid holidays/year
- leaves of absences for disability/maternity, military, personal, paternity, bereavement, and jury duty
- paid health insurance for employees, spouses, and their children age nineteen and under
- paid life insurance and an accidental death policy
- participation in a pension plan

HOURLY WORKERS
- no vacation
- no tuition reimbursement
- no paid leave
- ten paid holidays/year
- no paid leave

- paid health insurance for themselves after one year on the job

- paid life insurance after one year

- participation in a pension plan
- a quarterly bonus based upon attendance[*]

---

[*]The quarterly bonus was awarded as follows:
— Individuals with 100 percent attendance received a $200 bonus;
— Individuals with a 99–98 percent attendance received a $160 bonus;
— Individuals with 97–96 percent attendance received a $120 bonus;
— Individuals with a 95 percent attendance received a $100 bonus.

- 6.67 hours of accrued paid vacation each month,
- tuition reimbursement of up to $600 per year,
- a maximum of three paid administrative leave days per year,
- ten paid holidays per year,
- leaves of absence for disability/maternity, military, personal, paternity, bereavement, and jury duty,
- paid health insurance for themselves, their spouses, and their children age nineteen and under,
- paid life insurance and an accidental death policy,
- participation in a pension plan.

Ruth and Henry, on the other hand, brought only their welfare recipiency, inner city residence, and lower-class status to Development. Those characteristics hadn't translated into much of value. They and the other sixteen men and women who arrived at Development via its training program, as well as nine other African American and Puerto Rican employees, had hourly positions, a subordinate rank confirmed both in their daily interactions with supervisors and in their biweekly pay checks. Categorized as hourly workers, these twenty-seven men and women earned a starting wage of $4.25 an hour with benefits or $5.50 without. They were granted no paid sick leave or vacation, were not eligible for a leave of absence for any reason, and did not receive tuition reimbursement. (Chart 1.2 contrasts the benefit packages of Development's two categories of employees.)

JUSTIFICATION

While official justification for this wage and benefit schism was difficult to obtain, unofficial explanations abounded. They all addressed perceived abilities or lack of abilities. James Taylor, Development's Human Resource manager, talked about the hourly workers in terms that echoed British anthropologist Victor Turner's work on liminality. Liminality, as Turner (1974, 232) wrote, is a state in which one "becomes ambiguous, neither here nor there, betwixt and between all fixed points of classification." To Taylor, hourly workers were in an undefined place; no longer clients, they were also less than professional, responsible employees. "I don't know if hiring former clients is a good idea," he explained.

> They do well, but often backslide. They never lose the feeling they're clients. Sometimes I think there should be a third stage. They just get comfortable here; when they get too comfortable, they start sliding back. (James Taylor, Human Resource Manager, Development)

He argued that since hourly employees were still unfinished, they required a separate status, with policies that encouraged and reinforced appropriate workplace behavior. Bill Perkins, the company's director, held a not dissimilar image of the hourly employees. He explained,

> You always have folks who are still fragile. As to work, with self-respect, they're still fragile. Sometimes they get here working, feel good about themselves, feel they can do more than they can. It's like me, as golf coach, trying to recruit kids. They think they're great, but they're not. It's maintaining that balance. Their expectations exceed capabilities. Sometimes, you're so into the client, you forget about the employees' needs and development. (Bill Perkins, Director, Development)

Perkins could justify Henry's and Ruth's lack of full worker rights by arguing that they were neither ready nor able to assume full worker responsibilities. As Development's patriarch, Perkins saw himself as balancing employees' expectations with their shortcomings.

This discourse about former welfare recipients had followed Henry and Ruth from training to work at Development. It echoed at the uppermost levels of management where decisions about the organization of training and work were made. Managers, relatively free with their comments about the hourly employees they supervised, tended to frame all former welfare recipients as inexperienced, with neither work histories nor commitment. Ray Smith, Ruth's and Henry's boss in the kits department, openly asserted that "eighty-five percent are here in a job; they wouldn't last in a job anywhere else." A small, weatherworn man in his late fifties, Ray was more at home in the urban garden he had carved out of an abandoned lot behind the old INCLINE CARPET building than in the kits department itself. But while he rarely visited the warehouse operation, he didn't hesitate to offer his read on the problems he experienced with his employees. "Did you see my sign?" he asked, alluding to the sign he had fixed to the time clock announcing that any employee arriving more than fifteen minutes late would not be allowed to work that day. Smith declared,

> You can't come in here at ten or leave at two without telling me why. This is not a country club. They go to the clinic during work so they don't have to pay the doctor twenty-five dollars, but then they lose forty-five dollars of work. How do they think I do it? They have two fifteen-minute breaks and half an hour lunch. You can arrange just about anything over the phone.
>
> The number one problem is latenesses and absences. That's one of the things our mission is to correct. If you can get someone to come five days a week and on time, that's a bonus. This place is a little loose. I won't stand for any belligerence. They expect leniency. They're minorities, they're poor, this is a training project. They think you're in a spot. I don't feel that way. We need to limit the amount of nonsense. Discipline is good for people; they enjoy it. One of the problems, it may be a language barrier, when you tell them to do something they say okay, they nod, but what you get is half between what you want and what they think you want. What you get is somewhere in between, slap dash and half ass. (Ray Smith, kits department supervisor, Development)

Ray was a tough man, as he proudly proclaimed, who had worked hard all his life, and he expected the same from those around him. In his eyes, his hourly workers demanded, rather than worked for their due, a posture that signified both laziness and irresponsibility. Within this manager-construed framework, monthly bonuses were offered as an inducement to help "fragile folks come [to work] five days a week and on time." Almost in unison, Ruth's female co-workers in the kits department explained how Development's bonus system worked.

> Every ninety days, if you're staff and hourly and you're here and not late, you get two hundred dollars. If you're absent once, they deduct twenty dollars [from the $200], but I don't really know, they take out some amount. They even take out taxes. And if you're late for four times they put it as an absence. They get really hot if you're late or leave early. But the bonuses are good. They come in handy. (Edith Jenkins, Noreen Diaz, Maria Lopez, kits department, Development)

With salaries averaging $4.50 an hour, the women looked forward to the extra money. Not openly internalizing the message of the bonus system, they were only concerned that the bonuses were issued too late to get the bank before it closed for the weekend. "They won't give us the bonus checks on time," Edith complained. "Bill takes his time [signing the checks]. We can get them [only] after twelve."

Conceptualizations of Development's hourly employees as lacking both work ethic and work experience were supplemented by a somewhat less harsh portrayal concerning a lack of self-esteem. In a conversation with Helena Gay in the wood paneled office she shared with three other counselors, Helena asserted:

> You have to think about people who work at a place where they don't get benefits. Maybe low self-esteem, no high school diploma. Someone else wouldn't settle. Even like the secretary. She has a lot of skills. I ask her why don't you apply for another job. She says no, it's nice here. People don't think that they can do something else, or that they can learn a lot more. (Helena Gay, counselor, Development)

Joan Chance, a city worker who managed a homeless project that was housed at Development, agreed with Gay's appraisal. African American herself, Joan's comments are a reflection of economic status rather than race.

> People who stay at Development are too insecure about their own capabilities to look for another job. People here have low self-confidence. They don't think they can do anything else. (Joan Chance, Homeless Project Manager, Development)

Yet despite these psychological analyses, decisions about salaried and hourly employees were neither totally humanitarian nor completely arbitrary at Development. They were instead financially convenient. The agency would not have been able to find and secure counselors had they not been paid livable wages and assured adequate benefit packages. Bill's friends and social contacts occupied other salaried positions, and he felt the need to be fair to them. However, people such as Ruth and Henry were expendable. They came to Development from the welfare office in cohorts of fifty, three times a year, and members of each cohort were always begging for jobs. If Ruth or Henry left the company, finding warm bodies to fill their vacated positions would not be difficult.

EXCEPTIONS TO THE RULE

There were a few exceptions to this pairing of former welfare status to low wages and minimal benefits. Three graduates of Development's supported work program, Juan Martinez, the warehouse manager, Donna Hastings, a bookkeeper, and Enid Castro, Development's receptionist, had been granted salaried status. While specific rationale for their more valued standing differed, like their salaried colleagues, social capital also played a part in each of their stories. Juan, Donna, and Enid each had an advocate who advanced their position within the company.

Juan Martinez had his own way of explaining his rise at Development. Born, educated, and employed as a teacher in Puerto Rico, Juan was in his late forties when we first met. He carried himself with the composure of a mature Latin man. Juan explained,

> In Puerto Rico I was an assistant manager in a supermarket. I also was a schoolteacher. First I was a teacher. I got a license. Because I'm a diabetic, I thought a job in the supermarket would be a more relaxed job. Something happened in my family, forced me to come here. My son died, he was sick nine years ago, and the doctors said there was no cure. We thought we'd come here to see. (Juan Martinez, warehouse manager, Development)

Juan registered with the welfare office when he arrived stateside, and his case manager sent him to Development as "a volunteer." "I stay six months," he explained. "I do a good job here. They thought it was a good idea to hire me."

I was a reliable man. I was here every day. They don't have to be on
my back. Don't have to keep telling me what to do. Only tell me one
time a week to do something. (Juan Martinez, warehouse manager,
Development)

Bourdieu's notion of capital is again salient in Juan's story, but it was
his cultural, as much as his social capital, that justified his status.
According to Bourdieu, cultural capital is "legitimate knowledge of
one kind or another" that is valued in a particular setting (Jenkins
1992, 85). Juan's bachelor's degree and teaching experience gave
him the kind of cultural capital that was honored at Development
and with his skills, experience, and attitude, he knew he would be a
valued employee. Juan had also been a tough negotiator, accepting a
position at Development only after management's third offer. But
also important to Juan's story was his friendship with James Taylor,
the agency's human resource manager. Taylor provided the social
capital Juan required. As Taylor explained, "Juan become salaried
mainly because he just said I can't do this job on an hourly salary. We
based his salary on his previous position. I didn't ask. I just made the
decision."

Donna Hastings, an African American woman with a rounded figure and halo of frizzy hair, had a somewhat similar story. In her late
forties, Donna had participated not in Development's supported
work, but in a CETA-funded program for displaced homemakers.[3]
She explained that Development had on occasion received funds to
run training programs for target groups other than TN recipients.
"Most of us had kids, and now we needed to get into the work
force," she continued.

The training was for clerk typist. When we came in, we had a teacher
who taught us how to learn the typewriter. Every two weeks one person was in finance. The woman there, Dottie, would show us how to
do the time cards, payroll, a lot of paper work. (Donna Hastings,
bookkeeper, Development)

Donna was well liked during training, and once hired, she acted as
surrogate grandmother to the younger staff members. She sent each
a birthday card for instance, according to a schedule she carefully
maintained. As an employee, she also pursued additional training,
relating a story that was different from that of her peers.

Once I came here work wasn't familiar. My boss suggested I go to
night school or take a class. I got a certificate, I don't remember the

name of the school, it's at Fifteenth and Oak. They gave me the basics of setting up balance sheets and the rest Mike [Smalls, the supervisor in accounting] will tell us, or he'll set it up and we'll fill it in. By
working with him, I get a sense of what to do. (Donna Henderson,
bookkeeper, Development)

But Donna's relationship with her supervisor, Mike Small, Development's comptroller and the director's best friend, was at least as important as her training or her newly forged workplace friendships.
Mike's assertive advocacy undoubtedly helped her cause. With his
support, Donna built up the social capital that salaried employees
required, and over her ten years at Development, she quietly slipped into that more secured status.

Enid Castro was the anomaly here. A Puerto Rican woman in her
early twenties, Enid did not have the mature stance of either
Donna or Juan. Wildly dressed in brightly patterned Spandex with
one of an array of exotic hats, from fedoras to Moslem skullcaps,
covering her razor shorn hair, Enid always made a striking appearance in Development's front office. None of the hourly workers
knew exactly how Enid had acquired her salaried status. Ruth and a
few of the other women credited her appearance. "They must have
liked her looks," Ruth contended bitterly. But more likely, Enid's
status could be explained by a combination of her appearance, her
bilingualism, her newly earned GED, and her ability to do a fair job
as receptionist. With no prior work experience, Enid had had little
capital to spend when she arrived at Development. "In eighty-
eight I dropped out," she related. "I dropped out in grade twelve,
five months left. Until ninety when I came here, all I wanted to do
was watch soap operas." When her case manger at the welfare office
gave her a referral to Development's training program, Enid had
been dangerously close to the precipice into which many poor
teenagers in the United States stumble.

I got here through the welfare office. I didn't have kids. I could work.
They put me here. I was lazy when I started working here. I had to
psych myself up. But that's a thing of the past. That was a sad thing,
but I'm over that. (Enid Castro, receptionist, Development)

Upon arrival at the agency, her path also diverged from that of her
inner-city colleagues. The majority of Enid's training had occurred
as part of an informal relationship with Miriam Velez, Development's former receptionist. Miriam had guided and encouraged Enid
through what the Russian educational theorist, Leonid Vygotsky,
called the *zone of proximal development*, that space through which we

need a teacher or more skilled colleague to guide us. Miriam's assistance in helping Enid conquer her initial fears of the agency's telephone system is a good example of this learning process. As Enid explained,

> I was terrified of these phones. Miriam was training me when she was the receptionist. They ring so much. I was nervous I would lose a call or I wouldn't take an important message. Miriam helped. She explained what to do. She showed me how to take notes to remember who was on which line. (Enid Castro, receptionist, Development)

Enid also attended formal training sessions on the practicalities of clerical work conducted by Mary Spencer, the wife of Development's lead counselor and a secretary at the local community college.

> In the class they told us always have a pen and pad ready. We was taking a clerical class; Ben's wife came in to teach it. She just teaches you about a lot of stuff. . . . When a need comes up, she would come. Someone in the back, maybe James, heard people were being kept on hold on the phone too long, about ten minutes. So Mary, Ben's wife, came in to give training on the phone. (Enid Castro, receptionist, Development)

While even this small deviation from Development's basic supported work model required extensive negotiation with the agency's director, Spencer eventually arranged the workshops and facilitated one every six months. She taught

- basic telephone and office skills, so they know how to answer the telephone and to ask a caller whether he or she wanted to hold, to call back, or to leave a message;
- basic punctuation and things like the abbreviations of the names of the states;
- basic letter writing, as in how to set up a letter (Mary Spencer, secretary, local community college)

Furthermore, Spencer asserted, "They benefit from having a real teacher to ask questions, to talk with." Albeit short in duration, the workshop, like the informal mentoring, resulted in a training experience that differed greatly from the one Development had offered Henry and Ruth. The combination of formal classes and informal on-site mentoring provided Enid with the support necessary to master the specifics of work and to progress from novice to competent receptionist. "It was this place, they pushed me. I dropped out in grade twelve, but I got my GED here." Because Enid was simultaneously challenged and supported, the sustained belief in and recognition of her potential translated into practice. She had become a good receptionist, and she was proud of her work.

But in addition to this more focused training, Enid's "looks," and her other attributes, Enid also had an advocate in James Taylor, Development's human resources manager and her supervisor. He pushed her salaried status through bookkeeping without the director's knowledge. Like Donna and Juan, Enid's story is an indication that at Development, capital was not confined to a particular characteristic. It was instead a melding of variables that included educational levels, contextualized abilities, and especially social contacts.

PERCEIVING INEQUITIES

Other than these few exceptions, most men and women who moved from welfare to work at Development found themselves in the bottom of a peculiar, bifurcated work situation where two pay and benefit packages and two sets of workplace rules reflected employees' histories and routes to Development. Henry, Ruth, and their hourly colleagues were not unaware of the inequities that were packaged as personnel policies. Henry asserted, "Everyone tells me I'm crazy for working here." As illustrated in field notes of June 1992, Henry's critique was widely shared in the kits department:

> During one of my first conversations with Ruth Fallows and Barbara Wilson in the kits department, they talked, in grudging terms, about their wages and benefits. Barbara pulled a personnel booklet from her desk. "I say if we been here a year he [the director] should give us a week vacation, personal days, sick days. This place is ring around the rosie. They just say gimme, gimme, gimme. They don't give you nothing. They don't thank you." I asked if she perceived a difference in the treatment of hourly and salaried employees. Barbara replied, "A big difference." Ruth offered, "All we're asking for is sick days. They [salaried employees] take off anytime they want." Barbara continued, "I've never been anyplace where they have two different policies." (June 19, 1992, field notes, Development)

While the quality of health-care coverage and the low wages were the topic of their constant complaints, the lack of paid sick days posed a real problem for the hourly employees. Noreen Diaz developed asthma during my later visits, and her illness was a harsh reminder of the difficulties incurred by the lack of paid sick leave.

> On one of my visits to Development's kits department, I was told that Noreen was in the hospital. Ruth told me Noreen had pneumonia, but she had been to work yesterday. "She looked dead," added Henry. I asked if Noreen would get paid sick time during her hospital stay, since at this point she had worked at Development for three years and was titular supervisor of the kits department staff. "No, no paid sick days." Ruth responded, "That's why she didn't go [to the hospital] earlier. She had to pay her rent."
> Nearly two weeks later, Noreen was back at work. Attaching labels printed with the words "Roving Robots" on cardboard boxes that were stacked six high against the wall, Noreen explained that she had had bronchitis, which developed into asthma, and so now had to be careful about dust in the warehouse. Noreen had asked Bill to be paid for the two days she was in the hospital, particularly since "I left from here," as she asserted. "But he said 'no, there's nothing I can do about it.' I told him why? We all work here." (August 31, 1993, field notes, Development)

Barbara Wilson also found herself testing Development's policies for hourly workers. Barbara had been the first official employee in the kits department. "The kits was originally a sideline," explained Ray Smith, her supervisor.

> I had two helpers, and we used to do it in our spare time. Barbara came in as one of the first folks up there. She really was a fireball. I said okay, that's good. Edith was next; they worked together pretty good. (Ray Smith, Kits Department supervisor, Development)

But despite Barbara's four years with the agency and her reputation as "a fireball," her job was put at risk when she became pregnant. Smith explained Development's maternity policy as "No maternity leave. Getting pregnant is her responsibility, her decision. If and when she decides she's not pregnant, she can come back. If there's a job, she's welcome back." While I had a hard time believing that Smith would be so casual about a relatively senior employee, Barbara had assumed the worst. "When I go out, I'll have to go on welfare," she told me. It turned out she was right. There wasn't a job waiting for Barbara after she delivered her daughter that August. Josefina Burges, brought in as Barbara's replacement earlier that spring, remained in the kits department in her place. In an attempt to get her job back, Barbara brought an Equal Employment Opportunity Commission (EEOC) suit against Development. She did not win. Bill Perkins, Development's director, explained his version of the events:

> EEOC, we were sued through them for sexual discrimination, one of the women went out for a pregnancy, was out for a longer period of time, so we had to let her go.
>
> The EEOC investigator told me, "Even with something like this, this place is great. I know you don't understand." I don't. I don't understand why I or any company has to go through this. The investigator told me, "You're not going to like this, but I need more information. You have to show me there's a male who is in the same situation."
>
> I asked other hourly workers, has anyone been hurt for a long time and not been brought back? How about so and so? We found someone, ten years back. They said that was okay. They sided with us. It wasn't racial or sex discrimination. She clearly got advice from someone. What are folks trying to do? (Bill Perkins, director, Development)

When I stopped by Barbara's apartment after her unsuccessful litigation, it was empty. Her phone had been disconnected, and she had left no forwarding address. Barbara had been right all along. After four years of work at Development, the company's policies left her jobless and with few alternatives to welfare.

The lack of avenues for redress was another confirmation of Ruth and Henry's lowly status at work. Barbara was forced to resort to the legal system because no official channels existed through which she or her colleagues could be heard. They were never invited to company meetings; they had no regular contact with Ray Smith, their supervisor; and after James Taylor, the director of Human Resources, left for a position with another agency, they had no one to whom they could turn. Even Development's director confessed:

> If you asked me about one area of improvement, the toughest thing for me is having meetings, getting the staff together. I told the architect we need more space for meetings. Now all we have is the office out there and the cafeteria. That area should be stronger. Now I meet weekly with core staff, and I hope the news percolates down. (Bill Perkins, director, Development)

Perkins attributed the silencing of worker voices to a lack of physical space for meetings. In practice, however, no avenues for redress existed because Development was his company, and all news, money, decisions, and power moved one way, down from him. The agency had been his vision, and it grew from his imaginings. "This is Bill's company; I couldn't change Development," asserted one hourly worker. Bill himself took to saying, "I used to think of myself as father. Now I think of myself as grandfather." Blending his role of employer with that of parent, Perkins assumed and enjoyed a patriarchal stance. Yet in the same way that the training program and social organization of work were rationalized as providing these "hardest to serve" men and women with the structure and support they needed as new workers, at Development this paternalism had become yet another justification for separating staff members and underpaying the men and women who had been on welfare in the past. By positioning former welfare recipients as hourly employees who required more parenting, more guidance, and more explicit positive and negative reinforcement, Bill rationalized and maintained existing gaps between the haves and the have-nots.

NEGOTIATING AND NAMING

Henry's expectations, like his job performance, had been high during his first few months at Development. After only a few weeks on the job, he had been awarded fifty dollars for his creative re-use of boxes. During my first trip to Development, he talked with pride about the cost- and time-saving innovations, pre-packing items or re using inverted boxes for instance, that he had introduced into the department. When I asked him about his creativity he explained, "That's what I said on my resume, cost-saving innovations, and they bought it."

One year later, Henry's initial expectations and optimism had dis sipated, and he settled into a state of muffled despondency. He had been hired as kits department supervisor, but the supervisory role and its respective status had still not materialized. Henry began to talk of himself as "stock boy" and "messenger boy," roles that he felt vastly minimized his capabilities. The following is from field notes of July 1993:

> The temperature was a sweltering ninety-five degrees when Henry and Ruth took their first break of the afternoon to smoke on the stoop outside. Pat Prescott, their newly appointed boss, walked past them as they smoked. Unhappy about a management change in which they had no voice, and in hindsight feeling loyal to Ray, the supervisor whom Pat had displaced, Henry and Ruth seemed to scowl at Pat without looking directly at her. Hostility was thick in the air.
> As she passed, Pat said, "Excuse me, I don't mean to interrupt

what's going on here, but have you seen Ray?" She added that she needed to talk with Ray about the printing of a brochure, and that she had seen him a few minutes ago, but couldn't find him now. Henry responded that they hadn't seen him. Pat, looking directly at Henry now, asked, "Can you do me a favor? Can you tell Jean [a management consultant working temporarily at Development] that Sister Eileen is here? She's in a meeting and I think it's better if you interrupt them than me." Henry, with a note of incredulity in his voice, asked, "You want me to give her a message?" When Pat responded with, "Yes please," Henry looked up at the sky, seemed to wince, and repeated "Sister Eileen?" for confirmation.

After Pat disappeared around the corner, Henry asked rhetorically, "Now I'm the messenger boy?" Ruth suggested, "Just say you forgot," and Henry continued, "I ain't tellin' her nothin'. Let her fire me. I ain't her messenger boy." After venting their frustration, Henry and Ruth were quiet. They sat smoking their cigarettes, the smoke curling above their heads like visible manifestations of their anger.

About five minutes later Jean walked by. Ruth elbowed Henry and whispered, "Tell her." Henry gave Jean Pat's message and explained to me that he hadn't realized Joan was in the nearby garden. He thought she was in her office.

As we walked back into the old factory building after break, Ruth commented that Pat would probably fire them "for insubordination or something, anything to deny us unemployment." Muffled silence ensued, continuing inside as Henry filled boxes with BBs and Ruth sat, staring into space. I commented on Henry's work and about his expectations of supervising the department. He responded, "I thought so too. No, I'm just a stock boy here." (July 29, 1993, field notes, Development)

A year after his date of hire, Henry's role as supervisor had still not materialized. He began to deal with dashed hopes and workplace conditions he believed to be both inequitable and disrespectful by grumbling and giving Pat the cold shoulder.

AN IMPERFECT FIT

As Henry discovered, the workplace imposed official roles that were not always a perfect fit. In fact, there were plenty of ill fits at Development. Development's hourly employees brought previous experience to their work at the agency, yet most struggled openly to maintain a sense of self in a context in which they felt minimized and even denigrated. Like Henry and Ruth, it was in their conversations and everyday practices at work that the hourly workers' feelings about themselves and their work were manifested. It was in their actions and talk that their resistance to the low-status positions from which they could not escape was made most visible.

Basing their assertions on the demographics of Development's Archives Department, at times the men and women framed the agency's policy bifurcation as racism. The Archives employees were all salaried, and the question regularly raised by hourly employees was, "Why are they all white?" Barbara Wilson asserted that the Archives Department "will only hire you if you're white." Enid Castro, who had been initially hired on a temporary basis to input data in the Archives Department, had her own story to confirm Barbara's allegation.

> "It's a long story," Enid began. She was at her desk in the reception area as she narrated, and Ronnie James, hired from training as the agency's maintenance man, periodically stopped his sweeping to add related details. Enid continued, "I don't want to say anything, but it's something racist. I was working up there when they got accounts from two new companies. Dick [the supervisor of the Archives Department] wanted more input. I was at the computer all day long. They'd give me grief when I had to go to the bathroom. The other three people up there, at least two of those guys were men from the training program. They gave us all a lot of trouble. Dick is very sarcastic. When I was done, they wanted to have me fired."
>
> Ronnie interrupted. "Some of the guys from the back were working up there, moving boxes. They had to sign out to take a break or go to the bathroom. There's something goin' on there."
>
> "What Ronnie told you, that's true," insisted Enid. "They had all these guys sign in and out. The girls on the first floor too. And they didn't even work for them and they had them signing in and out. And they [the salaried employees] don't have to do that upstairs. They're like a little family up there. You can ask anybody in here, they'll tell you the same thing. They think they're better than everyone else."
>
> Ronnie teased Enid that she might be sent back up to Archives to work. "I wouldn't go back up there for anything," she responded. "It's not worth it to me. Ben [a counselor] won't send clients there anymore." (June 22, 1992, field notes, Development)

Although allegations of racism or sexism, as Barbara asserted in her EEOC suit, were often contested by individuals in power, they were regularly voiced by those who were denied access to resources and opportunities. The accusation of racism, however, was not necessarily as straightforward as either Barbara or Enid believed. The Archives Department employees were certainly all white, and the department's exclusionary practices may have appeared to be based upon race. But being white was not sufficient to secure salaried status at Development. Henry and Ruth were both white, yet they, like their colleagues of color, found themselves locked in low-wage, low-status positions. In practice, race combined with other factors to open or close doors at Development. Yet race had become a password for inequality and inequity, and the company's African American and Latino hourly workers asserted that the agency's separate and unequal policies must have had something to do with the color of their skin.

Against this background of segmented employee policies and perceived racism, Development's hourly workers grumbled and engaged in what social scientists Michael Adas (1986) and B. J. Tria-Kerkvliet (1986) call everyday resistance. Because Development came to mean different things to different people, this resistance was enacted unevenly across employees, reflecting a match or mismatch of supervisors' beliefs about an employee's potential, an individual's perceptions of his or her own capabilities, and the opportunities afforded in the workplace. For Enid Castro and Donna Hastings in clerical, for instance, Development was a safe hold, a haven in a storm of speculation and possible loss. For Henry Thompson, Ruth Fallows, and Barbara Wilson in the kits department, however, Development was a place where racism was encouraged and classism justified an inequitable social order. The reality was that in practice, Development was two different workplaces, one in which employees were respected and supported family members, and another in which workers were neglected and mistreated. It was an organization in which women without direction or workplace experience had been guided and supported during training and work; where they had been afforded an opportunity to learn and use skills in challenging situations. As Enid Castro asserted, "It was this place; they pushed me." Development was also an organization that treated men and women in recovery with respect, tolerating their relapses, and perceiving them as more capable than they themselves expected or perhaps even deserved. Their success at staying straight and sober varied, yet all six men and women in recovery approached work at Development with optimism. "They put me in the right direction here. I like them for that," explained Andy Johnson, a weatherization technician who had lost a previous job as a registered bricklayer to drugs. Ben Spencer, Andy's case manager during training, added that sometimes "Andy relapses. One time he asked me to keep his [salary] check for him, because he knew if he had the money he'd mess up." Sam Jessup, the crew supervisor who had been recruited by Development straight from his inpatient treatment program, asserted, "This is like a family. People feel they belong, people who don't belong anyplace else." For Andy, Sam, and their colleagues in treatment, Development was a place where they came to be respected and liked. In their experience, professional respect was rare, and well worth the tradeoff of a lower salary.

Henry, Ruth, and the other women in the kits department had also come to Development with high hopes. As previously mentioned, Henry had been hired to be department supervisor, and Barbara Wilson, his African American friend and colleague, had started working in the kits department with the hope of moving downstairs to a clerical position. Just twenty-one then, she had worked in several area department stores after finishing high school, but these jobs had all been temporary. Barbara had wanted a real job, but real jobs were scarce for young black women, even those with a high school diploma. She had initially welcomed the opportunity that Development provided; four years later she was still counting rubber bands and bagging batteries upstairs with Ruth and Henry. She complained, "I thought that this was motivation, that you'd move downstairs. But I think you have to be beautiful and dress nicely." Like Henry, Barbara was disappointed, frustrated, under-utilized, bored, and convinced that managers perceived her as far less capable than she either expected or deserved.

In keeping with this argument, the agency's Puerto Rican employees moved from one point on the continuum to another depending upon the congruity of their expectations about work, their beliefs about their own capabilities, their perceptions about fairness, their actual position within the social organization of the workplace, and their mood on any particular day. Tomas Lopez, for instance, participated in Development's training with his wife Maria, and was later hired as an hourly worker at the company. Tomas certainly recognized the frustrations encountered by his colleagues. But given his limited English skills, Tomas was content with the responsibility and compensation he received as work-crew supervisor. Josefina Burges, Barbara's replacement in the kits department, was similarly content. At twenty-one, Josefina had only worked for two years in a cafeteria in Puerto Rico. Arriving on the mainland just six months before our first meeting, Josefina's English was limited, and with no education past a diploma from her high school in San Juan, she knew she was fortunate to find steady employment of any kind. Noreen Diaz fell somewhere in between complaisance and frustration. Noreen's English was far better than Josefina's, but she had come to the company with only a seventh grade education and three years' work experience at a toy factory twenty-three years ago. Noreen cer-

tainly grumbled about workplace conditions, yet her complaints
were muted by her appointment as the department's personnel supervisor. She proclaimed with some pride that, "I'm the supervisor
here, the boss." Even though this titular responsibility, a reward for
her focused and steadfast work, did not come with salaried status, at
times it mediated her complaints.

Maria Lopez, Tomas's wife and Ruth's and Henry's colleague in
the kits department, had a story of interest here. During her training
at Development, Maria had been assigned to provide clerical support to the Human Resources manager, and after training, she was
hired to work as an assembler in the kits department. When we met
one year later, she was clearly unhappy working in that capacity. On
Fridays she would complain, "Soon it will be Monday and that's
what I hate," adding, "I hate to come here. . . . I hate thinking about
coming back to work on Sundays." But several months later, midlevel supervisors recognized her talents and potential, and promoted
her to the position of office manager. The promotion transformed
Maria from a disgruntled and stoned-faced assembler to a challenged and stimulated secretary. I noted the change in the following
field note entry:

> I saw Maria in the hall today, two months after her promotion. She
> showed me a resume that she had just finished typing for a client, and
> talked about revised job search plans. She had a job interview at
> Brand and George, a center city law firm, a few days ago. "They of-
> fered me a job. I talked with Tomas [her husband, who is also em-
> ployed at Development]. He's looking for a job. I want to wait to see
> what he finds. He told me to wait a little while, since it's not an emer-
> gency. He may get something up this way, then I'd be going the op-
> posite way. . . . I've learned a lot here. I do all the reports. . . . Ben [a
> counselor] keeps telling me I need to move on, get a better job, but I
> think I'll wait. I'm thinking about working part time and going back
> to school for accounting. That's what I want to do." Maria smiled as
> she continued down the hall toward the copier. (July 29, 1993, field
> notes, Development)

Maria remained Maria, but her demeanor changed dramatically. Her
new status at work gave her such a positive sense of self that even
when she was offered a better paying job with a law firm downtown,
she decided to remain at Development. Maria's upgrade was unique
at the agency, yet the shift in her connection to and her sentiments
about work illustrate a fundamental relationship between social
structure and personal agency that played out at Development.

These matches and mismatches related to the ways men and women negotiated the company's social organization. The women working as clerical support, as well as hourly employees in recovery for substance abuse programs, voiced virtually no complaints about company policies. Ruth, Henry, and their colleagues in the kits department, on the other hand, made little effort to hide their dissatisfaction.

RESISTANCE

Resistance took several forms in the kits department, and most were equally indirect. It was the women in the department, rather than Henry, a self-professed workaholic, who slowed their work pace as a means of taking ownership of a situation that was in other ways outside their control. Many days Ruth and Barbara worked only as much as they felt was absolutely necessary, spending the remainder of their time reading magazines, newspapers, or paperback books, making telephone calls, and polishing their nails. Since they essentially supervised themselves, they were able to monitor their own speed, basing their pace upon the seasonal demands of the work. Used during the school year, the educational kits required hurried assembly during the month of September. The dismantling and inventory of returned kits parts, however, were unhurried and could be spread over the rest of the year. This seasonal schedule, coupled with a lack of direct supervision, allowed the women to slow down or speed up work as they chose. This slowing down was an ambiguous phenomenon. If it was resistance, it was a subtle form, reflecting a time-cost analysis common among low-paid workers who intuitively adjust their work speed to their level of pay. At times, trainees at Development functioned in a similar fashion. Watching a training crew hand sand a hardwood floor during a morning assignment, for example, I noticed an African American woman sitting out her stint. Fully cognizant of my status of guest rather than supervisor, she didn't hesitate to explain, "I already worked my $4.25 worth today," referring to her daily stipend as a trainee in Development's TN program. The time of day was not as important as her calculation of a work to pay ratio. In her mind, two hours on her knees rubbing the wooden floor light with sandpaper was an equitable exchange for the $4.25 stipend she would receive for the day's work.

The agency's supervisory staff had a very different take on worker slowdowns. Ray Smith, the kits department supervisor, viewed Ruth and Barbara's work pace as problematic. He related:

The kits were originally a sideline. I had two helpers, and we used to do it in our spare time. Barbara came in as one of the first folks up there. She really was a fireball. I said okay, that's good. Edith was next, they worked together pretty good. The problem was the work slowed down. Noreen came in, she's sort of a tattletale, said people weren't working. Unbeknownst to them I had a key to the door upstairs. When I came up Noreen was working. Barbara was doing her nails, and Edith was listening to music.

I told them take three days off. I was surprised that they didn't quit. It was a slap in the face. (Ray Smith, Kits Department supervisor, Development)

Resistance, by its very nature, is not necessarily recognized by those in positions of relative power. While fundamentally oppositional, anger, frustration, or disappointment are often indirect and unfocused and may appear to be more like personal deficits than informed expressions of dissent. In attributing a slow work pace to poor work skills, Ray came to an accepted conclusion. He saw what he saw. Instead of working, the women were painting their nails and listening to music. Lacking a holistic framework from which to view the women's practice, Ray relied on what he knew best, Development's framework of positive and negative reinforcement. In this case, his response was punitive; the women lost three days' pay.

The resistance of hourly workers was also embedded in language. Ruth, Henry, Barbara, and Noreen grumbled and gossiped about one another, about the salaried employees, and about Bill Perkins, Development's owner. At times they commiserated with one another, bemoaning their fate and quoting vulgarisms about their lives. "Life's a bitch," asserted Noreen as we were getting off the elevator one day. "And then you die a fuckin' asshole. And you can say I said that," she added for my benefit, priding herself on her philosophical bent. In fact, most of the hourly employees, as well as several of their salaried colleagues, complained about Development's salary levels, personnel policies, and social organization. TriaKerkvleit writes at great length about this use of language as an expression of opposition.

The broad notion of everyday resistance means that language usages that would not qualify as avoidance protest might be forms of everyday resistance. Jokes, puns, and other play on words, verbal characterizations, and even swearing and complaining safely in the confines of one's family and friends can reveal disgust and indignation with the way things are compared to how they should be even though the latter may only be dimly conceived. (TriaKerkvleit 1986, 109)

In the kits department, verbal laments about "the way things are" were constant. "This place is shit list, no personal days, no vacation after one year. We need a union," complained Barbara. "It's not fair here, no paid vacation, no sick time. We're staff; everyone should be treated the same. I think it's prejudice," added Ruth. "Tim [a newly hired training crew supervisor] is crazy to work here. He did a good job, but you won't hear it. No one gets credit for anything here," Henry asserted. He later added, "Write down that we're hard working and Development doesn't recognize that." Perhaps the most telling use of language as dissent was the hourly workers' regular use of the title "Massa" to refer to the director when he was out of earshot.

Development's hourly employees also carved out a niche of equity for themselves by engaging in what management referred to as petty theft. Regularly browsing Development's homeless project, a space in the old warehouse building where the city stored used clothes, furniture, and other items that had been donated for the area's homeless population, Ruth, Barbara, and the other women sometimes purchased items at minimal cost or were given an item for free. But they also took items without permission. One week Carla Whitaker, a new employee in the department, told me she found a dress in the center that still had a $180 price tag on it. The next week the women took brand-new baby furniture that they said would serve as perfect gifts for pregnant friends and relatives. A few days after the furniture find, however, they were caught taking some clothes from the distribution center. Noreen rationalized the pilfering by linking the petty theft with subsistence. She explained, "If they gave to me, I wouldn't just take for me. I'd take for people who need it. They collect for people who need, but they should give to us before throwing things away." Given their own needs, the availability of items, and their perceptions of inequities, none of the women had trouble justifying their actions in terms of taking what they deserved. Anthropologist James Scott relates this behavior to what he calls "bread and butter issues."

> To require of lower class resistance that it somehow be "principled" or "selfless" is not only a slander on the moral status of fundamental human needs. It is, more fundamentally, a misconstruction of the basis of class struggle, which is, first and foremost, a struggle over the appropriation of work, production, property and taxes. "Bread and butter" issues are the essence of lower class politics and resistance. Consumption, from this perspective, is both the goal and the result of resistance and counter-resistance (Scott 1986, 27).

Surviving on $4.25 an hour, Development's former welfare recipients were just one rung above what might be called quiet desperation. They dealt with "bread and butter issues" on a continual basis, and like all individuals living in poverty, they found ways to make do. Finances forced Henry to live with his mother and Ruth to live with her brother Lenny. Edith Jenkins, renting a single room in a halfway house, complained that she couldn't afford a refrigerator and so had no way to store her food.

> "I'm tired of puttin' the margarine on the windowsill," she complained. She saw one she wanted in Development's homeless project for which Joan Chance, the project's manager, had quoted her a price of $75. Reflecting that she might pay in installments, Edith asked us if $75 was a good price. Noreen suggested bargaining. "Tell her 'I'm trying to improve my life. I don't have too much money, with my rent and bills.'" Noreen added that she hadn't had gas for two years in her apartment. She just got the gas turned back on, but now her stove was bad. She asked Joan, the center manager, if there was one at the center, but she didn't have any money to pay her and didn't think Joan would allow her to take a stove without paying. (January 6, 1993, field notes, Development)

The boycott of Development's annual picnic, however, was anything but a "bread and butter issue." In fact, the men and women compromised "bread and butter" in their resistance to managers' efforts to create a sense of workplace gemeinschaft.

> The company picnic, held at the end of August in a picnic grove outside the city specifically designed for office picnics, was one of Development's main social events of the year. Described by supervisory staff as an important event for the staff, Development paid for the food, picnic fees, and employees' salary for the day, and provided transportation. Yet despite the expense that the company incurred, not all employees were equally anxious to attend the function.
>
> One week before the company picnic, Ruth and Henry told me they were not going. Ruth hadn't gone the previous year, and she said she would take the day without pay if that were the only alternative. "I have something to do that afternoon anyway." Henry commented cynically, "Bill wants us to be a big happy family." (January 6, 1993, field notes, Development)

The director may have thought of Development as "a big happy family"; Henry and Ruth used their limited autonomy at work to disagree. Refusing to participate in the agency's social events became a metaphor for their unwillingness to pretend to be part of a family that treated them as poor relatives.

AGAINST EACH OTHER

They also turned their anger inward, cutting the deepest schism between Spanish and non-Spanish speakers. For most of my time at the agency, the divide across ethnic lines manifested itself most conspicuously in what I called the great radio war. Barbara presented the non-Latino side of the story. "They always speak Spanish all the time with their loud Spanish music which I think is so loud." I saw the playing out of the war for the first time during one of my earliest visits to the department.

> Sitting with Henry and Ruth in the large warehouse room that was the kits department, we talked about work and training experiences while the portable radio on the table blared Latin salsa. During most of our conversation, Noreen, Josefina, and Maria, the department's three Puerto Rican employees, worked together on the far side of the large room. When I asked about this separation and if the department was divided into two work crews, Ruth commented, "Not necessarily. They're just always together."
>
> Ruth excused herself and upon returning to the room told us that the other women were "in the back," referring to the distribution center on the other side of the warehouse. She turned off the radio and with it the loud Latin beat, an action Henry greeted with a firm "thank you." Ruth observed, "That quiet sounds wonderful."
>
> A few minutes later Josefina returned to this main room and Ruth commented under her breath, "Oh, I thought we could have some quiet." Prompted by a "huh?" Ruth assumed Josefina hadn't understood, and so she repeated herself. Josefina however, had no further response. She did not turn the radio back on; instead she left the room. (July 24, 1992, field notes, Development)

The radio war subsided only when Ray decreed that Walkmans, with their obligatory headphones, would be the sole source of music allowed in the department. But the frustrations of the non-Latinos continued, translating to grumbling about the Puerto Rican women's English-language ability and their "greasy" Spanish food. Ruth and Henry regularly objected to Josefina's minimal English, and Barbara complained that "Josefina, she don't understand. I don't know how she got hired. When Ray tells us something, they [the other Puerto Ricans] have to translate." To which Ruth added, "People like that should stay downstairs in GED." While the friction between Latinas and whites never completely disappeared, the division became less salient when the us/them paradigm shifted from one defined by culture and language to one that separated Edith Jenkins from the rest of the staff. The change was catalyzed by Edith's theft of money she had collected for Barbara's unborn baby. Edith had taken the lead role in the collection, approaching each employee with a request for a donation. Yet the money never made its way to Barbara.

> When I visited Barbara at her house, she told me Edith spent the money she had collected for Barbara's baby. "She mustn't have no conscience. How could she do somethin' like that?" Barbara asked. I told her I was surprised because I thought Edith was her friend. "She comes at eleven at night, when I'm asleep. Wakes me up to borrow money. She's on drugs, that's why she did it." (July 29, 1992, field notes, Development)

With no official channel to vent their frustration and anger, the kits department employees redirected the animosity they had shown one another to the new convenient other, and Edith's transgression made her convenient. Although she attempted to make restitution by making a partial payment of twenty dollars to the staff, Edith continued to assume pariah status at the workplace until January, when after working for the company for four years, she abandoned her job and disappeared from the neighborhood.

COOLING OUT

"Cooling out," as documented in sociologist Burton Clark's (1960) classic study of students in a community college, was another way of maintaining a sense of self. During my time at Development, individuals' emotional shifts, from initial excitement about new opportunities to ensuing disappointment and resignation, were apparent. Henry is a good example of this "cooling out." As mentioned earlier, when I first arrived at Development, he had just received a creativity award for his idea to re-use cardboard boxes, thus avoiding the purchase of new boxes and the costs of hauling the old boxes away. When we talked several months later, he was decidedly less enthusiastic.

> Seated at a table at one end of the room, Henry used a graph, drawn in marker on a piece of paper that he had taped to the table, to cut pieces of string. He looped string against marks on the graph, cut one end, and then the other. I watched him, fascinated by his intuitive math abilities.
> I asked if he had submitted any more cost-saving ideas to management, and he quickly responded with, "Why? I don't get appreciated anyway." Although "they made quite a big thing of it," he asserted that the $50 bonus that accompanied the creativity award was only a tiny fraction of the tens of thousands of dollars Development had

saved from his idea to re-use cardboard boxes. "That's the last time I'll say anything. It's not appreciated," he said with resignation in his voice. (January 6, 1993, field notes, Development)

Another piece of Henry's "cooling out" was his adoption of a "wait and see" philosophy.

> According to Henry, he and his colleagues in the kits department each received a $100 to $150 Christmas bonus, along with an hour-long speech delivered by Bill, the agency's director. I commented on what seemed to me to be relatively generous Christmas gifts. "Sure, but the big guys, like Mike, he gets $2,000," Henry claimed. "Bill holds up an envelope saying I've got $10,000 here for all of you. Sure. He said he was going to help the hourly workers, better benefits, more money. Nothing we haven't heard before. I'll stay awhile. See if anything happens." (January 6, 1993, field notes, Development)

Ruth voiced a similar philosophy. "There is nothing to do right now. But I don't mind, I think of this as like a break." With few, if any, alternatives on the horizon, "wait to see" may have been frustrating at times, but it was also self-sustaining.

The hourly workers occasionally attempted to take direct action to improve workplace conditions, but as Barbara asserted, "People are scared that they'll lose their job or stuff like that." In a previous effort to organize over an earlier release of paychecks, they found an advocate in James Taylor, the director of Development's Human Resources Department. Edith explained,

> James is my buddy, he'll listen to you and help. He'll try to do something. When we wanted our checks at twelve o'clock, we told him. He spoke to Bill; he talked to him and Bill said it was okay. (Edith Jenkins, kits assembler, Development)

Although this advocacy approach was somewhat effective for both the individual and the group, James's departure from the agency a few months after I arrived exaggerated the divide between hourly employees and upper management. He left a vacuum that undoubtedly contributed to the morose spirit that became increasingly apparent during my last several visits to the site.

STAYING

Given their dissatisfaction with life at Development, it was difficult to understand why these hourly workers didn't look for other jobs.

But contrary to assertions about low self-esteem, they remained not because they were happy at the company, but because in the postindustrial America that they occupied, jobs were scarce even for those with abundant academic credentials; good jobs seemed inaccessible to those without. Ruth and Henry might have been offended by the treatment they received at Development, saddened by their dashed hopes, and dissatisfied with their lot, but they were clear that no other options existed outside the agency. As Ruth asserts in the following conversation, "It's depressing being rejected."

> A hot, Friday afternoon, payday at Development, I sat with Ruth in the kits department as she counted thermometers and rubber banded them into groups of twenty. Edith approached, sitting down in the chair next to Ruth's desk, and told us she was depressed. Her paycheck was already spent, and she hadn't even received it yet. Ruth nodded in agreement, explaining that she was upset this morning when she realized how small her check would be.
> "Why do I stay here?" she asked rhetorically. I told her that's what I was wondering. "Looking for another job is depressing," she responded. "Filling out applications, being rejected. It's depressing." (July 24, 1992, field notes, Development)

The lack of other options forefronted everyone's rationale for staying. There were "no other jobs. It's hard to get a job in the city," Ruth explained. Although they had participated in a program that had the goal of "develop[ing] good work habits while simultaneously building up employment credentials necessary for . . . successful competition in the labor force" (Maynard 1984, 213), Henry and Ruth had earned neither credentials nor certificates at Development. Fewer than half the Kits Department employees had either their high school diplomas or an equivalent. Noreen explained that for people like her, looking for a better job was a frightening proposition. "People are afraid they won't have what employers ask for, high school diplomas and all sorts of things," she declared. "Sometimes it's hard, particularly since you're often asked for a high school diploma, and other things you don't have. So that you're afraid to approach employers since you know you won't have what they want." Noreen had only gone to seventh grade some twenty years ago in Puerto Rico, and while she occasionally talked about working on her GED after work, she never found the time. It didn't help that Development's Learning Center was only accessible until 4:30, and according to Noreen, "four o'clock to four-thirty [the time between the close of the Kits Department and building lock-up] is a very short time."

For Noreen, as for other low-skilled workers, the world outside Development was full of risks. An often related anecdote about Miriam Velez, Development's previous receptionist, and her experience with work outside Development's walls served as a warning of the dangers of this uncharted terrain. While the story circulated back to me several times, the first time I heard it was when Enid Castro explained why she stayed at Development. According to Enid,

> Development's convenient for me because I know what I got to do; I know my tasks for the day. Almost everybody says that you should start looking for a better job. But Miriam got a job for twice as much, and it didn't work out. Her boss was gay. She had to deal with that. She was working with Women in Transition; it just turned into women into transition. She lasted there three or four weeks, left the job, and then what? No job, but she had rent to pay, bills to pay. (Enid Castro, receptionist, Development)

Miriam took a risk, and according to her friends and colleagues, it brought her nothing but financial and personal insecurity. Given the harsh and even hostile nature of the job market, the risk of leaving Development was too great. Ruth explained, "There's no work out there. You'll go on unemployment and welfare." They had already been there; they knew that unemployment was short lived and that welfare was inhospitable at best. According to economists Barry Bluestone and Benjamin Harrison, these men and women made what was the most rational of economic decisions. They stayed.

> Workers with jobs will seldom sacrifice them in order to move even when other locations offer higher wage rates or lower unemployment. In economic terms, staying rather than moving is a "normal good"; unless there are extraordinarily compelling economic reasons for moving, people generally prefer to remain where they are. (Bluestone and Harrison 1982, 192)

Despite their frustrations, Development was safe in its familiarity. As they told me again and again, Development was "convenient. . . . I know what I got to do."

So they stayed, their long-term retention evident in the agency's termination rates. Over an eighteen-month period, only two of the twelve employees who left Development had come from the welfare rolls, and neither had left for another job. Edith Jenkins resumed the crack habit that she had tried to kick throughout her four years at Development. "Drugs," she confided. "I went back since you been here. I have some character problems I can't get rid of. I believe there's a God, so he'll take care of me, one way or another." By January 1993, drugs had won the battle. One afternoon Edith walked off the job and didn't return. Over her four years at Development, Edith's tenure had been consistently tumultuous. Her personnel file was "huge," she explained, putting her hands six inches apart to indicate its size. "If I stay here until the year two thousand, I won't be able to lift it. I've been on probation two or three times. I'd understand if they'd fire me. I'd say okay, you're right. I'll get my things." Yet even with her "huge file," Development's managers had trouble giving up on her. Ben Spencer, Edith's case manager when she was in training, was well schooled in matters of substance abuse. He explained Edith's final departure.

> She left, couldn't take the pressure. I was always on her. She couldn't do it, just walked away. Bill [Perkins, Development's director] liked her. I don't know why. And I had to tell Ray [Smith, the kits department supervisor] to fire her. She was gone a month, and he still hadn't fired her. I said fire her. (Ben Spencer, case manager, Development)

Barbara Wilson also left, but as mentioned earlier, her departure was not of her own volition. Despite her attempts to return to Development after giving birth to her daughter, her leaving quickly became a paradox to her colleagues in the kits department. They mourned her absence, yet talked of her "escape" with envy. "She's lucky, she got out," Henry confided. "Everyone told us not to work here during training. I thought different, but we learned soon. And now we're stuck."

Stuck in a job that offered neither access to a career ladder nor equitable working conditions, Henry was simultaneously frustrated with Development's lack of opportunities and disconcerted by his own inability to access a better-paying job. Choosing to remain, Ruth, Henry, and most of their hourly colleagues found voice, sanity, and solace in their grumbling, slowdowns, and rebuffs. They "struggle[d] to affirm" themselves in what they perceived as "unfair treatment and conditions" (TriaKerkvliet 1986, 108). A useful metaphor in thinking about the experiences of these former welfare recipients at Development is that of wearing a coat that was too large, too small, or a perfect fit. The social identity imposed at work was one of many coats that Henry, Ruth, Edith, and Barbara wore throughout their lives. The fit was not always guaranteed, and they did what they could to gain some comfort. Although linguistic, ethnic, and class differences impeded Enid's and Donna's assimilation into the agency's management structure and culture, they were comfortable with the clerical roles they occupied, and their feedback on Development was positive. Respected, well liked, and challenged, the identity jackets they wore were a good fit. The fabric was a bit thin and didn't always keep out the cold, but they were happy with both the size and color.

Henry and Ruth, on the other hand, were far less satisfied with the ways they were perceived and treated at work. Their work roles felt confining and their skills were undervalued, yet they knew they had no certification with which to purchase a more respected identity at another workplace. They had to be prudent to avoid the cold. They kept their tight coats, and they shivered and complained. They pulled at the sleeves, tore at the material, patched torn seams, commented with jealousy about the garb of their salaried co-workers, and stole shreds of material to patch their coats. To continue with this metaphor, despite their efforts they got no warmer.

FULL CIRCLE

At Development, each "expression" of hostility, to use anthropologist Michael Adas's term, was costumed as something else, and in the eyes of their superiors, was seen as something deficit. In hindsight however, I realized that the men and women's oppositional behavior had always been in plain view. When I arrived at Development, the uneasiness expressed by James Taylor, Development's human resources director, concerning the company picnic was the first hint that something wasn't right. From my field notes of January 1993:

> James Taylor explained that just before last year's staff picnic, several hourly employees approached him to ask how he thought Bill Perkins, the agency's director, would feel if they didn't attend. Upset by their query, James told them that if he were Bill, he'd fire them for not attending. "And I'm the low key one," he added.
>
> Later, he conjectured that perhaps their hesitancy was related to a discomfort they may have felt in leaving the neighborhood. (January 6, 1993, field notes, Development)

But Taylor's version was only one side of the story. It was only after spending several months with men and women who found themselves in opposition to the social identities imposed upon them in the workplace, that I began to identify these interactions as resistance. Yet rather than perceiving the hourly workers as dejected and angry, those in positions of relative power described them as incomprehensible, odd, or self-punitive, attributes that provided continued rationale for Development's supported work and its patriarchal workplace policies. The apparent reticence of Ruth, Henry, and their colleagues to leave Development, their lack of involvement in social activities, and their work slowdowns were confirmation, in the eyes of their salaried co-workers and supervisors, of their peculiarity, frailty, and perhaps their deep-rooted indolence.

We come full circle in this pedagogy of deprecation. Development's model of deficiency was enacted in messages embedded in its training program and the social organization of its workplace. In both training and work, the agency treated the former welfare recipients as "less than." When men and women resisted official labels of worth in their everyday practices at work, their resistance was perceived as confirmation of beliefs about merit and potential. In the process, imposed identities became real and Development's model of deficiency was justified and sustained.

Chapter 2

Church Hall and Single Mothers on Welfare

They don't react the same way. They're not too educated at all. I spoke with one girl; she said she thinks I was cursing at her when I was encouraging her. Their language is very street language. I can't think of the word now, but she thought I was cursing her.

—Ann Miller, licensed practical nurse, Church Hall

Without the workshops, [the women] most likely would not be hired, since they don't know how to present themselves or adequately fill out an application.

—Debra Waterman, trainer, DPW's Job Development Unit

I really like it here. It's very nice here. But I think we deserve more respect. We each do important things. If we keep their bottoms dry and warm, it's less work for you. I think nursing is racist. This is the only place I've worked, but I think nursing is racist. We do more work for less money.

—Katie Simon, nurse assistant, Church Hall

GETTING THERE

Dina Haskell and Joan Ford worked as nurse assistants at Church Hall, a for-profit nursing home nestled in a tree-lined upper-middle-class neighborhood on the northern edge of the city. The facility's three-story stucco building, blacktopped parking lot with spaces for fifty cars, and outdoor patio were set back from the busy street on 4.7 shaded acres. A blue cloth banner, its large white letters spelling out CHURCH HALL LOVES ITS RESIDENTS, hung over the double glass doors of the building's canopied entryway. The neighborhood, where carefully manicured lawns encircled suburban ranch

69

and split-level houses, was a far cry in terms of distance and economics both from Development's litter-strewn streets and graffiti-covered walls and from Dina's and Joan's inner-city homes. But despite its pleasant surroundings, there were never enough applicants to fill Church Hall's nurse assistant needs, what with the round-the-clock care the facility provided for its elderly residents and the rapid turnover of nurse assistants industry wide. Church Hall's solution to this labor shortage brought Dina and Joan from the welfare office to the workplace and frames this story of poor African American women, mothers and caregivers, and their negotiation of work and children, dangerous inner city neighborhoods, and the foreign environs of the suburbs.

Church Hall embodied an often-advocated antipoverty strategy, the linking of inner-city job seekers to available jobs outside their communities. Grounded in a hypothesis sometimes called geographic mismatch, the employment strategy was based upon the belief that jobs for the unemployed were available but were located in areas neither known nor accessible to inner-city dwellers. In this particular story, the Department of Public Welfare (DPW) assumed a matchmaker role for the nursing home. DPW case managers publicized Church Hall's job openings to welfare recipients on their caseloads, and the Department's Job Development Unit offered a five-day orientation to work to prepare applicants for interviews at Church Hall. Dina and Joan were among the more than 140 women who had applied for the nurse assistant positions and the twenty-one who had been hired through this arrangement with DPW.

Joan Ford, an African American woman with freckled cheeks and black hair pulled back tightly in a knot, was thirty when we met. Dressed in her neatly pressed nurse assistant uniform and talking with her arms wrapped around her body as though to keep herself warm, she explained that she alone supported her two young sons, occasionally by resorting to welfare, but mostly by working in area nursing homes. She had experience in four other facilities, dating back to her teenage years. "I have a lot of experience, all in nursing homes," she explained. "I went to school to be a nurse assistant. PTC . . . for six months.[1] I was a straight A student, on the President's list." When Joan had completed training, she quickly discovered that because her studies at PTC hadn't come with state certification, they didn't translate into a job. Finding herself back on welfare with a $3,000 tuition loan to repay, she welcomed her case manager's referral to Church Hall. "It upsets me that I found out on my own about going to PTC. I didn't know no better," she volunteered. "The best I can do is start paying on that loan."

At twenty-eight, Dina Haskell was also a single mother, in her case, raising three small girls, ages two, four, and eight, on her own. A tall, thin, African American woman, Dina moved constantly as she talked. Crisply uniformed with her Church Hall name tag prominently pinned to her chest, she made beds, changed residents' diapers, and emptied catheters, and her work history reflected this industry. After high school, Dina had attended a state university down South for one year and then worked in a series of jobs, including receptionist in a doctor's office and bookkeeper at a furniture store. When her first daughter was born, she juggled two jobs, as a part-time private duty nurse and a claims processor for an insurance company. But after her second daughter was born, she went on welfare and soon found herself in a downward spiral of poor single motherhood, with no income, too many children to support, and for a few months, without a place to live. "And then I end up having another baby. . . . But when I decided to go back that's when I said all right, now I need a trade." Like many of the women at Church Hall, Dina had been thrust into the role of caregiver at an early age. "My grandfather got sick first, and no one had the stomach to actually change him and all those things, and I ended up doing it," she explained. "And so then I thought about work in health care." After making her decision known to her DPW employment training counselor, Dina waited nearly a year for an opening in a nurse assistant course. She explained:

> They had this new thing; they started this new program. You have an ETP (Employment Training Program) worker and I said okay, find out who my ETP worker is. This is what I want to do. So at the time they didn't have nursing, they had computer class or food services or . . . I said no, I don't want to do nothing else but be a certified nursing assistant. They said we do have one class, but when I was interviewed, it was full. So I had to wait like three more months later. But then I did get accepted.
>
> It was for three months; it was hard to a lot of people. It was hard because of the fact that you had an English class, you had a math class, and you had everything based on nursing. You didn't just have as far as a nurse assistant. You had everything based on if you were actually being a nurse. (Dina Haskell, nurse assistant, Church Hall)

Although she was hired immediately after training, moving off welfare was not as easy as Dina had thought. She continued:

I was hired straight from [the class] to Golden Glove Nursing Home.
I was only there six months, cause I was coming from my mother's
house. I was in the process of moving. I knew I was gonna move, but
I didn't have all my priorities as far as my kids straight. So what I did
was I resigned, 'cause I was taking out a lot of days, but I just went
out and resigned and told them what I was experiencing. And if I
wanted to come back, I'd let them know. So they were fine with that.
(Dina Haskell, nurse assistant, Church Hall)

Her case manager at welfare referred her to Church Hall. "Church
Hall," Dina explained, "You passed the workshop class, and then
Church Hall would pick up the ones that were most experienced
with home health care. I was a chosen one, and I started working
here."

SINGLE MOTHERS AND WELFARE

Church Hall was owned by a health care consortium, which had purchased it (along with four area hospitals), as an investment from Ron
Driver and his family during the economic boom of the late 1980s.
The Drivers were from the city; they had owned Church Hall for
nineteen years. Ron had practically grown up at the facility, and he
had stayed on as director after it changed hands. Driver oversaw 150
people, all non-union, who were divided across nine areas (i.e., nursing, physical therapy, social service, laundry, office support, food
service, activities, environmental service, and maintenance),[2] two
floors, and four wings. Of the 130 members of the nursing staff,
ninety were nurse assistants, seven were registered nurses (RNs),
and thirty-three were licensed practical nurses (LPNs). Together
they provided a home for 240 residents, 90 percent of whom were elderly and ailing from Parkinson's Disease, Alzheimer's, strokes, or
other ailments. It was Dina's and Joan's job to attend to the residents' most basic needs. They made beds, helped with toiletry,
moved people to lunch and back to bed for naps, got them up, fed
them dinner, and readied them for bed at night. They comforted
them and liaised with family members. They listened to residents'
complaints, settled disputes, and documented their activities and
physical well-being. As a staff physician explained, "The aides are
the backbone of this place. They're the ones that lift the residents,
wipe their heinies. It's different from a hospital, and each wing is
different."

I learned early on that Dina, Joan, and nearly all the women that worked as nurse assistants at Church Hall had been single mothers at one time in their lives, and that the identity defined the way they were perceived and treated by both DPW case workers and their supervisors at the nursing home. The concentration of single mothers at Church Hall stemmed at least in part from cultural assumptions about work. The job of nurse assistant itself has long been gendered. Women self-select into nurse assistant positions, and men select out. As Debra Waterman, DPW's trainer, explained, "We had some men in there. Of fifty-one trainees, one man did show." But this convergence of single mothers at Church Hall was also an outcome of the state's implementation of the Family Support Act of 1988, the federal government's previous solution for reforming welfare. Grounded in the belief that the welfare system fosters dependency among poor women, the Family Support Act was designed to prevent long-term reliance on Aid to Families with Dependent Children (AFDC), the welfare category for needy individuals with one or more dependent children under age eighteen. The Act increased federal funding for job-training programs, child care, and transitional medical benefits, and its Job Opportunities and Basic Skills Training Program (JOBS) required state and local governments to offer education, training, and employment services to individuals most likely to become long-term AFDC recipients. As Irene Lurie and Jan Hagen (1993, 147) explained in their evaluation of the JOBS program, "To meet the targeting requirement [for JOBS services], recipients in the target groups are given priority in the queue to leave the enrollment pool." Target groups were comprised primarily of women:

- individuals receiving AFDC for any thirty-six months of the previous sixty months;
- custodial parents under age twenty-four receiving AFDC who have not completed high school or worked less than six months in the previous twelve months;
- a member of an AFDC family in which the youngest is within two years of being ineligible for AFDC. (County Assistance Office 1992, 50)

Each state tailored JOBS funds to best meet the needs of its constituency, with most money funding academic and job-training programs that averaged six months in length. The local welfare offices in this state utilized a portion of the funds to organize units focusing specifically on job development, training and resources, literacy education, and teen parenting.[3] DPW's Job Development Unit (JDU) was given the responsibility of developing links with area employers; its staff both responded to employers' requests for qualified applicants and canvassed for job openings through direct mail to employers. Church Hall was one of more than fifteen companies with which the JDU collaborated in 1991 and 1992. In this translation of policy to practice, the Family Support Act's focus on single mothers connected Joan and Dina to available nurse assistant positions at Church Hall and set the stage for the construction of an identity of single mother on welfare in both training classes and at work.

Mothering was indeed a large part of both Dina's and Joan's lives. They woke early to drop children at friends, relatives, or at day care centers before work, worried about them during the day, and conducted endless arrangements for their after-school care. Joan described the morning with her two small boys. "I have to get up at four-thirty in the morning to get the kids ready and be out the door by five-thirty. That's why I took three to eleven [shift on] weekends only," she explained. She relied on mothers, friends, and community agencies to negotiate the demands of being a full-time mother with a full-time job. So did Lynn Brown, Joan's colleague at Church Hall, who was raising a six-year-old boy and eight-year-old girl on her own.

> I have to get up now at four-thirty. I leave out of the house at five-fifteen. I have to get me a car. My children are in school. My mom helps me. Now I have to drop my kids off at seven o'clock. (Lynn Brown, nurse assistant, Church Hall)

The Sisters of Mercy were part of Dina Haskell's extended family. When Dina found herself homeless in the 1980s, the church had helped her move into temporary housing.

> I was on welfare at the time and I met a church. Not a church, a shelter, Project Rainbow. I know a lot of the sisters there in the shelter, and they really gave me a sense of direction. They watched my kids, I got them in their day care, and while I went to school, they would watch them and welfare would pay. The Sisters help me now too. The Sisters of Mercy. They help me with my rent and food. (Dina Haskell, nurse assistant, Church Hall)

In assuming nurse assistant positions at suburban Church Hall, however, the women's identity of working mother underwent a drastic mutation. Race, economic status, and inner-city origins amplified gender. Dina and Joan were black, urban, and poor; they had children, but they had no husbands. Both DPW trainers and supervisors at Church Hall fused these characteristics into an image of African American women, irresponsible for giving birth to babies they couldn't afford, and fierce from life in a dangerous inner city. They were different, alien. "They don't react the same way," asserted a licensed practical nurse (LPN) at Church Hall.

> They're not too educated at all. I spoke with one girl, she said she thinks I was cursing at her when I was encouraging her. Their language is very street language. I can't think of the word now, but she thought I was cursing her. (Ann Miller, licensed practical nurse, Church Hall)

"Their lives are different from ours, unfortunately," explained Nia Gates, the facility's personnel officer. She was referring to the fact that while 95 percent of the facility's supervisors, the Licensed Practical Nurses (LPNs) and Registered Nurses (RNs), were whites from working-class neighborhoods bordering Church Hall, 90 percent of the nurse assistants, including Dina Haskell, Joan Ford, and Lynn Brown, were African Americans from the inner city. According to Maryann Clark, Church Hall's director of nursing, "Out of the ninety nursing assistants, we may have ten assistants who are white, and that's the highest percentage we've had in twenty years." On the other hand, all seven RNs and all but two of the thirty-three LPNs were white.

At Church Hall, the distance between city and suburbs was vast. In terms of geography, Dina and Joan traveled to and from the facility's suburban location by bus or car pool, often spending two to three hours a day in the commute. In terms of culture, the span often seemed too wide to cross.

TRAINING TO COMPENSATE

To both DPW's job trainers and the supervisory staff at Church Hall, these differences, of geography, race, and economics, came to signify a lack of training and work experience, and DPW's five-day orientation to work and Church Hall's subsequent certification training were designed to address these deficiencies. Like Development's model of supported work, both training and work attempted to fill the women with the "legitimate knowledge . . . the language use, manners and orientations/dispositions" that was required by the market place (Jenkins 1992, 85).

In practice, the assumption that Dina and Joan lacked knowledge of the workplace was contradicted by Church Hall's job announcement and by the women's real-life experiences. According to the job order (Bostwick 1992), Church Hall sought applicants with

- one to two years of nurse assistant experience in a nursing home within the last five years;
- the ability to read and write clearly and concisely for documentation purposes;
- good physical health and clean personal habits;
- a high school or GED graduate preferred but not required.

State certification was considered a plus, but was not required.

The women's experience consistently met or surpassed these criteria. Joan had both work experience and training. Dina had even more. She had attended a state university for a year before completing a three-month nurse assistant program and working as a nurse assistant at Golden Glove nursing home. Despite the women's experience, however, DPW's five-day orientation to work functioned as compensation for a perceived lack of knowledge of the workplace. According to Debra Waterman, DPW's employment trainer, the seminar was her prescription for the women's financial problems. Referring to notes she had made earlier on a piece of typing paper, Waterman, a small white woman, serious in her dark business suit and tortoise shell glasses, described the five days of training. Some of the changes Waterman sought were cosmetic, the kind of suggestions offered to all new job seekers (e.g., appropriate clothes for a job interview, best responses to interview questions). But also implicit within DPW's training paradigm was a priority on the employer's perspective. During the first day, Debra and Joan sat around the conference table in DPW's wood-paneled training room and identified barriers and strengths in a manner reminiscent of Development's counseling sessions. The next four days of the orientation moved from introspection to packaging and marketing; the women completed real applications, talked about references, and practiced interviewing skills. Waterman stressed that each of these activities was designed to encourage the women to reflect on the employer's perspective. In practicing interview skills, for instance, she provided sample questions and asked, "Why this answer? Would the answer encourage the employer to hire you?" And in a final exercise of the session, the participants acted as "the employer." "You're now an employer," she described. "And you choose from the ten people who apply for a position as a mail room clerk. How do you weight their responses? How are you selling yourself?"

To Waterman, the practical experience that Dina, Joan, and the other women brought with them to her seminars was inconsequential. Employers represented official knowledge, and she assumed the role of employers' emissary. The educational theorist Michael Apple posed what he called a *contentious question* that is of relevance here. Writing about the ownership of knowledge in schools, Apple (1993, 46) asked, "Whose knowledge is of most worth?" Within DPW's training paradigm, the answer to Apple's question is easy. After all, according to Waterman, "Without the workshops, they [the women] most likely would not be hired, since they don't know how to present themselves or adequately fill out an application."

For Waterman, the five-day orientation was a time to both inculcate norms and package the women according to employers' specifications. For the women, however, the orientation was a jump-start back into a job market from which they had had an extended absence. Despite the minimal space allotted for their own voices, they remained positive about Waterman's sessions because she reconnected them to work. Joan commented, "It was good . . . it was all right. A week training class, workshops, how to apply for jobs . . ." Dina concurred. "The class was very good. Some of the things I knew, since I went to college. But some of the things I didn't know." Donna Dixson, another former welfare recipient working at Church Hall, provided the most succinct description. "It was good, it helped me. I didn't work for a year. A long time."

Church Hall's supervisors had yet another take on the orientation; for them it was an inexpensive yet effective mechanism to screen nurse assistant applicants. According to Ron Driver, the facility's director, "People are screened much better. To try to get references on the lower level is very difficult. At least we have the screening mechanism [in place]." The screening took place on several levels. Part was self-regulatory. No one was turned away from the orientation, but as Waterman confessed, "We weed, actually they [the applicants] weed themselves out." This weeding was evident in a consistent decrease in attendance from the first to last day of each of the orientations facilitated from November 1991 through November 1992. Chart 2.1 documents the number of people who began each of the three orientations, the number who completed, and the number who subsequently obtained employment at Church Hall.

Chart 2.1. Screening Points to Church Hall

Cycle	Date of Training	Starting	Completed*	Number hired*
1	11/91	15	4 (26.6%)	4 (26.6%)
2	2/92	29	9 (31%)	4 (13.7%)
3	11/92	17	9 (52.9%)	3 (17.6%)

*Percentages are based on the total number of individuals who started each cohort.

The chart illustrates that fewer than half of the original applicants completed two of the three orientations. Some decided they did not have appropriate credentials to obtain employment, others realized they were not interested in working as nursing assistants.

Another important piece of the screening process was the interviews that Nia Gates, Church Hall's personnel officer, conducted on the last day of each orientation. As Gates explained,

> [T]he counselor who's worked with the women can tell me about latenesses, absences, willingness. At the end I go over them with the counselor, who agrees ninety percent of the time. A lot of it's desire, background, body language. I hate to use the word attitude. I hate that word. But a lot of times that willingness comes through. I've done this for a long time. You get a sense of people. You learn over the years what is reality. A lot of times the people who talk the most aren't the best. (Nia Gates, personnel officer, Church Hall)

Attendance, attitude, and desire, the talk here mirrors the discourse that surrounded DPW's orientation. Gates claimed she had a "sense of people," and that she knew when she felt comfortable with a particular applicant. At this gate it wasn't the women "weeding themselves out," but an official gatekeeper screening for character traits desirable in lower-rung workers. "I think a nursing facility is more difficult than any other facility," Gates explained. "[It's] twenty-four-hour care. You're never going to get people with a lot of education, so we've started to look for willingness." Her screening, distinguishing between the "deserving and undeserving poor" (Katz 1989), was stringent. Of the twenty-nine people who attended the session with Dina in 1992, and the nine who completed, four were hired. "They were looking for people with two years' experience," Dina explained. According to Church Hall's director of nursing, the process served as an effective screen. "Usually the ladies who come through the [DPW] program seem highly motivated," she asserted. "They want to do the work. At least in the beginning."

What was not made explicit, however, was that self-screening also took place after the women began work at Church Hall. Six months after the first sixteen DPW recruits had been hired at Church Hall, for instance, only Dina Haskell remained at the facility. DPW's job developers couldn't talk about this point of departure because they conducted no followups on the women they referred to Church Hall. The JOBS program did not require DPW job developers to re-port job placements or to base their own success on the job retention of former welfare recipients. Although DPW case workers arranged funds to pay for day care, health care support, uniforms, and a month's transportation to Church Hall for Dina, Joan, and their colleagues, they conducted no followup on the women's progress, and so were unaware of the women's workplace activities after their initial date of hire. "We don't do any followup, since the contractor tells us everyone is doing well," explained the Director of DPW's Job Development Unit. In part because DPW's job developers wanted to believe that moving women off welfare and into work was enough, in part because they acted within a self-imposed paradigm that privileged the employer's voice, and in part because the unit was understaffed and worked within a limited budget, they didn't know that a few of the departed women had found work closer to home, that several others had joined health-care agencies where the hourly rates were better, or that others had simply disappeared. I discovered their absence in my initial contacts with Church Hall; however, I didn't understand the meaning of their flight until many months into my observations. Their absence also became an important part of Dina's and Joan's stories.

BLENDING IN

Within a few weeks after I came to Church Hall in July 1992, a new cohort of women arrived from DPW, and Donna Dixson, Joan Ford, and Lynn Brown joined Dina at the facility. As the most recent hires, Joan, Lynn, and Donna immediately became the new girls, introduced to life at Church Hall with slow and systematic deliberateness. Church Hall's personnel officer explained, "They have two days of training with a professional Registered Nurse (RN). They go on the floor two weeks with an Licensed Practical Nurse (LPN). They don't start with a full caseload [of patients]; they start with two patients, and they're never left alone for two weeks. Then finally they get a full caseload. If they're not state certified, they come back down for fifteen more days of training."

For these women, moving off welfare played out somewhat differently than it did for Henry and Ruth at Development. First, no one in Church Hall's management clearly remembered who came from where, and no one really cared. Arriving from their inner-city homes to Church Hall's yellow and white striped canopy entrance, Joan and Lynn merged so completely with the nurse assistants on staff that the facility's personnel officer had no record or clear recollection of which women had come from the welfare rolls. "I'd have to go back through the records and check," she offered. She added that even though some women came to Church Hall's glass double doors through DPW's initiative, others by cold-calling the facility, and others by responding to a want ad in the newspaper, "once they're here, they blend in with everyone else."

This blending was due in part to the fact that the women all came from the same place. While they may have arrived at Church Hall's doorstep by different paths, in the lush, shaded suburbs around Church Hall, they all looked the same. Most were African American, most were from the inner city, and all were poor. In an attempt to make ends meet, they lived with relatives or in subsidized housing in some of the city's worst neighborhoods. Dina and her three daughters found housing for "low-income families" with the assistance of the church. The house was "in a bad neighborhood," in Dina's words, with streets strewn with litter, walls covered with graffiti, and corners occupied by omnipresent drug dealers. Other women lived in similar circumstances. Gladys Hopkins, at Church Hall two years prior to Dina's arrival, told me that in her neighborhood she felt forced to carried a knife in her sock.

> I have to take a bus a quarter to five. It's dark. I was mugged two times. I came in with my eye hanging out. I don't know what I'll do with it there [pointing to her ankle]. In my neighborhood you have to have something to protect yourself. (Gladys Hopkins, nurse assistant, Church Hall)

A life of poverty was even more complicated when children were involved. Phyllis Hampton, working as a nurse assistant downstairs on Joan's floor, explained that she worried about her daughter all day while at work.

> I've been callin' all day to see if my daughter went to school. They took the phone off the hook. She goes to Southern High School. After

the shooting [at the school] she said she wasn't going back. It's dangerous. My sister went there. It was dangerous then. (Phyllis Hampton, nurse assistant, Church Hall)

Race intensified this economic disparity. Theirs was a different life from that of their white supervisors, most of whom had moved to the suburbs around Church Hall to escape the very inner city in which the women lived. Ron Driver, the facility's director, explained these cross-cultural relationships.

We hire a Licensed Practical Nurse, with one year of school, no management training, very little supervisory or management training. Now you say we're going to sit you behind a desk, in charge of eight to ten staff. Most people like that left the city for the suburbs when the blacks moved in. I know about that. I'm from the city. We moved out here to get away from the blacks. And then they come here, and find they're supervising blacks. (Ron Driver, director, Church Hall)

Dina, Joan, and the sixteen other new girls were all foreigners to Church Hall's white suburb. By "blending" with the other nurse assistants, their racial differences were emphasized rather than mediated, and they became a mass of objectified other, members of the indistinguishable inner-city poor.

Like DPW's orientation, Church Hall's training pedagogy was shaped by this group identity. The training was based upon the assumption that these poor inner-city women brought few skills and little knowledge with them on their long bus rides to the facility. For Church Hall's supervisory staff, this inner-city badge of difference demanded what the Brazilian educator Paulo Freire (1970) called a banking method of teaching in all of the nurse assistant training conducted on site. Since knowledge worth knowing was that represented by institutional representatives and official texts, no space was allotted for the women's local knowledge or expertise. At Church Hall, as in DPW's training rooms, information flowed in only one direction, from instructor to student.

CERTIFICATION TRAINING

Church Hall's much-prized certification training is a good example of this banking model of education in practice. The training was the facility's calling card. It was what drew Joan to the nursing home, and it's what DPW job developers cited as the value of its link with the facility.[4] Since the passage of the Omnibus Budget Reconciliation Act (OBRA) of 1987, the state requires all nursing assistants to be certified to "ensure that nurse aides have the education, practical knowledge, and skills needed to care for residents of facilities participating in the Medicare and Medicaid programs." In order to become certified, the women were required to complete the following activities successfully within four months of their date of hire:

- a seventh-five-hour training program and at least 37.5 hours of practical training under the direct supervision of a RN or LPN (The state's mandated content of nurse aide training in the state is listed in Appendix C);
- a written or oral examination for nurse assistants, presently administered by Educational Testing Service;
- a Clinical Skills examination, conducted by an examiner from Red Cross (Center for Occupational and Professional Assessment 1989).[5]

One of twenty-two nursing homes and six educational institutions citywide that certified nurse assistants, Church Hall followed OBRA's mandated course content, but was allowed to carry out the training as its trainers saw fit. Evita Gomez, Church Hall's principal trainer, relied heavily on both handouts and a manual entitled *How to be a Nurse Assistant* (Johnson-Pawlson and Goodwin 1990) in her training sessions. A few weeks after their date of hire, it was Joan Ford and her two friends Donna Dixson and Lynn Brown who attended Gomez's classes on care theory. She lent them copies of the manual, and during the six days of theory class they worked through the text, from front to back, with five other newly hired nurse assistants. In Gomez's class, the text functioned as reference, and she was navigator, editor, gatekeeper, and timekeeper. The following, from field notes of April 1993, illustrates her training strategy.

> 8:00 A.M. on day four of the theory classes, the eight nurse assistants, seven women and one man, all African American except Donna Dixson, sat around a rectangular table in the small training room. Evita Gomez, a small self-possessed woman wearing brown-rimmed glasses and a tailored suit, leaned against a desk facing the students. I sat on a metal folding chair in one corner of the room, watching, listening, and taking notes on the training session.
>
> Gomez passed a sign-in log around the table, while at the same time announcing, "Let's start, turn to page one hundred and seventy-two. Donna, why don't you start?" Joan, at the head of the table asked "what page" and Gomez repeated "page one hundred and seventy-two." Donna read aloud about arrangements in the dining room,

while the other seven students studied their own texts. The loud sound of a lawn mower competed with her reading. After about two minutes Gomez stood up in front of the desk, saying, "Okay, stop. The things that you need in the dining room, the important thing is you check the . . ." Lynn Brown filled in the space with "card." Gomez continued, "And if you don't know the resident, check the bracelet. You all in Hammond Hall[6] have a different dining room arrangement. You must make sure the resident gets the right tray. If a resident is a diabetic and gets the wrong tray, you could get in trouble. Also the nurse must be there." Cynthia Hudson, at the other end of the table asked, "the charge nurse?" But instead of addressing Cynthia's question, Gomez pointed to a chart on the wall, a white poster board with purple writing underlined in brown marker.

REMEMBER

Infection	Control
	Dignity
Safety	Communication
Privacy	Promote
	Independence

*Keep all these factors in mind when
caring for your residents!!*

She began talking about the importance of covering residents in order to avoid food stains. "If not, when residents go out in the hall, visitors will see the stains. That's very important, food stains. That's very important, the resident looks the way you want him to look." And then, ". . . When you test on Heimlich maneuver, she's going to watch for safety." Cynthia asked, "Are we going to practice that Heimlich maneuver?" Gomez answered, "in the lab," and nodded to Donna. Donna understood the nod as a signal to continue, and began to read about a resident not liking food. Gomez corrected her pronunciation of the word "frequently" and then told Cynthia, "Cynthia, you read." Cynthia responded, "I feel like I'm goin ta' sneeze and it won't come." Lynn advised her, "Just read till it comes." Cynthia then began reading about a feeder tube. After about a minute Gomez stopped her with an "okay." She wrote "gastrostomy tube" on the board and said "everyone say it." They did. Almost as an aside, Gomez explained that when feeding a bedridden resident, the head of the bed should be elevated to ensure a patient's aspiration. "Never leave a bed flat. The fluid they're eating can go into the lungs, and that's very dangerous." Tasha Simpson, across from Cynthia, asked, "That's the tube that goes into their stomach?" and Gomez responded "Right. . . . Now tell me what's the name of the position?" In unison several of the women responded "fowler." Gomez wrote "semi-fowler" on the board while saying, "Also residents who don't eat much need good mouth care." Tasha asked, "How do you spell that?" and Lynn pointed while she said, "It's on the board."

Gomez continued, "Now we have the continuous feeder. I don't want to get into that too much, because we'll get off the track." She nodded to Cynthia, who began reading about a well-rounded diet. Gomez interrupted again, saying "Okay, before you go on, I want you to look at the well-rounded diet. I want you to take note of well-rounded food groups." Donna looked up from her book and asked, "Do you want us to put their names down?" Gomez responded, "I want you to write down each group and some examples. You will be tested on it." Head down, each student began to write. (April 16, 1993, field notes, Church Hall)

Broken only by a forty-five-minute lunch break, the class continued in the same vein for the next three and a half hours. Returning from lunch, Gomez continued to lead. But instead of relying solely on the text, she showed the trainees a fifteen-minute video on food supplements and led them through the correction of yesterday's quiz aloud. She directed their practice taking a pulse and counting respiration, and they took and reported each other's pulse rate. Gomez never gave up control of the session, nor did she let it wander too far from the focal topic. Regulating the pace of the reading aloud with admonitions such as "slow down a little bit, you're reading awfully fast," she restricted what she perceived as tangential conversations or questions based upon personal experiences with something like:

Okay, let's go on. I'm sorry to hurry you, but we're on the clock. We have to cover this material today. We'll talk more about that more when we talk about the urinary tract. (Evita Gomez, nurse assistant trainer, Church Hall)

After the six days of theory, Joan, Donna, and Lynn, along with their five classmates, proceeded to the second half of the training, six days of clinical instruction on the floor. Aided by a senior nurse assistant who acted as preceptor, they were assigned the joint care of eight elderly residents. Throughout their clinical days Gomez hovered, appearing on the wing without warning, watching and correcting the women as they shaved a male resident, filed a woman's fingernails, assisted the barber, made beds, and moved elderly patients. "I have a whole check list of criteria I check them on during training," she explained. (Her check list of skills appears in Appendix D.)

According to Joan, the opportunity to obtain nurse-assistant certification far outweighed her lack of voice during training. She knew that in order to continue working as a nurse assistant, she had to become certified, yet certification had eluded her in the past. Many of her colleagues had been in the same situation. Ninety-two percent of Joan's nurse assistant colleagues at Church Hall, including all the women referred by DPW, had been employed in at least one other nursing home. Yet only nine came to the facility certified. Like many of these women, Joan had attempted to obtain her state certification by enrolling in a proprietary school and had been duped by the school's advertising. Lynn Brown, her friend and colleague, had a similar experience. She explained, "When I graduated from high school, I went to PTC Training Center. I got a certificate from that. But the paper that I had doesn't matter anywhere. It's not worth anything." Although the school's diploma was not equivalent to the state's certification, Lynn was obligated nonetheless to re-pay her school loan. It was "two thousand dollars; with interest now it's three thousand dollars," she complained.

> I wish I had been through this [certification training] before I got the loan. Well, the only thing I can do is warn other people. You see what I did, I was lazy, trying to find the easy way out. But they don't listen. (Lynn Brown, nurse assistant, Church Hall)

Their experiences catalyzed a growing public concern over proprietary schools' manipulation of low-income men and women and made Church Hall's certification training even more valuable to the women (DeWolf 1992). As Tasha Simpson, a nurse assistant at Church Hall, asserted, "Let me say this is the only place that offers training while you're on the clock." Ophelia Adams, another nurse assistant, added that not many homes in the inner city offered certification. "You have to come out to the suburbs."

Church Hall not only offered the women the opportunity to become certified, but it also covered the cost of the training, including the trainer's wages, six days' wages for the women while they were in the classroom (and off the floor), and the $105 testing fee. It is no wonder that the women were able to overlook the training's banking orientation. Through DPW's link with Church Hall, they not only reconnected to the job market after a prolonged absence, but by gaining their certification, they also guarded their place in the labor

force and protected what labor economist Lester Thurow called
their "market share."

> Education becomes a good investment, not because it would raise an
> individual's income above what it would have been if no others had
> increased their education, but because it raises his income above
> what it will be if others acquire an education and he does not. In ef-
> fect, education becomes a defensive expenditure necessary to pro-
> tect one's market share (Thurow 1975, 97).

Yet while the women's initial appraisals of the banking initiatives of
both DPW and Church Hall were positive, as the next section illustrates, their enthusiasm about the facility quickly waned. Regardless of the trainers' attempts to inculcate a version of "official
knowledge" and the women's own best efforts at receiving it, they
soon realized that they would always be perceived and treated as
though they were uneducated, unknowing, and lacking within the
workplace itself.

THE WORK

Dina's and Joan's initial comments about Church Hall were over-
whelmingly positive; they were happy to work at a facility that was
clean and where the residents were well cared for. Joan explained
that she liked Church Hall, because

> nobody's on your back, getting you to get your work done at a certain
> pace. Everyone helps here. I think this is one of the best places I've
> worked. They're not on top of you all the time. And everybody here's
> just nice; everybody has a positive attitude. If you're always pres-
> sured, it makes you want to quit.
>   There's not so many bedsores. . . . They offer different schedules.
> I didn't get that at the other nursing home. Here you can pick week-
> ends only. You just have a choice of hours. I like the benefits package
> here—sick days, vacations, health care. If they have good people,
> they don't want to lose them. (Joan Ford, nurse assistant, Church
> Hall)

But Joan's sentiments soon changed. After just three months at
Church Hall, she confided, "I don't like it, but don't tell them.
There's not enough people. There are never enough people. The
only thing to do in this place is go on for more schooling." Her turn-
around was quick; very little time had passed between "Everyone
helps here. I think this is one of the best places I've worked" and "I

don't like it, but don't tell them. There's not enough people."
Although getting back into the workplace had initially seemed like a
big first step, Joan soon found herself stuck on the bottom of the facility's work ladder. Despite her efforts in DPW's orientation, in
Church Hall's own training, and in her work on the floor, she found
herself overworked, overburdened, and unable to shake the identity
of inner city, of poor black single mother, as "less than."

Like Ruth and Henry at Development, it wasn't the work that reminded Joan of her lowly status at the facility. She had known that a
nurse assistant's work was hard. It was the kind of job African
American women have been doing for the past two hundred years.
As bell hooks (1990, 42) writes in her essay "Homeplace,"

> Their lives were not easy. Their lives were hard. They were black
> women who for the most part worked outside the home serving white
> folks, cleaning their houses, washing their clothes, tending their chil-
> dren, black women who worked in the fields or in the streets, what-
> ever they could do to make ends meet, whatever was necessary. Then
> they returned to their homes to make life happen there.

Like all the women at Church Hall, Joan was accustomed to taking
care of "white folks." She had worked as a nurse assistant in other facilities and knew the responsibilities of a nurse assistant: waking,
bathing, diapering, dressing, and feeding "about eight to ten patients."

For those on day shift at Church Hall, work started early. At 7:15
each morning dietary staff brought breakfast trays up to the floor on
large aluminum carts, and nurse assistants distributed the trays to
their assigned residents. Residents able to feed themselves ate
breakfast in their rooms; nurse assistants fed residents who needed
help moving spoon to mouth. One morning, I watched Carlita
Henry, a nurse assistant from Haiti, feed Sophie, an elderly white-
haired resident, in the TV lounge. Carlita sat on one of the room's
green leather couches and Sophie was in her wheelchair about six
inches away.

> The breakfast tray, with scrambled eggs, toast, and oatmeal, rested on
> a small table attached to the front of Sophie's wheelchair. The old
> woman was bone thin, as she ate her head drooped down so her chin
> seemed to rest on her chest. Carlita, on the other hand, was alert and
> attentive. Doe-eyed with her hair braided and pinned up into a
> crown, Carlita was slow and methodical. She focused on Sophie as
> she carefully cut the crusts from the bread, doubled a piece, and put
> it in Sophie's mouth. She talked to the woman the entire time, en-
> couraging her to eat. "Okay Sophie, open your mouth. That's right,

that's my baby. Chew, Sophie. Chew the bread. That's good, isn't that good?" Carlita cut off a piece of the scrambled eggs with the fork and put the fork to Sophie's mouth. She continued her chanting, "That's a good girl. That's good, isn't it, Sophie? That's right, have some eggs."

I asked if Sophie talks. Carlita shook her head and said, "No. But Sophie likes to eat, don't you, Sophie," drawing us both into the conversation. Carlita then exchanged the fork for a spoon, filled it halfway with oatmeal, and put it to Sophie's mouth. "How about some oatmeal? You like oatmeal. That's good, Sophie."

Sophie's arms were bent up and inward, permanently stiff during the meal. But her mouth moved continuously, chewing and swallowing the oatmeal and waiting for Carlita's next spoonful. (March 2, 1993, field notes, Church Hall)

Although very ill or very old, residents evidenced a continuum of awareness. Some were able to walk, albeit slowly, and function on their own, while others were completely bedridden and required total care. Sophie was somewhere in the middle. Care correlated with a resident's condition, and assistants such as Carlita put much thought into the negotiation of that care.

Work in the total care unit was undoubtedly the most difficult in the facility. Standing against the wall one day, I watched Gladys Hopkins complete her after breakfast activities, bathing and dressing residents, in the total care unit. Gladys, in her late thirties, was a woman with hard edges. Small, dark, with strong hands and a strong back, Gladys had grown up poor, and had never found her way out of the inner city. She had worked at Church Hall for three years and was working overtime in the intensive care area. "I don't like this wing, I'd be depressed if I worked here all the time," she explained. "But I can use the money, you know what I mean."

After putting sheets on the empty bed nearest to the door, Gladys moved to the room's second bed, where a white-haired woman seemed to sleep, completely still, under a dark blue blanket. "This is Faye," Gladys related, "she's in like a coma."

Gladys worked quickly and smoothly, her movements a well-rehearsed dance with a mute, inanimate partner. Gladys was in the lead in this waltz. She took a large metal container from the corner of the room, put one end into the side of the mattress, and as she pushed back the container's handle, she inserted air from the container into the mattress, making it bigger and fuller as it inflated. Gladys put the air gun back into the corner, went into the bathroom, and returned with a bowl of water and a bar of soap in her hands and a washcloth and three towels hung over her arm. She put the bowl and soap on the table and hung the towels across a chair next to the bed. Pulling down the blanket, she peeled Faye's nightgown down off her shoulders, out from her back, and then slipped it off her other arm and then laid it on the chair. Thin and paler than white, Faye was a limp rag doll in Gladys's hands. Gladys laid a towel under Faye. She spread out one side, rolled Faye onto the half of the towel that was flattened, and spread out the other side, adjusting Faye's body so that the woman lay in the middle of the towel. Then Gladys washed Faye. Starting first with the right side of the woman's body, she wet the washcloth in the bowl, wet and soaped Faye's shoulders, and continued down her body, wetting and soaping breasts, stomach, hips, between legs, legs, and feet. She dried Faye lightly, and covering her with a towel, she emptied and refilled the bowl in the bathroom. Returning, Gladys removed the towel and repeated the washing on Faye's left side. Gladys chatted as she worked, explaining that when she started working at Church Hall, Faye had been alert. "This isn't hard work. I can do a patient in ten minutes. I'm taking it easy now because I'm bored."

Finishing with Faye's inert body, Gladys covered her with the towel, emptied and refilled the bowl, and returned to wash the woman's hair. She wet the short white pixie-cut hair with the washcloth, soaped the hair, and then wiped it wet with a rinsed washcloth. She dried the hair with a towel, and took a clean nightgown from the top drawer of a wooden bureau that stood against the wall near the foot of Faye's bed. Removing the towel from under Faye by rolling it on one side, moving Faye off the towel, and then taking the towel off the bed completely, Gladys began to dress Faye in the nightgown, first one arm, then the other. She moved Faye's body, lifting her shoulders, buttoning the front of the gown, and smoothing it down and under her legs. What seemed to be only a few seconds later, the nightgown covered the woman's body. Gladys then straightened out Faye, so that her legs were unbent, flat on the sheeted mattress. Gladys then pulled up the top sheet and blanket to cover Faye and tucked the sides of the sheet neatly under the mattress. She returned the soap to the bathroom, emptied the bowl into the bathroom sink, and wiped it dry with one of the towels. She gathered the wet towels and last night's nightgown, bundled them into a loose ball, and put them in a hamper in the hall.

After nearly twenty minutes of continuous movement, one room was finished. Gladys left for the next room and I loitered in the hall, watching the beginning of the daily parade of wheelchairs sauntering to the lunch room for the midday meal. (December 23, 1992, field notes, Church Hall)

Gladys's work was mechanical; she followed a procedure she knew well. Caregiving was tailored to each resident, yet the steps in the process, the waking, feeding, bathing, and dressing were morning activities facility-wide.

Joan Ford, like the other women, knew that the work of a nurse assistant was not only difficult, but that it was by its very nature dirty and unpleasant. Most residents wore disposable diapers, which the assistants changed twice a day and twice a night. Other residents had foley's, or catheter bags, hung under their wheelchairs. Joan told me about Linda Jones, a nurse assistant on her floor. "Linda was fired for not cleaning residents. You know that's part of the work, cleaning behinds. If you don't want to do it, get another job." And she introduced me to Teresa Sanchez, a Puerto Rican woman working as a nurse assistant upstairs in Wing Three, who told us both about a recent incident with one of her regular residents.

> Last week, one of the residents was in the bathroom. It was Gerald-ine. She was wiping herself with a rag and when I came in to get her she threw the rag at me and the water and shit got all over me, all over my face. I had shit on my lips. I was so upset I had to walk out. I said where's the clean towels. Geraldine was ringing the buzzer. Elizabeth [the LPN] asked me if I had Geraldine and I told her what she did. I told her I'm not going back in there. She should go. She wouldn't go, so I had to go back in. I couldn't leave her in there. I was so mad, I could have abused her. I wouldn't, but that's how mad I was. (Teresa Sanchez, nurse assistant, Church Hall)

The nurse assistants all had stories about residents such as Gerald-ine. Sometimes the stories included feces and other messes; other times they included verbal or even physical abuse. The following is from field notes of April 1993:

> I stood at the nursing desk, near five nurse assistants who had gath-ered when they heard that Cynthia Hudson, a young nurse assistant on the wing, had cut her arm on Lillian's wheelchair. An LPN had al-ready washed and bandaged Cynthia's arm; now the women were both advising Cynthia and weaving tall tales about the Injury Center, where she might be waiting "half the night" to complete insurance forms and be examined. Sally, a resident who had an endearing way of always being hungry, wandered by. "I'm hungry, honey," she said to me. "Can't you get me something to eat?" Henrietta Jessup, one of the senior aides, turned to me and said, "Don't let her fool you. She's mean." The women repeated a litany of Sally's epithets. "Ugly" . . . "fat" . . . "fat ass." Tesha Brown, one of the assistants, said, "She tells me my ass is a big as a basket." (April 21, 1993, field notes, Church Hall)

Some of the residents' remarks concerned race. The vast majority of the women and men who made Church Hall their home were white, and based upon their ability to pay the facility's $3,600 to $3,900 basic monthly fees, it seems they were also fairly well off. Most were unaccustomed to and somewhat uneasy with the dark-skinned women who surrounded them at Church Hall. Here they were, in their twilight years, totally dependent upon these African American women for their most intimate care. Sick, tired, with little to no control over their lives, or in most cases even of their bodily functions, they all too often took out their frustrations on their caregivers. As Maryann Clark, Church Hall's director of nursing explained,

> What the nurse assistants have problems with is that there are patients' rights, but they don't have rights. You're going to be verbally abused by residents. You can't be abusive. You may be hit. Duck. I try to give them real ways to deal with problems. They leave the area. In orientation they're all taught how to deal with patients, how to cope. There's in-service and the floor nurse knows how to handle it. We don't allow closed doors, to protect them, the patients. Some of them have imaginations, you wouldn't believe. They can say anything. (Maryann Clark, director of nursing, Church Hall)

The women who stayed did learn to cope with residents. Many became attached, and like Carlita and her Sofie, called them "my babies." As Gladys Hopkins explained, "I don't have children. This is like having children."

It wasn't the work but the lack of support from supervisors that reminded Joan Ford of her status at Church Hall. While in an ideal world each nurse assistant was assigned "eight to ten residents," the reality was that the facility was always short staffed, and a caseload of fourteen residents per nurse assistant was far from unusual. The rationale for staffing problems varied. As Linda Donaldson, an LPN at Church Hall asserted, "Short staff is a problem everywhere. I think it's upper management, cutting costs to make a larger profit." However, Kathy Hicks, another LPN, blamed the nurse assistants themselves. "Sometimes we do schedule enough, but people call out and we can't replace them." Yet while LPNs, RNs, and nursing assistants all recognized short staffing as a problem, the hierarchy of work at the facility remained constant. Nurse assistants may have shared work and helped one another, but their supervisors, the facility's RNs and LPNs, never pitched in to help out. LPNs, one assigned to each wing, treated patients according to physicians' orders, distributed medications, and supervised nurse assistants. Each RN, in turn, managed an entire floor. The impression, both mine and the nurse assistants, was that neither LPNs nor RNs considered assisting with the daily demands of patient care to be part of their jobs. Instead, they distributed medicines and completed records. As Joan asserted, "That's right, all they do is write reports and stand by those medical carts."

LOCAL KNOWLEDGE

The rank ordering of personnel at Church Hall played out in several ways, all reminding Joan and Dina of their subordinate status at the facility. Like workplace responsibilities, knowledge was segmented hierarchically at the facility. Although certified nurse assistants were intimately involved with their residents' daily welfare, their knowledge was neither recognized nor validated at the institutional level. Nurse assistants were not included in care meetings convened to monitor residents' status nor were they afforded any other regular input on resident care. Mary explained, "They have care meetings for the family, charge nurse, physical therapist, but nurse assistants aren't involved." The problem was that nurse assistants' knowledge was local. It concerned the everyday of residents' lives and was composed of particulars, not medical diagnoses. The following field notes excerpt illustrates this local knowledge:

> Mary Winston, an African American woman in her early thirties, had been working at Church Hall as a nurse assistant on the floor above Joan's for the past nine months. The Souths, one of the few married couples residing at the facility, were two of her regular residents. As we walked down the hall one afternoon, Mary told me that an elderly white man and woman had approached her and had introduced themselves as Mrs. South's brother and sister-in-law. They wanted to find the Patient Assistant Coordinator, who was responsible for resident wardrobe needs. Mary redirected them, "I take care of them. I know what they need," and she proceeded to make a list of the South's clothing needs on a half sheet of paper, Mrs. South on top and Mr. South on the bottom. Perusing the list, the brother-in-law asked, "Does he wear short sleeve or sleeveless T-shirts?" and Mary offered "short sleeve." The man mentioned to his wife that he had some extra T-shirts at home.
>
> Later that same day, I heard Kathy Hahn, another nurse assistant on Mary's wing, talk about residents' clothing needs from inside a resident's room. "We need shirts," she announced to no one in particular, as she catalogued the clothes in the resident's drawers. Afterward in the hall Kathy explained to me that she regularly brought in

her clothes for her residents. Al, one of her male residents, was wearing her socks that day. Mary chimed in from across the hall, "We all do." Coming out into the hall, Mary continued on the topic of clothing. She related that she overheard a charge nurse talking on the telephone to the brother of one of her residents. When the nurse hung up, Mary said she asked her, "Why did you tell them he needs pajamas?" As though in a chorus, both Kathy and Mary lamented, "They wear gowns." (December 2, 1992, field notes, Church Hall)

In addition to material needs, the women also took note of residents' skin tone, speech capabilities, idiosyncrasies, moods and mood changes, toiletry habits, and physical condition and made monthly recordings of residents' weights and vital signs. As Pam Griffin, the charge nurse on Mary's wing, asserted, "We depend on the nurse assistants. They're the ones. They let us know. They're the ones who see the patients every day." Yet while the women were depositories of information about their residents' material needs, they had trouble finding anyone other than Pam who would listen to them.

The distinction, separating local from official knowledge, was important because it explained and justified the facility's rigidly defined hierarchy. LPNs and RNs, not nurse assistants, were the professionals at Church Hall. They were involved in care meetings, dispensed medications, and talked in medical jargon about "impacted patients," "decubitus ulcers," and "lesions." Nurse assistants, on the other hand, had intimate knowledge of their residents, but not of their medical diagnoses. When I questioned the women about the specifics of a resident's illness, their most common response was "I'm not sure, I'd have to look in her [medical] chart." Yet while medical charts, stored at the nursing desk at each wing, were available to nurses and nurse assistants alike, nurse assistants rarely had or took the time to review them. I talked with Dina about access to this information one afternoon after work, and from her vantage point, caring for fourteen elderly residents a day translated into an enormous workload and little time for followup research on the residents.

> *Frances:* Do you get a sense of what's wrong with the patients you have now?
> *Dina:* No. Like a lot of them, you can't sense what's wrong with them, you don't really know until you take time out and read the charts.
> *F:* And you can do that?
> *D:* Yeah, you can read their charts.
> *F:* Do people usually do that?

D: Yes, yes. No, see, let me stop. People don't normally, no. Nursing assistants don't normally. Cause you don't have the time to read the chart, unless you're on your break or you, say, for instance, you're doing, like everyone has to do a daily report on what they did to a patient and so, the flow sheets. So if you're ever doing a flow sheet and you might want to figure out, you have such and such. Well, what's wrong with them and then you pull it then, it's good to do it that way.

F: But I've never seen anybody do that.

D: No, they normally don't have the time to do it. And you don't really actually know. You can kind of sense what's wrong with the residents, but you don't know unless you pick up their charts.

F: Aides are involved in the care plan team meetings, is that right?

D: No. Cause I know when I was at Golden Glove nursing home, we, I was only there two weeks, I had to go to the Care Plan. I was like, Oh my god, 'cause I was that patient's nurse. They should [do that here] 'cause I got to know the family, to know the patient and you learn more about the patient.

(July 12, 1993, interview, Church Hall)

At Golden Glove, Dina had been an active participant on care teams, and that experience forced her to become more involved in her residents' care. At Church Hall, however, participation was far more ambiguous. Dina found no official space for her voice or her knowledge. Medical records were available for her perusal, but the onus for knowing was on her. And like the other nurse assistants, she found that her days left her little time or energy to take the responsibility to make her local knowledge official.

A PROFESSIONAL HIERARCHY

The segmentation of responsibilities and officially sanctioned knowledge at Church Hall paralleled differences in formal education, cultural group membership, and wages. Race and economic status compounded variations in educational levels, which, while relatively small, became significant. Each of the facility's seven RNs had at least two years' post–high school education, and the thirty-three LPNs had one year post–high school training. The ninety nurse assistants had earned their high school diplomas and had either participated in a short-term training program at a proprietary school or were previously employed as a nurse assistant in another facility.

The result was vast differentials in wages. The starting salary for an RN was $18 an hour and for an LPN $12.50 an hour. An uncertified nurse assistant, who often had only six months less schooling than an LPN, earned a starting wage of $5.25 an hour, which increased to $6.00 an hour after the aide passed the certification test. Consensus on the floor was that the assistants' pay was low, particularly for the weight of their workload. "Too much work, too little money," was the refrain among nurse assistants. Gladys Hopkins said she started at $3.00 an hour four years before.

> We get fifty cents a year raise. It barely keeps up with inflation. People are coming to work, welfare is making them. With kids it's hard. You have to pay rent, day care. (Gladys Hopkins, nurse assistant, Church Hall)

Like Gladys, nurse assistants all talked about the difficulties of making ends meet on their salary. Their biweekly checks provided neither a cushion for emergencies nor discretionary income for niceties such as decorations for the walls at home. As I walked down the hall one afternoon with Dina, for instance, she commented that Wing One "looked nice." The hall was decorated with large framed nature scenes. "Every time I go down there I see a new picture," Dina reflected. "They're beautiful. Those are the kinds of things I can't afford working here." Even at $6.00 an hour, the women's salary kept them well below the poverty line.[7] Not only could Dina ill afford the niceties of decorations for the wall, but without the continued support of the Sisters of Mercy, she would not have been able to pay rent or buy food for herself and her three daughters.

The facility's benefits played an ambiguous role in these official constructions of worth. Unlike wages, at Church Hall vacation and health care policies were consistent for all full-time employees. In our initial conversations, the women waxed positive about Church Hall's benefit package of

- nine paid holidays;
- paid vacation after one year;
- 2.5 hours of paid sick time every two weeks;
- a leave of absence for personal sickness, family illness, maternity, military leave;
- term life Insurance after the full-time employees' ninety days probationary period;

- partial medical insurance after the ninety days probationary period.

When I met Lynn Brown a few days after she started work at Church Hall, she told me

> I heard the benefits here are great. I can get benefits for my kids, that would be great. I heard they give you bonuses. If you're here a whole month you get a twenty-five dollar bonus. They truly motivate you to be here. There's no excuse for you not to be here. Except for things that you can't control. (Lynn Brown, nurse assistant, Church Hall)

But the health care coverage that was initially appealing became more complicated when Lynn realized that $133 was deducted from each biweekly paycheck for the coverage of her two children. As illustrated in field notes from January 1993, insurance and health care quickly fell under Lynn's rubric of things "you can't control."

> A Monday afternoon, Teresa Sanchez and Charlotte Kingston, two nurse assistants on Church Hall's second floor, talked about cars while completing their daily resident forms at the nursing station in Wing Three. Teresa said she was thinking of selling her old black Cadillac, although "only black guys want to buy it." She explained to me, in an aside, that she had no car insurance because she couldn't afford to pay the premiums. We talked about the cost of insurance, and Teresa added that having $133 deducted from every paycheck for health care coverage of her seven-year-old exhausted her extra cash. Charlotte suggested Teresa go on welfare, but Teresa quickly objected. "They give you so much trouble. They want to know everything about your life. I have to get another job. I have to make more money; that's what I have to do. I'm living hand to mouth." She added that she had had no insurance when her son was born, and that the hospital had hounded her until she finally signed a form they had sent. Charlotte, one of the few assistants without children, commented that she still owed the hospital $2,000 from four days she spent there recovering from an asthma attack. As a new employee, Charlotte had gone to the hospital even though her health care coverage had not yet begun. Now she was stuck with a debt that she couldn't pay. (January 25, 1993, field notes, Church Hall)

Working overtime was one way the women augmented salaries and paid bills. The facility was always understaffed, and so they worked double shifts, from two times a month to two times a week at time and a half their hourly rate. "You can do it if you know you're working for something," said Charlotte. "My mom says I live here."

Overtime improved wage levels, the extra hours resulted in hard-working, underpaid women working even harder, in equally stressful conditions.

DIFFERENT, STRANGE, AND EVEN DANGEROUS

But as the following vignette illustrates, no matter how long or hard the women worked, they could not dispel the identity of different, strange, and even dangerous that was ascribed to them by supervisors.

> Church Hall on a spring Sunday, just a few weeks before Easter, the facility's walls were bright with cardboard cutouts of rabbits and baby chicks. Wandering through Wing Two, I found Linda Donaldson and Kathy Hicks, the LPNs who supervised the wing each weekend, at the nursing desk. Both were white, Linda had long red hair, and Kathy, more squarely built, had short dark blonde hair. We chatted and when our conversation meandered to the topic of overtime, Linda brought up the nurse assistants.
>
> "They have to work overtime. For the money. But what I can't understand is then they come with hairstyles and these long fingernails. They spend their money on that. You see my nails." She held up her hands to show us her unpolished, uneven, short nails. "I wouldn't work. Would you?" she asked Kathy, who responded, "Well, I keep sayin' I'm gonna get my nails done. But my washing machine is broken, the kids need shoes. . . . If it makes them [the nurse assistants] happy."
>
> They continued talking about the nurse assistants in the same distanced way. "They're fired for abusing residents, for being on drugs, for stealing, for being in prison. They check, but some people get through. One girl, well I can't tell you about that . . . we've had a knife fight here," Linda said. She continued, "Some of them take three buses. And some of the nurses here . . ." Kathy took up her sentence with, "We're not like that. I'm only here every other weekend. I just want to get along and get things done." Linda continued in a lowered voice, "And then, you see, there aren't too many whites here. Kathy and I are out in the parking lots [after the shift] with our Mace." Kathy repeated, "But we're not like that, are we?" Linda, as though explaining, said, "Especially when you're not used to solving problems by fighting. I wasn't allowed to fight as a kid." (April 4, 1993, field notes, Church Hall)

Hard-working or not, to Linda, Kathy, and their LPN colleagues on Church Hall's supervisory staff, Dina, Joan, and the other women from the inner city remained strange and perplexing. Their condensed, inexact stories of knife fights, drug abuse, and resident abuse cast the women as tough and frightening enough to warrant precautions in the dark parking lot at night. Each LPN had her own anecdotes about the women. One explained, "Last week a girl from Wing Three got in my face. She don't even know me." Another added, "I got attacked by an aide, I was out of work seven months." Indelibly marked by a melding of race, language, inner city origins, and culture, Dina, Joan, and the other nurse assistants at Church Hall found themselves boxed in by perceptions of difference that reverberated throughout the institution's walls.

A LACK OF RESPECT

Finding both work and the opportunity to become certified had been godsends to women who were desperate to get off welfare and back into the workforce. While Joan Ford and Dina Haskell had skills and prior work experience, they had not been able to put the pieces of a job, state certification, and day care together by themselves. With DPW's help, they became nurse assistants again, and with the certification Joan acquired at Church Hall, she was also assured the continued possibility of work. As the previous section delineates, the women all had positive first impressions of the facility, praising it for its cleanliness, camaraderie, responsive scheduling, and benefits package. The section also describes their experiences in a training program that privileged official knowledge over their local knowledge and a workplace that was constructed around and dependent upon the women's low-paid labor. While the particulars of the women's stories differed from those I heard at Development, the argument concerning dissonant perceptions of identity and potential continues to be relevant. But at Church Hall it was not just Joan, Dina, and the women referred from the welfare office who resented what they perceived as a minimization of their skills and experience at the facility. It was the nurse assistants en masse. Clustered together in a place where race, socioeconomic status, and inner-city origins marked them as different and ultimately, deficit, and where their voices and local knowledge were afforded no space, the women carved psychological and physical spaces for themselves by complaining, grumbling about, and arguing with supervisors. When they had no more will to fight, they left the facility for greener pastures.

As the following field note entry illustrates, a perceived lack of respect for their work was fundamental to their complaints:

I hadn't met Katie Simon, Allie West, or Helen Blackman before I ran into them at Church Hall's Wing One nursing station. Katie was the talker of the group. A large, African American woman whose face seemed to shine a perpetual smile, she explained that for the past four years she had worked part-time at Church Hall while holding down a job as a school bus driver.

"I really like it here," she explained. "It's very nice here. But I think we deserve more respect." Lowering her voice just a notch she added, "We each do important things. If we keep their bottoms dry and warm, it's less work for you. I think nursing is racist. This is the only place I've worked, but I think nursing is racist. We do more work for less money." (January 15, 1993, field notes, Church Hall)

Katie's critique of the facility was not atypical. Aware and resentful of the stratification of job responsibilities and credentialing, the women were explicit about their frustrations in private conversations with me and in talk among themselves. They complained that their certification, an emblem at least to them of their commitment to their work and to their patients, was not given due respect.

Lunch time in the dining room in Wing Two, the room was bright with January sun, and the tables all decorated with winter center-pieces of red poinsettias and white mums. Alice Burton and Barbara Young, two nurse assistants on the floor, fed two wheelchair-bound residents as we talked. The women, both African American, had been at the facility for a combined twelve years, and the lack of respect they felt from their supervisors still stung sharply.

In talking about the LPNs who supervised their wing, Alice related, "Some of them are okay, I'm not sayin' all of them are like that, but none of them down here help." Barbara added, "I've actually had one nurse say to me, 'I don't answer call buttons. You can answer if you want, if you don't want to answer go back to school and get an LPN license.' As though our certification isn't worth anything. We may be bottom of the ladder, but you can't say our certification isn't worth anything." (January 5, 1993, field notes, Church Hall)

Stress from overwhelming workloads compounded this perceived lack of respect. Nurse assistants did not have an easy job. Although developing a fictive kin relationship with "their babies" kept many women at the facility, the work was hard, dirty, and stressful. Exhausted after a long morning, Lynn Brown complained, "Of all the jobs I've had, nursing assistant's the hardest. Just change shoes for one day. On my feet all day . . . I'll tell you why, because of the workload." "I've already had sixteen patients today," asserted Sophia Hudson, a senior nurse assistant on Church Hall's first floor.

Cari Jones, a nurse assistant on Dina's wing, added, "With all the regular stress, that makes it worse. We have a lot to do in the morning."

CARVING SPACES

The women's frustration with working conditions, coupled with a lack of legitimate channels for protest, spilled over into their interactions with LPNs and RNs, and at times, into the ways they dealt with the residents. Their resistance was unplanned and unorganized at Church Hall, and to the LPNs, it looked more like disrespect than a protest of unfair treatment. A verbal exchange between Terry Whitman, the white RN on the second floor, and Jane Turner and Teresa Sanchez, two nurse assistants on Wing Three, reflected this resistance positioned as disrespect.

> Terry approached the nurse assistants at the Wing Three desk saying, "Well as long as everybody's here, I should tell you. Evita [Gomez, the nurse assistant trainer] says no one's allowed to sit on a resident's bed to feed them." As though on cue, the women erupted into an outburst. Jane stammered in her search for clarification, "What do you mean . . . . Do you mean . . . how are we supposed to feed those patients that can't sit up?" When Terry suggested standing, both Jane and Teresa objected with, "Now you're talking about regulations. If the state comes in and sees you standing feeding patients, you'll be out." Pam Griffin, the LPN assigned to the wing added on the women's behalf, "If you're standing, you can't see if the person is choking." Pam, moving close to Terry now, added, "How are you going to tell if the patient's choking?" Terry mimed bending down, insisting, "I can see." Pam groaned at Terry's miming and with some resignation in her voice commented, "Oh never mind." Terry allowed, "Well, you're taller than I am. In that case it might be different."
>
> Terry walked to the medication cart next to the nursing desk and began preparing pill dosages for the floor's residents. She muttered to no one in particular, "I'm just trying to watch out for all of you, so you don't get into trouble. This is a RN who looks out for you. I'm just telling you what Evita told me." In a slightly lowered voice Pam suggested, "Next time you have an announcement, have Evita come up." Terry responded, "But that's an RN's job," insisting that it was her responsibility to pass these mandates to her nursing staff. Pam countered with, "Well, you just seem so upset."
>
> As Terry disappeared down the hall behind her medicine cart, Jane and Teresa rolled their eyes, complaining, "These orders come down from people who don't feed the patients. Passing out meds isn't giving them breakfast in the morning . . . . She thinks everything she

says is right . . . . They don't even feed the patients." (November 13, 1992, field notes, Church Hall)

The interaction filled the air with an hostility that was thick, and that I came to recognize as commonplace at the facility. Both nurse and nurse assistants believed the interaction illustrated a basic lack of respect. Responsible for actual resident care, Jane and Teresa felt their input was unrecognized. Terry, on the other hand, complained later that, "I don't like the way these girls talk to me. They have no respect."

FEW OPTIONS

The women had few options, however, for improving the working conditions that caused them so much frustration. Management did not hold meetings at which they could discuss wages, salary increases, particulars of their benefit package, or supervisor relationships, and no other avenues for airing complaints were made available in-house. The union offered a ray of hope, and during my months at Church Hall, the Health Care Local made several attempts to organize the facility's nurse assistants. The women viewed the union's approaches with hope, but were convinced that its chances for success were negligible.

> As I started down Church Hall's back hall in one of my many strolls around the facility, I spotted Pam Griffin, the LPN on the wing, talking in hushed tones with Mary Winston, a nurse assistant. Pam prompted Mary with "tell her, tell her," as they pushed me into one of the resident's rooms. Mary explained that union representatives had been in the parking lot that morning, handing out fliers and asking nurse assistants to contact them. She contended, "A union's good," and Pam added that the union "helps people stick up for each other."
>
> Mary continued, "We're all afraid to do anything. I know from my last job they can't fire you from trying to get the union in. But they'll find something else. I've been here a year. I want to stay here long enough to get my vacation. They give you trouble with that. And unemployment. They'll fight you on that. Make sure you put that in your notes. We're counting on you." (March 19, 1993, field notes, Church Hall)

The Local's organizing efforts were not successful during my visits to Church Hall; the women's fears and management's entrenchment gave union representatives little room to maneuver. In a place where

few alternatives for change were envisioned, I found myself positioned as a default savior. My notes were scattered with women's ex-
hortations to include their grievances in my findings and to make
certain that I send my report to the president and first lady. "Hillary
Clinton would be very interested in hearing about this," they told
me. But short of relying on the union or me, both poor risks at best,
no other avenues existed for changing the current social organization of the workplace.

They believed change was improbable, and so the women talked
instead about ways to escape their subordinate status. One possibility was to move up within the facility. Vertical moves did exist for
nurse assistants, and in theory, the facility prioritized hiring in-
house. "Basically we post all positions available, and everyone's welcome to apply," explained Nia Gates, Church Hall's personnel
officer. Two women in the facility had gained some notoriety not
only because they had moved up from their positions as nurse assistants, but also because they had received financial support from
Church Hall for their moves. Liz Bishop started as a nurse assistant
at Church Hall in 1984. She returned to school a year later and upon
graduating as an LPN in 1986, she moved into a quality-assurance
position within the facility. "Initially [while in training] I continued
to work," she explained. "I returned to Church Hall. I was on con-
tract for two years because they paid for my tuition." Brenda Turner
had also started work at Church Hall as a nurse assistant. She soon
found herself wanting more, and so she researched career options,
and found a supply clerk training course that fit her needs. The facility paid half her tuition for the eleven-week course and adjusted
her work schedule so she could attend the Friday training sessions.
After training, Brenda was transferred to Church Hall's Central
Supply, where she organized, monitored, maintained, stocked, and
distributed supplies from the supply room in the facility's basement
to the floors above. Like Liz, Brenda's training had been financed
before the facility's change of ownership. But despite the almost
mythological quality of these moves, during my visits to Church
Hall only one of the eleven positions posted, the Patient Relations
Liaison position, was filled by a nurse assistant. Given the more than
eighty nurse assistants employed at the facility, this internal social
mobility represented a 1 percent chance of promotion over the
course of a year. Since the buyout, the facility had provided no funds
to help women upgrade their work roles.

Because neither structural improvements nor in-house advancement was likely, the women came to see school as their only option.
Talk about planning to go back to school, hoping to be in nursing

school next year, and even applying to go back to school was a constant conversation among the women. As Joan asserted, "The only thing to do in this place is go on for more schooling." Over and over again I heard women at the facility offer, "I'd like my RN. And I was a straight A student"; and, "I want to go back to school. I won't do LPN. I'd go for my RN"; and, "Ever since I was a little girl I wanted to be a nurse. I want to go on to RN." Given the $6.50 to $10.00 wage differential between LPNs and nurse assistants, and the $9.00 to $12.00 between RNs and nurse assistants, their plans made sense. Like the welfare recipients in Catherine Pélissier Kingfisher's (1996) *Women in the American Welfare Trap,* "the women's talk about education represents a status quo approach." Kingfisher writes,

> Protagonists in a status quo narrative accept and are willing to perpetuate the dominant system of which they consider themselves to be potential, if not actual beneficiaries. In this case, the dominant system consists of mainstream models of achievement and success. In short if a minimum wage job was not the answer to welfare, a well-paid job was, and the way to get a well-paid job was to get an education . . . . As striking as the ubiquity of the perception that education was crucial to "making it," however, was the frequency with which the women began but did not complete educational programs. (Kingfisher 1996, 27)

This incongruity between belief and reality certainly held true for Dina Haskell and her colleagues at Church Hall. While the women all talked about going to school, they also complained about a lack of both money and time. Thirty, or 34 percent, of the nurse assistants at the facility had studied in a nurse assistant track at a proprietary school within the area. Still paying back loans, they were unwilling to incur more debt. Gladys Hopkins had studied at National Institute, a local proprietary school downtown. Gladys related that she was having difficulty repaying the last $900 of her $2,500 loan, and had sent in a double payment two months ago, assuming that her check would cover a two-month period. "I told them not to call my work," she complained. "But they called here and said I owe them. They said they thought it was just double payment, and I still owed for the month. They made my credit bad." Given the financial difficulties that she incurred post-training, I asked if her studies had helped her with work. "Yes . . . no . . . no . . . yes," she replied with hesitancy. "I think the best is when you're trained at work. I am savin' to go for LPN after I pay off my loan. I want to learn more about medicine. I know some medicines, but I want to learn more." Even with this clearly articulated goal, however, Gladys was against asking her supervisors at Church Hall for help with tuition. "I want to do it myself. I don't want to feel like I owe them." Gladys's loan and her reaction to borrowing more money was commonplace. Everyone at the facility talked about saving money and making plans to start school. Lynn Brown had defaulted on her proprietary school loan payments, and so was temporarily unable to access PELL grants or other school loans to continue her studies at the local community college. Lynn explained,

> I'm still going to college. I went to community college for a year. When I went to enroll, I had my classes registered, but they told me I couldn't use my grant. I had to have twelve consecutive payments on my loan. I already made twelve payments but now they have this new law. I had to pay again. I'm gonna' have to start payin'. I was takin' general studies at the time. Maybe I'll study RN. I'm undecided. (Lynn Brown, nurse assistant, Church Hall)

The women explored all possibilities. Dina even talked about going back on welfare to access the additional support she needed to return to school.

> I talked to all the important people in my life and decided I want to become an LPN. I don't know much about schools. I got to settle my loan first. You know, I defaulted on my last loan, when I went to Norfolk State for that year. I heard you can pay it off, even five dollars a month. And you have to pay for six months before you can get another loan. Or a grant. I was thinkin' of going to John Mellisant, that LPN program in town. But I don't know how I'll do it. I'll probably have to go back on welfare to go back to school. (Dina Haskell, nurse assistant, Church Hall)

In addition to funding, time was also a concern. As mentioned earlier, most women at Church Hall regularly worked double shifts to earn extra income, and overtime demands, combined with familial responsibilities particularly burdensome for single parents, left them fatigued and without time for school. "I'm interested in psychology," offered Nancy Henderson, a nurse assistant on Dina's wing who supported three young children on her own. "But where am I gonna' get the time or the money?" she asked. For most women, this dilemma of time and money was unsolvable, and without easier access to funding and the support of a strong kinship network, school plans remained talk. As Carol Nelson, Church Hall's physical therapist, asserted, "I hear a lot of talk about going back to school, but it rarely seems to happen."

PROTESTS OF DENIAL

In the absence of official channels to air and address their concerns, the women were left with few alternatives to improve their lot. Overworked, frustrated, and increasingly angry, leaving the job began to look more and more like their only avenue for change. The women's flight was an example of what anthropologist Michael Adas calls a protest of denial (1986, 68), when individuals "quit positions that are no longer considered tenable or abandon particular social systems altogether." And quit they did. Like the industry in general, Church Hall experienced a rapid turnover of nurse assistant staff. According to the director of nursing, the average length of time a nurse assistant stayed at Church Hall was "probably six months." A more formal review of staffing over a one-year period revealed a facility-wide turnover rate of 180 percent, which translates to a turnover of the entire staff of nurse assistants nearly twice every year. Dina's colleagues from welfare were no exception. One and one-half years after the DPW/Church Hall collaboration brought twenty-four former welfare recipients to Church Hall, twenty-one, or 88.5 percent, had left the facility. In fact, four months after her initial comments of, "I think this is one of the best places I've worked," Joan was gone. "Joan, she came in at seven o'clock," explained Church Hall's nursing director. "The nurse gave her her assignment. She said she didn't like it and left." Joan's leaving wasn't a big surprise to anyone who knew her. She was clearly unhappy at Church Hall. Watching her interact with her supervisors, both African American and white, I realized that it was not race that was Joan's problem, but status, her own low status in the workplace.

It was the start of the afternoon shift, and Joan was at Wing Two nursing desk. She was working a double shift, day and middle, and had just finished her 7:00 to 3:00 duty. As Joan talked about the schedule with Rose Banks, the LPN in charge of the wing and one of the few African American LPNs at the facility, I perceived her growing discontentment.

Joan asked, her voice rising as she spoke, "You mean I'm not goin' to lunch until seven o'clock?" Rose pulled the schedule from the desk, looked at it, and said, "Let me finish. We'll go by the schedule. If you want to change and everyone agrees, you can go earlier." Joan continued, "Why we go so late?" She looked at me, shook her head and rolled her eyes. Rose answered, "Because this is the three to eleven shift." Joan had been working since seven A.M., so to her, a seven P.M. dinner apparently seemed late.

The discussion shifted to staffing. Only four nurse assistants were

on the wing, and each was assigned fifteen residents. Both Joan and
Cari Jones, another nurse assistant on the shift, began to complain.
Joan said, "I've been here all day. I'm not doin' extra people." To
which Rose responded, "We all have to chip in. If you don't like it,
maybe you shouldn't be working." Rose made a phone call and in less
than five minutes, Pat Sherwood, the RN on middle shift, approached the desk. Pat confirmed that only four nurse assistants
would be on the shift. To Joan, she repeated Rose's earlier admoni-
tion. "If you don't want to work, you can punch out now. Let me
know."

Joan rolled her eyes again, waited a minute and then said, "I'm
leaving at nine o'clock. And I'm only gettin' people up." Cari added,
"I'm leavin' at nine o'clock." Pat responded, "If you both leave at
nine o'clock, that'll be a problem for me too. You need to tell me
now." Joan and Cari conferred quietly for a minute, and decided that
Joan would leave at 9:00 and Cari at 10:00.

When I saw Joan later, she shook her head and commented on the
earlier exchange. "That ain't right." (March 26, 1993, field notes,
Church Hall)

After four months on the job, Joan just decided she had had enough.
Charlotte Kingston, her friend in physical therapy, conjectured, "I
know Joan. She walked off. She was in last week to pick up her
check. She didn't want to work in Wing One. I think that was the
problem."

Also initially positive about Church Hall, Lynn Brown had Joan
beat by a month. "Here people are nicer to you," Lynn first told me.
"It doesn't make the job so tough. I like it here. It's nice." But three
months later, Lynn was fired for fighting with a male co-worker. He
had been bothering her, wouldn't leave her alone. One afternoon
during lunch in the dining room, things heated up. Lynn grabbed a
butter knife, the man pulled out his own knife. No one got hurt, but
both were fired on the spot. As a staff nurse explained, "You can't do
that around residents." Dina agreed, telling me, "Some people can't
control themselves. Both Lynn and the guy left. Automatic termination. There's not a guard around here. A resident might get hurt."
No one really knew why Lynn blew up. She had received high
praise during her initial months at the facility and seemed upbeat
about both the work and the facility. Although Lynn wasn't someone
who seemed so incendiary, personal antagonisms can blow up
quickly, and the facility's zero-tolerance policies didn't allow for any
flexibility in decisions about hiring and firing.

Employees at Church Hall, whether on the nursing, food service, or environmental staff, had opinions on why women like Joan and Lynn left. Most attributed at least partial responsibility to the facility's low salaries. And according to the results of three surveys on nurse assistant wages, they were right. An analysis of wages across sixty-six nursing homes validated the women's complaints; nurse assistants at Church Hall were paid considerably less than their counterparts at other care facilities in the state.

- An annual wage survey, conducted by Pennsylvania Association of County Affiliated Homes (1992), identified the starting salaries of nurse assistants at forty-five county homes in the state. The salaries ranged from $4.45 to $8.66 an hour, and averaged $6.49 per hour. Thirty-one, or 68.8 percent, of the forty-five homes paid their certified nurse assistants a wage higher than Church Hall's $6.00 an hour.
- To collect information on the starting salaries offered by Church Hall's competitors, I conducted a supplementary telephone survey of twenty-one nursing homes, selected randomly from the sixty-three local homes listed in the *Directory of Nursing Homes* (Mongeau 1991). Starting wages for nurse assistants in these twenty-one facilities ranged from $4.50 to $10.41, and averaged $6.61 an hour. Twelve, or 57 percent, of the homes surveyed paid more than Church Hall's $6.00 an hour.
- A third survey of starting salaries of twenty-seven graduates of a local PIC-funded nurse-aide certification program found wages ranging from $5.57 to $9.75, and averaging $6.51 an hour. Nineteen, or 70 percent, of these graduates earned a rate higher than Church Hall's $6.00 an hour.

The difference between Church Hall's starting salaries and those offered at comparable facilities meant that once certified, Dina and Joan received an average of $1,123 a year less by remaining at Church Hall, a difference equaling nearly 10 percent of their total salary. In addition, they also incurred considerable expense traveling up to two hours each way from their inner-city homes to suburban Church Hall. A transit pass cost both $58 a month (that is, an additional $698 per year) and an enormous amount of time every day. While the opportunity to re-enter the job market and become certified had drawn women to Church Hall, once certified, remaining at the facility cost them money. Interesting, while Ruth and Henry found themselves trapped at Development because they had not earned the additional certification needed to access better paying employment, Joan and Lynn's certification encouraged their flight.

The economist Lester Thurow called training such as Church Hall's nurse assistant certification "general training," because it is of value not only to the facility itself, but also to other companies within the same sector. According to Thurow (1970, 91–92), when a company provides general training, "the individual would pay for it by accepting wages below his marginal product." As reflected in the following field note excerpt, insiders at Church Hall confirmed Thurow's assertions about "general training."

> Charles Smith, from housekeeping, sat in the residents' lounge in Wing Two waiting for his shift to begin. He reported to me that two nurse assistants quit this week. " I think they just come to get certified," Charles asserted. "Maybe that's why they don't pay 'em as much as these women think they should. Because they also offer training." (March 26, 1993, field notes, Church Hall)

In other words, although the women benefited from the facility's paid training, they paid for it in lower wages and transportation costs. At the same time that low salaries, compounded by a lack of voice and respect for their work, frustrated the women, the general nature of their newly earned certification enabled them to leave Church Hall for jobs that paid better and were located closer to home. Liz Bishop, an LPN responsible for quality assurance, explained, "Several [women] left recently. They got their certification and found a job closer to home. There's also the possibility of more money if they go to an agency." Referring back to the metaphor of wearing a workplace identity, the women at Church Hall flung their social identities aside, believing that their newly earned certification would enable them to purchase one of a better size, a coat cut of finer cloth, elsewhere.

Low salaries and distance to work may have prompted women to seek out work that paid more and was more conveniently located, yet not all women left Church Hall. Feelings of hope, disappointment, and accompanying practices of accommodation and resistance were neither absolute nor exclusive. Why Dina Haskell, Nil Harper, and Donna Dixson chose to remain at Church Hall while their colleagues and friends left remains unclear. Senior nurse assistants equated this differential turnover to age and luxuries of youth. "Young ones don't stay," asserted two assistants in their late forties. "They don't have responsibilities like us." Henrietta Jessup, a nurse assistant at Church Hall for nine years, added, "There's a handful of us who stay. . . . I have a child. I have a house. I have bills. I need the job." That explanation may have applied to Donna and Dina. As sole support for their children, they carried the weight of ample responsibilities and so believed they could not afford to leave. But Nil Harper, twenty-three and still living with her parents without children of her own, was an exception to these claims about age and responsibility. In practice, tenure at Church Hall may have had more to do with a match or mismatch between each woman's beliefs about herself and the opportunities afforded her than to either age or responsibility. Perhaps like the high school dropouts in Michelle Fine's *Framing Drop-outs* (1991), women who left the facility were more self-confident, more sure of their options, or more comfortable with the risk of leaving. Those who stayed, women such as Dina, Nil, and Donna, on the other hand, were happy to find even the small amount of security that Church Hall provided.

VIEWING PRACTICE IN PIECEMEAL

In interviews and less formal discussions, the facility's upper-level management recognized both low salaries and the attitudes of supervising nurses as cause for some concern. Ron Driver, the facility's director, talked about the need to pay his nurse assistants a livable wage.

> I know I recognize with stability comes customer satisfaction. The people who supervise them last longer. I always say in a department you have to depend on a handful of people. Some people want a revolving door; they don't have to pay pension. The salaries are lower. I believe in cost of turnover, it's one hundred to fifteen hundred dollars per person. You're better paying somebody eight or nine dollars an hour. I'd like to see zero turnover. (Ron Driver, director, Church Hall)

Maryann Clark, the facility's director of nursing, focused on the role of supervising nurses:

> It's the attitude of the charge nurses. If they pitch in and help, make a couple of beds, people will want to come to work in the morning. If they are barking all the time, the nursing assistants don't want to come. I wouldn't want to come to a place that barks at me. I don't bark and they couldn't. When I worked the floor, I never let anyone leave without saying, "Thanks, good job." Even if it's been a horrible day.
> LPNs get no managerial training in school. If they go to a hospital

it's okay. They work under RNs. Here the RNs run the floor. . . . I say
it's common sense, treat people like you like to be treated. They [the
nurse assistants] can become very resentful of that white lady who's
telling me things. (Maryann Clark, director of nursing, Church Hall)

The organizational changes required to distribute power and voice
more evenly within the facility were not complex, but in practice,
they were low on management's list of priorities. The immediate
cost of raising wages, for example, outweighed any longer-term sav-
ings that might result from decreased turnover. As the facility's personnel officer asserted, "I don't know if a raise in salary is possible,
given the number of aides required." While profit was rarely mentioned, profit was important to Church Hall's new owners. Keeping
salaries low meant larger profits for management, and after all, finding a new body to replace an unhappy nurse assistant was not difficult. Poor women with caregiving experience were plentiful in the
city. Management training for LPNs and scheduling modifications
to allow nurse assistants time to participate in care committees had
also been discussed, but no changes had been implemented.

Supervisors and managers recognized the rapid departure of
nurse assistants, but they neither viewed the women's flight as a
problem, nor did they perceive their strained interactions as a manifestation of women's opposition to workplace policies. Supervisory
staff instead talked about the nurse assistants' leaving as an industry-
wide problem, and at the same time regarded the women as lacking
patience, tolerance, and middle-class finesse. Like Development's
managers, they encouraged their attendance at work through a system of bonuses. And like Development's managers, they viewed
practice in piecemeal fashion. Supervisors who heard women assert
their own knowledge found them defiant or ignorant of the social
order. "They don't react the same way; they're not educated at all,"
asserted one LPN. And as Terry Whitman, the RN on Church Hall's
second floor, commented, "I don't like the way these girls talk to
me. They have no respect." When supervisors saw frustrated and
angry women regularly abandon their jobs, they perceived them to
be irresponsible and immature. "Many young girls leave once
they're certified," explained a supervisor. "Some people don't have
the right attitude." But because managers attributed both job abandonment and interactional dissonance to either the idiosyncratic behavior of irrational individuals or the perceived cultural deficits of
women who were different from themselves, the bonuses they
adopted to encourage attendance and their informal advice to nurse
supervisors to improve communication were ineffective. As a result,

despite best intentions, rapid turnover and communication glitches were constant throughout the course of this research. Although anthropologist Michael Adas writes about peasants and elites in Southeast Asia rather than nurse assistants in the northeastern United States, the following quote from his article "From Foot Dragging to Flight" (1986) is thematically relevant. Adas (1986) asserts that the challenge is to view practice systematically, not in the discrete fashion of Church Hall's senior staff.

> Because they are embedded in established institutions and on-going exchanges between patrons and clients at various levels, serious analysis of peasant defenses and avoidance protest forces us to deal with *whole* social and political systems, rather than concentrating on peasant conditions and responses to vaguely delineated and caricatured elites. It requires that we examine in depth the on-going interaction and day-to-day contests over scarce resources between elites and peasants, taking into account the impact of institutions and ideologies on these processes. (Adas 1986, 66)

An analysis of "whole systems" would have made the relationships between local knowledge and silencing, and between official knowledge and resistance, clear. Instead, nurse assistants, both those referred by the welfare office and those who came to Church Hall directly from a proprietary school or through their own cold calling, were perceived as members and even reproducers of the inner-city poor. Lacking the markers of official knowledge, they were denied a voice both in training and at work. Frustrated by this lack of validation, the women, like the hourly workers at Development, wrestled control of their work through discourse and physical flight. And through that process, like the hourly workers at Development, they too assumed the role of "other" to which they had been delegated.

Although their oppositional behavior might be interpreted both as an expression of power in the midst of powerlessness and as an affirmation of identity by women who felt minimized at work, the outcome, in terms of improved conditions, was not significant (Giroux 1983, 285). Most women moved to other nursing homes that paid only minimally more than Church Hall. Others found work in agencies that paid a higher hourly wage but did not ensure a regular full-time schedule. But few found a way to move up. Like poor women throughout the United States, without an investment in additional education, Joan, Lisa, and their colleagues found themselves relegated to a revolving door of low-level positions, advancing neither professionally nor economically (Harris 1997; Edin and Lein 1997; Schein 1995; Zucchino 1997).

Chapter 3
Concordance Steps and Southeast Asian Refugees

As employees they're outstanding. You have to put a fire extinguisher next to their sneakers. They have a different attitude about jobs. The others haven't seen the other side. They're very protective of their jobs. That's their nature. We could and are probably learning from these Cambodians.
　　　　　—Pete Somelski, floor supervisor, Concordance Steps

You can't impose your will on them [refugees]. They won't take a terrible job just because you tell them. Funders who think refugees should do fast food work think refugees are industrious, they will do what you ask them to. It's not true. They'll do what you want if it's what they want to do.
　　　　　—Bill Dougherty, woodworking training program director

The boss is good, they talk sweet. When make mistakes they say okay. I have a very nice boss, a nice man.
　　　　　—Chan Monivong, CNC operator, Concordance Steps

REFUGEE AS IDENTITY

Chan Monivong, Koung Sisowath, and four other Cambodian men who worked at Concordance Steps were part of the wave of Southeast Asian refugees that entered the United States after the Vietnam war. The men had traveled long and far before arriving at Concordance's thirty-five-man wood shop, where they built spiral, circular, and straight stairs of walnut, pine, and mahogany for custom homes.[1] From prewar Cambodia where they spent their childhood, they fled the Khmer Rouge regime, first to Khao-I-Dang, a refugee camp in Thailand's Prachin Buri Province. After years of waiting in the limbo of refugee life, and countless interviews with and applications to the camp's United Nations (UN) refugee officials, they were transported to this large east coast city and supported for their first eighteen months in the United States by checks from the Department of Public Welfare (DPW).

Four of the men had been farmers or rural laborers in Cambodia. Moeun Daun, Chan's colleague at Concordance, explained, "After school there, in Cambodia, I was a miner. Just a short time. And after that I'm a farmer." Chan and Koung, both from urban middle-class families, were exceptions to the socioeconomic profile of refugee as agricultural worker. Chan Monivong was forty-two, dark haired, squarely built, and serious in demeanor. When he was young, his father, as Chan had explained, owned "two businesses, and buy and sell sheep. He had three hundred employees working." Chan had studied law in Cambodia before the country erupted into civil war in 1975. Now he was a refugee with a wife and three young children to support. Chan explained, "Here I make money to support my family. I need to work hard to learn. Before I never work with my hands." Koung Sisowath was much younger than Chan. Twenty-nine when we first met and dressed in jeans and T-shirt, he looked every bit the postadolescent American. His father had been a professor in prewar Cambodia and his sister was a journalist in Cambodia. Koung was still a boy when the war broke out. His parents were killed, and he escaped Phnom Penh, spending several years alone in the jungle before reaching a refugee camp in Thailand. "I'm there for four years, with men chasing me with guns." The youngest of the Cambodian men at Concordance, Koung was no longer son nor brother but not yet husband nor father. "I think about getting married. But our way I must pay for everything, maybe ten thousand dollars. I'm thirty now, normally Cambodian men are married by the time they are twenty-one." Because he had been so young when he first came to the United States, Koung spent his first few years not only on welfare but in high school, where he majored in hotel services.

Despite their experience and economic status however, once in the United States Chan and Koung were viewed as no different from their four countrymen. They were all Southeast Asian refugees, and in the eyes of most U.S. citizens, that identity made them hard working, dedicated, and focused on the future. Listening to their stories about their past, watching their present, and talking with them about the future provided a window through which to view life postwelfare for refugee men in the United States.

A POLITICAL HISTORY

Similar to Henry and Ruth at Development and Dina and Joan at Church Hall, culturally based perceptions about identity ground the men's stories. Henry and Ruth were the *hardest to serve* of the welfare population, and Dina and Joan were single mothers on welfare. As such, they were all deemed deficit in middle-class norms. But Chan and Koung, on the other hand, were seen through their refugee identity, an ambiguous persona embedded in the social, political, and economic context of their arrival. Asylum seekers can be perceived as either positive or negative additions to the status quo, and during Chan and Koung's first years in the United States, the social identity of refugee was manipulated by both the Right and the Left to justify two very different orientations in government policy. This co-opting of identities by opposing constituencies reflects the fluidity of socially constructed identities and highlights the role both local actors and local events play in shaping poverty prescriptions.

Chan and the other men who found work at Concordance were part of the one million Southeast Asian refugees who flooded the United States between 1975 and 1982.[2] They arrived at a country that was shifting from "the reform-minded social movements of the 1960s" to "the right wing resurgence of the 1980s." The writing of critical theorist Michael Apple provides a background for these changing times.[3]

> The dislocations of the 1960s and 1970s—the struggle for racial and sexual equality, military adventures such as Vietnam, Watergate, the resilience of the economic crisis—produced both shock and fear. "Mainstream" culture was shaken to its very roots in many ways. . . . Traditional social democratic "statist" solutions, which in education, welfare, health, and other similar areas took the form of large-scale attempts at federal intervention to increase opportunities or to provide a minimal level of support, were seen as being part of the problem and not part of the solution. Traditional conservative positions were more easily dismissed as well. After all, the society on which they were based was clearly being altered. The cultural center could be *built* (and it had to be built by well-funded and well-organized political and cultural action) around the principles of the New Right. The New Right confronts the "moral, existential, [and economic] chaos of the preceding decades" with a network of exceedingly well-organized and financially secure organizations incorporating "an aggressive political style, on outspoken religious and cultural traditionalism and a clear populist commitment." (Apple 1993, 25)

Within this historical scenario, publicly constructed perceptions of Southeast Asians' motivation and resilience had been welcomed by an emergent conservative coalition of the New Right. Coalition members set as their goal the dismantling of the welfare state, and they used these ethnically based portrayals as justification for a decrease in funding for refugee training programs (Apple 1993; Omni and Winant 1986). Alfred Russell, the state's Refugee Program manager, reflected these beliefs in his claims about Southeast Asian refugees.

> With refugees there's absolutely no recidivism. You can't argue that refugees come back on assistance. It's so rare, [there are] many studies to support that. The recidivism was very low. We went back quite a ways, went back and looked at were they on before, once they got off, they don't want to get on. It's not something chronic with refugees. Once they leave public assistance, they want to get going. They work hard to keep moving. (Alfred Russell, program manager, State Office for Refugee Affairs)

Through this confluence of circumstances, men such as Chan and Koung had become pawns in a political battle. Federal and state governments preferred inexpensive, immediate placement of refugees into entry-level jobs, while refugee program personnel demanded longer-term training that required greater funding commitments, but resulted in better-paying jobs.

The history of this political battle of wills began with the 1975 passage of the Refugee Assistance Act, which funded English language and employment training for Southeast Asian refugees in the United States (Mason 1986). The funding climate was altered in 1982, however, by the release of a General Accounting Office (GAO) study of resettlement programs. Emerging from the Reagan administration's political and cultural milieu, the study, *Greater Emphasis on Early Employment and Better Monitoring Needed in Indochinese Refugee Resettlement Program* (General Accounting Office 1983), maintained that training programs were not only not necessary for refugee employment, but that they ultimately prolonged welfare dependency. In response to the report, federal refugee assistance was reduced and eligibility for cash and medical assistance was cut from thirty-six months in 1982 to eighteen months by 1987. With the cutback in federal funds, responsibility for refugees fell to the states, and ultimately resulted in large-scale public-assistance cutoffs, mass migrations of refugees across states, and high refugee unemployment, and "served to restrict most refugees to jobs in the secondary labor market requiring little or no training" (Mason 1986, 17). Again quoting the state's refugee manager,

> Eighty-six was the first time Refugee Cash Assistance from the federal government put a 6-month max for training, only if you could also show a reasonable gain in employability wages. We must abide

by that. We have no separate regulations whatever. Our program was 100 percent federally funded. The state pays an awful lot to keep people on welfare after the 6 months. In '86 the states had 36 months reimbursement. Starting in '86 funds were rationed to 31 months, in 1987 to 24, then 18, 12, and last year to 8. Between '86 to '92 the maximum time on welfare dropped from 36 to 8 months. That's all states got in terms of welfare reimbursement.

   At the same time there was an equally dramatic increase in refugees. In 1986 we had 1200 refugees, we have 4400 now. There's a large number on general assistance. We went from 100 percent federal funding at 8 months [after arrival] to 100 percent state funding. A lot of refugees still need assistance after 8 months. Before, 50 percent were self-sufficient. We're approaching 50 percent at 8 months in terms of employables. But there are still a lot of refugees. They cost the state a ton of money. (Alfred Russell, program manager, State Office for Refugee Affairs)

Caught in a political tug-of-war between training program providers and government officials, and between state and federal governments, Chan and Koung's fate in the United States hung in the balance.

ADULT LEARNERS

Culture and difference are negotiated on the local, as well as on the political level, and in practice, Chan and Koung's stories were shaped as much by the training program to which they were referred as the larger political climate. After exhausting his shortened, two-year tenure on welfare, Chan, his DPW case manager's referral in hand, traveled by subway to the midtown offices of Vocational Employment Services (VES), the only agency in the city that offered training for refugees on welfare. Koung's final destination was the same, but his path took a slightly different turn. After graduating from high school he found a job working the reception desk at a nearby Sheraton Hotel. He was happy, but the money he earned wasn't enough to pay the rent. He sought help from his refugee case manager, and she connected him with VES. From its ninth and tenth floor suites in the glass-enclosed midtown office building, VES offered both Chan and Koung hands-on woodworking instruction. Billing itself as "a unique Vocational English as a Second Language (VESL) training opportunity for refugees residing in the city," the agency offered its training to more than 250 welfare eligible émigrés from 1985 to 1992 (Vocational Employment Services 1987).

   Instead of following a model of training that assumed a deficit of middle-class norms, at VES Chan and Koung were perceived and treated as rational and able adults, served best by training that would both enhance their skills and connect them to jobs offering livable wages and comprehensive benefits. Fundamentally different from the beliefs espoused by trainers at Development and in DPW's Job Development Unit, this relatively unusual orientation was repeatedly linked to Bill Dougherty, the project's former director. Dougherty, an anthropologist by education, had done fieldwork in Southeast Asia. During our first conversation, he explained:

> I believe [the training model] was my doing. I have a background in Anthropological Linguistics. I have an interest in cultures. I think people don't think in cultural terms. Obviously we have to address programs within these terms. The closer cultures appear, the less people focus on cultural difference, but the greater those differences matter. There's a great paternalistic view of the foreign born and refugees. Employment practices and government are racist. They're based on a sense of superiority. It really shapes policy. But you can't impose your will on them [the refugees]. They won't take a terrible job just because you tell them. Funders who think refugees should do fast food work think refugees are industrious, they will do what you ask them to. It's not true. They'll do what you want if it's what they want to do. (Bill Dougherty, woodworking training program director, VES)

The unique circumstances of the program's funding supported Dougherty's convictions. The woodworking training was funded by what was then called a Targeted Assistance Program (TAP) grant through the state's Refugee Resettlement Program. Congress created TAP in 1983 in response to the intense lobbying efforts by refugee program personnel, state-level coordinators, and county officials over cutbacks in refugee training initiated the previous year. Unlike earlier federal funding structures that simply reimbursed states for all refugee-related expenditures, TAP grants, as part of government's efforts to tighten funding for refugee training programs, were awarded in response to proposals from counties with high refugee densities. According to Mason (1986, 22), TAP moneys were to "provide English language instruction, employment training, and employment services to promote self sufficiency in impacted counties." Because grants were awarded outright rather than attached to performance measurements, TAP actually freed program staff to experiment. As a result, VES staff members enjoyed an unusual amount of flexibility to plan, implement, and modify its refugee training program.

Most fundamental to their planning was the assumption that linking men such as Chan and Koung to jobs with livable wages required
both an appreciation of existing skills and an understanding of the
local job market. Chan and the other men were perceived neither as
empty vessels to be filled by the legitimate knowledge of texts and
teachers, nor as the embodiment of warped cultural norms. They
were treated instead as adults with experiences and skills gained
over a lifetime. According to Dougherty, "The programs that worked
best had some vague connection with skills people brought with
them. We tried to look at what kind of training would use the skills
that Southeast Asian and Ethiopian refugees brought with them."
VES staff members found that woodworking was a common denominator in the men's experiences. "Cambodian people mostly do this
kind of thing," Koung explained. "But not with a power saw."
Koung himself had built huts in the refugee camp in Thailand. "I
work for the, I don't know the name, for the UN." Nearly all the
Cambodian men had worked with wood in the past. Tang Preah,
working alongside Chan in Concordance's straight stair department,
concurred with Koung's assessment. "In Cambodia I cut big pieces
of wood lumber, hardwood, with a hand saw," he explained. Only
Chan Monivong, from an urban middle-class family in Cambodia,
had had absolutely no experience with wood at all. "I work hard to
learn everything in America, because I didn't go to college here," he
explained. "My brother was mechanical. I only watched. I didn't
want to get my hands dirty."

THE LABOR MARKET

The state's Department of Labor and Industry (DOL) projections,
however, did not support a training focus on woodworking skills. In
fact, like projections for most of the country, data from the DOL
showed a decrease in employment opportunities for woodworkers
and an increase in employment in the service sector. Other PIC
(Private Industry Council) and welfare funded programs reflected
this market analysis, with training for the poor clustered in areas
most closely related to the service sector. From 1985 to 1992, the
same years VES facilitated its woodworking training, for example,
local training programs for welfare recipients focused on the following jobs: security guard, paralegal, retail associate, dental assistant,
income tax preparer, computer technician, food server, maintenance
worker, customer service representative, nursing assistant, data processor, child care worker.

But for Chan and Koung, local dynamics won out once again. By basing their proposal on former clients' placements and conversations with local employers, VES trainers convinced state officials that woodworking was indeed a viable training focus. "We had job development meetings with employers," explained Dougherty. "We had talked to employers before and that continued before, during, and after. We added machines when we saw them in the shops. We were using practical knowledge from our clients about the job market." He continued:

> We looked at surveys, thought woodworking was a possibility, and the agency had placed some people on the lower level. People who did best had some skills, at least had worked with wood.
>   The economic forecasts were toward the service sector. People just took the economic forecasts literally, but our placements showed differently. Working with refugees, we saw it was clear there were non-service jobs to be had. There were some directories that showed woodworking jobs. During the time I was there, there was more job availability. In woodworking there was no training offered. When we looked, we also looked at construction. There were problems with the union, getting in at all, and also the problems of minorities getting in. Although eventually they did get some people in. We didn't have a lot of heavy duty labor market manuals and parameters. We could develop curriculum matching the local job market. Local government programs tend to want uniformity, so the model can be tested and used in many places. We were more flexible. (Bill Dougherty, woodworking training program director, VES)

Both trainers and job developments talked about their on-going consultation with local employers as key to VES work. Potential employers acted as consultants during the planning of the project and development of the curriculum. Local employers visited the training site, and VES's job developer and skills instructors regularly visited potential employers to coordinate skills training with workplace needs.

Despite the somewhat atypical training focus, the VES fifteen-week woodworking training program also fit the state's criteria. Less than four months in length, it was considered short in duration, had a low minimum academic skills requirement, and a realistic goal of full-time, permanent employment paying $5 to $6.00 an hour with benefits.

SKILLS TRAINING AND HANDS-ON LEARNING

Like many models of skills training, VES's woodworking was hands-on. But at VES, hands-on meant something different from either Development's supported work or Church Hall's clinical instruction. At VES, hands-on translated to the integration of doing with learning the skills needed to do. Chan and Koung were introduced to a new world, with its new vocabulary and specialized math operations, both in class and during the hands-on practice time. During their fifteen weeks of training, they built a grinder table, a hardware chest, a frame and panel box, stairs, a cutting board, an Ellis Island bench, and a credenza. They acquired the language they needed for these tasks by talking about jointers, dado heads, bevels, calipers, radial arm saws, and splines, and they acquainted themselves with principles involved in design and fabrication by calculating in metrics, manipulating fractions, and measuring angles in real tasks. Their days consisted of three hours of hands-on practice and three hours of vocational English as a Second Language (VESL), mathematics, shop theory, work orientation, and job search techniques, all synchronized by teachers who "coordinate[d] lessons and activities in ways which reinforce[d] vocabulary, shop skills, and the development of effective communication and problem solving techniques" (Vocational Employment Services, 1987, 7). Caren Kurtz, the project's job developer, described the VES training as both participatory and interactive.

> Reducing her voice almost to a whisper as though telling me a secret, Kurtz described the changes made in the woodworking curriculum to create a learning environment that more closely reflected the workplace. "We had a really good rapport with the companies. Very often the shop teacher would come to the job site, to see what kinds of things they were doing. Anything he could take back he did."
>
> "I don't want to betray Bill [the director], but the program design originally had discrete skills. The shop teacher said no, you got to do projects. People can see the process and the end result. That was one reason for success. People made incredible furniture, laminated cubbies for a day care. We built a lot for nonprofits, for a school for handicapped children, for day cares, a shelter, for the Y where the school was located, and for the school itself." Caren pointed to her bookshelf and desk of light wood and simple Shaker design, both made by a woodworking class. "I could go into raptures about the furniture."
>
> "People would make things, smaller projects, cutting boards to take home. Did you see the reception desk upstairs, with inlaid wood? They did that." She pulled out a stack of colored photographs from her desk drawer and sorted through them, showing me prints of

smiling men and women of all shapes and hues, holding striated wood grained chess boards. (January 13, 1993, field notes, Concordance Steps)

During training, Chan and Koung also learned first hand about the industry. "Students would also take field trips," added Kurtz. "They went to sawmills, Martin Guitar company, to arboretums."

JOB PLACEMENT

Job placement rates for VES graduates were high; between 80 percent to 85 percent of the men and women found work and remained on the job after ninety days at an average cost per placement of approximately $4,500. The majority of the placements were in woodworking, with a smaller percent in skilled assembly. Concordance was one of more than three hundred employers contacted through job developers' cold calls, woodworking instructors' networks, and existing agency links, and everyone agreed that this link was particularly fortuitous. As Chan explained,

> The first thing it's so hard to have the same language to talk and joke. The boss was kindly, the other people were kindly, and I was lucky to get another kindly boss and supervisor. . . . The boss is good, they talk sweet. When make mistakes they say okay. I have a very nice boss a nice man. (Chan Monivong, foreman, Concordance Steps)

According to Dougherty, marketing Southeast Asian refugees to members of the local business community had been relatively easy.

> Some employers were interested because it was refugees. It's possible employers wanted to help. But they may also think refugees were subservient. Among employers there's a definite belief about refugees, they would work, not give them any trouble. There are traditional biases in the workforce, and they affect hiring. We had a lot of experience pushing refugees. Some employers wanted a specific kind of refugee. They never said anything but based on their hiring practices, we could tell they wanted a Southeast Asian rather than an Ethiopian. (Bill Dougherty, woodworking training program director, VES)

Chan's and Koung's identity as refugees may have been an asset in VES's job placement efforts. Dougherty, however, was not as positive about the reception other job seekers would have received from the private sector.

The program originated in the south side of the city, the building was burned by an arsonist. It was moved to the YWCA on Barbara Street. People at the Y knew of African Americans in the community who knew about the program and were interested. We talked to employers, and they weren't necessarily interested in African Americans as woodworkers. Because of the labor market I don't know if it would have really worked. With PIC type [performance based] funding, it's not reasonable to require much more than the job markets would allow. (Bill Dougherty, woodworking training program director, VES)

Jay Hawks, Chan's "kindly boss," seemed to agree with Doughterly's assertion. Hawks described his company's workforce, six Cambodian men, one Pole, two Puerto Rican brothers, and twenty-five ethnic whites from the surrounding area, as diverse. However only one woman, the secretary in the front office, was employed at Concordance, and no African Americans had worked at Concordance since Hawks bought the company in 1985. Hawks justified the absence of African Americans on the shop floor by explaining that while he had tried to hire a few blacks, only six or seven had ever applied, and none were as qualified as the other men in the applicant pool. "Anyway," he continued. "there aren't a lot of blacks in the industry. In construction sites blacks only compose five percent of the workforce."

> The VES training program has a very different student body. In another world the Cambodians were almost middle class. We can deal with their problems. I don't know if we can handle drug abuse, low skills, no work ethic. A lot of things we can't handle, a lot of grief all the time. (Jay Hawks, owner, Concordance Steps)

Hawks's assertion was actually far from true. Although Chan and Koung had been from urban families, Concordance's other Cambodian employees, Peang Sothearos, Moeun Daun, Tang Preah, Sefan Ang, and the vast waves of Cambodians who came to the United States were not. They had been poor miners and farmers. According to Mary Carol Hopkins, the author of an examination of Cambodians' struggle, *Braving a New World* (1996, 132):

> Those who had some higher education knew French, not English, and so often those chose to go to France; consequently many of those who came to the US were those with little education or little choice. They came with a low level of literacy in their own language and almost no English. Few adults had any Western-style schooling, and many had no school experience at all.

But the veracity of Hawks's claims about the men, their being "almost middle class" mattered less to Hawks than his beliefs about what being a Cambodian refugee meant. Ethnicity and identity had melded for Chan and Koung in their move from welfare to Hawks's woodshop, as much, if not more than it did for Henry, Ruth, Dina, and Joan. The ideology around a refugee identity, rather than any real knowledge of the men's background, became their cultural capital in the labor market, and it proved sufficient to access what other men and women could not.

In a political climate molded by the New Right and its continued calls for cutbacks in social spending, however, the success of the VES woodworking training soon became too expensive, even for these deserving few. Alfred Russell, the state's Refugee Program manager used the woodworking training cost of "somewhere around $4000 to $5000 per person" to justify the program's termination.

> The woodworking training was relatively inexpensive for training but not compared with $800 for employment services. Our policy is a less directed policy; it's more a reactive policy. As reductions from the federal government came down, we put people straight into jobs. We can place people for under $1200 because of our accelerated job placement. Entry level, a lot of service, some small assembly type jobs. The average wage was $5.42, in the city it was $5.80.
> The entry wage for people coming out of woodworking wasn't higher. They were better prepared, but not better wages. They were pretty set entry wages, either union or non union. The program staff could not show any increased wages initially. But if you did longitudinal research, people were going to stay there [in woodworking jobs] longer from a 12-week program. (Alfred Russell, program manager, State Office for Refugee Affairs)

Chan's and Koung's identity as Southeast Asian refugees was negotiated in federal policy, in locally made decisions, and in what society chose to afford at a particular moment in history. Yet while finding themselves at Concordance rather than at Development or Church Hall may have been an accident of circumstances, this negotiation of social identities certainly worked in their favor. Caren Kurtz, the project's job developer, agreed with Chan's assessment of his good fortune:

> Concordance is a real find. It's at the higher end of stair building. There were a lot of possibilities for growth. Not like a year later you're stuck or you move on. Companies also had a broad range of pay. Some started at $5.00. Others started higher. Concordance started at $6.50 or $7.00. (Caren Kurtz, job developer, VES)

THE SOCIAL ORGANIZATION OF WORK

Concordance rented space in an office park about ten miles across the river from center city, along an old four-lane highway dotted by car dealerships, chain appliance and furniture stores, and shopping malls. The company was located six streets in from the entrance of the office park, toward the back of a row of low-slung brick buildings that housed the stair-building firm and five other companies. Concordance was basically one large warehouse with space divided into discrete work areas for drafting, straight stairs, circular stairs, rail department, sales, and installation. Wood was piled floor to ceiling against each wall, and stairs, in various stages, decorated the room's bare wooden floor.

Like all workers on the shop floor, Chan and Koung started work at Concordance "in the back, little stupid jobs," as one of their colleagues explained. For their first six months with the company, they moved wood and sanded balusters, short pieces of wood that eventually became supports for stair railings. According to Koung, "In school I learned how to make cabinets, and I learned about stairs on the job. New workers start slow on small jobs, learning all there is to know about each job. No one thinks you'll know everything."

His description of his entry into the company was not atypical. Tang Preah, for instance, started work on the baluster machine in the back of Concordance's shop floor, spending days inserting thin rectangular pieces of wood into the machine's saw, and standing over it as the wood was shaped into balusters. "For me I take about half year to learn all different kind of baluster. Make good baluster, make good stair," Tang explained. After six months, he moved to the straight stair department, where he worked as part of a team with Peang Daun, Sefan Ang, Moeun Daun, and Chan. Koung, on the other hand, had been assigned to the rail department after "start[ing] slow on small jobs." Jake Hansen, the rail department's supervisor, explained that "Koung was sanding balusters. I wanted him to work in the stairs. He said okay, and after a month he knew the work." Koung now made rails for spiral staircases. He generally worked alone at his neat work station to the front of the shop floor, and occasionally conferred with Jake about a particular piece of wood. The following is from field notes made while I watched Koung work.

> I approached Koung as he worked at his station on a three-foot piece of curved wood. He told me, "This is not fun," referring to his difficulty in maneuvering the cumbersome length of the wood, which was

only part of a long curved banister. He laid the piece of wood on a table next to his workstation, and put two two-foot pieces of wood, previously cut with an electric saw, end to end so that the smaller pieces touched each other and one was flush against the end of the larger piece. Together, the three pieces would become part of a banister.

Koung took a clipboard from the wall above the work station, flipped through the pages clipped to the board, found a sheet with some drawings on it, unclipped the page, laid it on the table, and studied it for a few minutes. He explained that the paper was part of a pattern for the rail, designed by Tim Brown, the company's computer programmer, and John Jacobson, its draftsperson. Koung took one of the smaller pieces of wood, laid it onto the pattern, and toyed with the wood, moving it around in an attempt to determine where to cut notches into the wood.

He took the pieces to Tang Preah in the straight stairs department to sand, and when he returned, he laid one of the pieces back onto the pattern. Koung marked triangles in ink onto the edge of the piece and a crown-like shape onto the other end, and then approached Jake Hansen for advice on the markings. From the consultation, Koung moved to an electric saw, and holding the wood steady, he cut notches into one end and cut the other so that the triangles protruded. Returning again to his work station, Koung sanded the edges with sandpaper, laid the wood edge to edge with the longer piece on the table, and slid them together so the notches accommodated the small triangles. The pieces fit firmly. Koung repeated the process with the second two-foot long piece of wood, cutting and sanding, and then sliding this piece onto the edge of the other two-foot piece. He removed the pieces, sanded the edges yet again, reassembled the pieces, disassembled them, and applied glue to the edges. Working with two pieces at a time, Koung pushed the edges together, held them first with his hands, and then clamped them with a brace he took from a drawer in his workstation. (August 3 and October 16, 1992, field notes, Concordance Steps)

While not tedious, Koung's work was slow, precise, and as he suggested, not always "fun." Each rail was individualized and demanded constant problem solving. Working on these often unwieldy rail designs was an unhurried process of trial and error. As Tim Brown, the company's computer programmer, asserted about this facet of the company's work, "The design dictates the speed."

Chan had a different history with the company. Despite his self-professed lack of experience working either with his hands or with wood, something about his distinctively middle-class and academic background made him stand out from the others. After his obligatory six months of sanding balusters, Chan had been selected to supervise the straight stair department. And when the time came to choose three men to operate the company's newly purchased computerized, numerically controlled lathe, more commonly known as the CNC, Chan was one of the three. According to Chan, Pete Somelski, the shop foreman, had chosen him as CNC operator because the job "needed someone who could handle mistakes, could stay calm. [I] learned slow, slow. It's not easy, little by little." During one of my first visits to Concordance, I watched Chan operate the CNC.

> The CNC was a large green machine, eight feet wide, twenty feet long, six feet tall, a metal monster sitting in the center of the shop floor. Chan divided his time between the straight stair department, the computer in the drafting station, and the CNC. On the days he operated the CNC, he worked to a fluid, yet silent rhythm, as though dancing to music only he could hear.
>
> Wearing plastic goggles, Chan took four pieces of rectangular wood from a box on the floor to his left and inserted them into the CNC. He programmed commands on a keyboard on the front of the CNC, pushed several buttons on the machine's control panel, and stood five feet back while a large rotating bit followed his commands. It descended from the top of the machine and shaped the wood into spindle shaped balusters. When the wood was shaped, Chan removed the pieces and inserted four other wooden rectangles into the CNC. Every now and then the bit got stuck. When it did, Chan turned off the machine and knocked the bit with a wooden hammer. He then removed the bit, and wiped it with a tool that he took from a tool box to the side of the computer panel.
>
> Chan pointed to boxes of shaped and unshaped pieces of wood on either side of the CNC, explaining that he shaped three hundred balusters yesterday. "Today maybe finish." He added that he did work for all three of the company's departments. The CNC took five minutes to shape the wood. Shaping it by hand took thirty minutes. (July 27, 1993, field notes, Concordance Steps)

Despite different paths within the company, both Chan and Koung found themselves postwelfare in the least hierarchical of all four work places. At Concordance, management was thin and autonomous teams (i.e., straight stairs, circular stairs, and rail) were responsible for the construction of the company's staircases. The organization of woodworkers into teams was based upon managers' perceptions of the men's' skills and limitations. As Jay Hawks, the company's owner explained, cultural identity loomed large in his decisions.

I almost always keep them [the Cambodian men] in the shop for two reasons. One, they don't function well except in a structured environment. They need to know what to do. They are around other Cambodians, to speak Cambodian. And two, they don't like to go out, they're afraid they might not understand, or that they'll have to make decisions they won't feel comfortable making.

Another guy here, a foreigner, he's Polish. He's the same. As long as you keep them doing the jobs they have to do, they do well. But don't send them out to do sales. (Jay Hawks, owner, Concordance Steps)

This talk about teams once again reflected stereotyped beliefs about Asians. According to Pete Somelski, Concordance's shop foreman, "They're [the Cambodians] very clannish. I find that they work best when they're together. Together as a team they work better."

Teamwork, however, was not absolute. The men functioned independently and in formal and informal groups, at times with the "rhythmic complementarity" of ballroom dancers, working in reciprocity on tasks initiated through work orders (Erickson and Shultz 1982, 96). They formed and re-formed themselves, asking supervisors and colleagues for guidance when needed and occasionally receiving unsolicited input and assistance from the floor. As Koung explained:

I work in the rail department by myself. Sometimes I work in the back, pulling out lumber and planks. There's always something there. When you need help, you can just ask anybody. If we see someone do something dangerous, we help. (Koung Sisowath, rail department, Concordance Steps)

Regardless of where Koung found himself, at Concordance, the work was always most important. The stairs, in their evolving states, were the common denominator, and shaping and manipulating wood was the focus, the challenge, and the practice through which the men related. The planks of mahogany, pine, and walnut stacked floor to ceiling on metal shelves, and the enormous circular staircase, arranged in parts and set in clamps in the corner, were in fact as much a part of Concordance as were the men. The language of the stairs, balusters, treads, risers, returns, helix, rabbets, bevel, rake, tangents, stringer, and soffits, was a language the men shared. It was the language of the industry, and one that united these men of diverse backgrounds, ethnicities, experiences, and first languages. The men worked with the wood as demanded; the construction and completion of each staircase was based upon a symbiotic relationship among the company's departments. In this way, much of the floor ran itself, with supervisory staff working alongside employees and acting as resource and facilitator. The company's owner related the fluid social organization to his beliefs about management. "Pete is a laid-back supervisor," Jay Hawks claimed. "I'm a laid-back manager. It's a two-sided coin. Back in the beginning I made the commitment. I think most people want to do a good job, if they're allowed."

CAMBODIANS ARE A LITTLE BETTER

Wherever they worked on the shop floor, the Cambodian men were perceived by their supervisors as hard workers, as almost better workers than their American counterparts. These images of Southeast Asians as industrious and focused on the future had preceded Chan and Koung into the workplace. Everyone at Concordance Steps believed that it was in the men's "nature" to be diligent and devoted, and these beliefs were echoed in both formal interviews and informal discussions throughout the company. The following conversation with Jay Hawks, the company's owner and director, and Pete Somelski, the shop foreman, reflected these sentiments.

> We talked in Jay's small office, the floor scattered with architect blueprints, and the desk with papers and books. Our discussion was informal, focusing on the men who came through the VES training. Jay, a white man in his mid-forties, looked more like a lab technician than a manager in his blue cotton jacket, Concordance Steps embroidered in red script on the right breast pocket. He related, "These are Cambodians. They're different. . . . They'll work weekends, overtime. They know very well what they're worth and they expect a paycheck." Pete, taller and thinner, with light brown hair cut shorter than Jay's, was Jay's shop supervisor, and he continued where Jay left off. "As employees they're outstanding. You have to put a fire extinguisher next to their sneakers. They have a different attitude about jobs. The others haven't seen the other side. They're very protective of their jobs. That's their nature. We could and are probably learning from these Cambodians."
>
> The praises continued with Pete commenting, "I heard the national standard is 80 percent of time on task on the job." Jay added, "Our Cambodians are a little better." Continuing with this thought, Pete asserted, "They give 120 percent every day and love it. The tendency for the locals is to wait until you tell them to do something." (July 15, 1992, field notes, Concordance Steps)

These opinions were not limited to the company's supervisors. As the following excerpt from a later set of field notes illuminates, they were repeated by the men's colleagues on the shop floor.

Late morning at Concordance Steps, I watched from the sidelines as Peang Sothearos, Moeun Daun, and Tang Preah, three of the Cambodian men assigned to the straight stair department, maneuvered a five-inch thick and fifteen-foot long piece of wood onto an electric saw that was permanently stationed in the rail department. The length of the beam, four pieces of plywood glued together, made it unwieldy. Even for three men, cutting the beam into the wall stringer it was intended to be would be awkward.

Resting the wood on a saw horse, Peang held one end and Moeun the other as Tang cut V's out of one of the beam's long sides. Finishing with one side, they slowly walked a full circle as they turned the beam around so that Tang could cut triangular-sized wedges from the other side. George Simpson, a young white man from the rail department, approached the Cambodians, and without asking, helped them hold the wood as Tang cut. Later he took one end as they carried it back to the straight stair department. After about five minutes, the three Cambodians carried another long uncut piece of wood to the saw. They moved it into position, and cut the same kind of triangular wedges out of this piece.

Later George confided, "I don't know if you've ever seen these guys working. There's five of them. You'd swear it was fifty the way they work." (August 3, 1992, field notes, Concordance Steps)

Of course it was no secret that the men were different, particularly in terms of their language and their histories. They spoke Cambodian outside work and fragmented English at work, they played a Cambodian version of Chinese Chess during lunch, and they all lived in close proximity to other Cambodian families just south of center city, some in a Cambodian neighborhood, others renting an apartment in a building in which at least one other Cambodian family lived. Chan was also active in a local Cambodian cultural organization. "I'm in charge of culture there," he explained. But difference in and of itself does not ensure censure. To quote linguist Del Hymes (1972, xxv), "Everything depends, not on the presence of variation in speech—there is always that—but on whether and to what extent difference is invested with social meaning." And because the men's identity as refugee worker, rather than their linguistic or cultural differences, was made salient at Concordance, their ethnic difference was not "invested with social meaning."

THE LANGUAGE BARRIER

Grounded in the belief that Chan and Koung were hardworking and dedicated, cultural differences came to be viewed at Concordance as strengths and preferences, rather than as deficits. This paradigm of difference was applied to the men's language skills. Their English was limited and their ability to communicate remained questionable. Pete Somelski, the shop foreman, confessed that he had initially resisted hiring the men because of their limited English. "The problem with the Cambodians, I was afraid of their lack of English," he admitted. "I need someone to understand. When I say turn off the saw, I need them to do it immediately." And earlier, during our first conversation, Somelski confided that his only real problem with the Cambodians was "trying to understand their English. We communicate through International Sign Language. Chan, his English's no better, but I'm understanding him better. When Chan's not there, it's difficult to communicate to the others." Somelski's assertions were true. No one hid the fact that even after an average tenure of three and a half years with the company, the men's English was still rudimentary. Yet managers and colleagues alike minimized these communication difficulties, and readily described a range of strategies they employed to communicate with the Cambodians. Jay Hawks, the company's owner, asserted, "Almost all the work orders are in numbers; they understand numbers. We are not grading these guys on language skills. We're paying them to build staircases." He even went so far as to find advantages in the communication difficulties.

> One thing about not speaking much English, they're much less likely to be distracted by chatter. They don't try to eavesdrop on office politics. The other big fault of the American workers, they bring unfortunate baggage. They've worked in another shop; they want to reinvent the wheel. That's not a problem with the Cambodians, their English isn't sufficient to suggest alternatives. They don't advise. (Jay Hawks, owner, Concordance Steps)

Tim Brown, the company's computer specialist and Chan's mentor on the CNC, talked about the ways he communicated with Chan.

> Chan's English is better than some of the others. You try to make unambiguous statements. I use pictures or just pick up and talk about the object. Do by example. Pick up a physical thing. (Tim Brown, computer programmer, Concordance Steps)

Jake Hansen, Koung's supervisor in the rail department, added:

> Koung, he really doesn't interact with those other guys. So he really
> has no need to speak Cambodian. It is sometimes a bit hard. With
> Koung it's not too bad. He's pretty much Americanized. Sometimes
> with Frank too, our shaper, he's Polish. You use your hands a lot, draw
> sketches, show them the actual thing. I've been with Frank for a long
> time. (Jake Hansen, rail department supervisor, Concordance Steps)

The problem of language was mitigated at Concordance. Although
in our conversations the men's English pronunciation was unclear,
their sentences choppy, and their vocabulary extremely limited, as
Hymes suggested, these linguistic "variations," like their cultural
differences, were not "invested with social meaning." Instead of
their limited English, it was the men's attitudes toward work that
were made meaningful. In fact, when I asked Pete what finally convinced him to hire the men from the woodworking program, he responded, "The results were immediate." Workplace performance
quickly outweighed any concerns Pete had about the men's inability
to communicate on the shop floor.

ERRORS ON THE FLOOR

This respect for and appreciation of the men persisted even when
they made mistakes at work. Foreshadowing a company-wide preoccupation about errors, during one of our first conversations, Jay
Hawks, Concordance's owner, leaned forward and lowered his voice
to explain:

> If we give a work order that's wrong, they'll [the Cambodian wood
> workers] build it anyway. If I put in a work order, mistakenly trans-
> pose the numbers, and give it to American workers, they'd say some-
> thing's wrong. If you give them [the Cambodians] the wrong order,
> they'll build it anyway. Americans won't. (Jay Hawks, owner,
> Concordance Steps)

When I asked Chan what happened when mistakes were made, he
explained, "They say okay, you build another one. Everyone make
mistakes, because no one is perfect." Koung described a similar
management style in the rail department.

> We go to our supervisor and tell them what's wrong. We try to correct
> or throw it away. But it is not a problem, because there's a lot of mis-
> takes, it comes from the salesperson. They write the work order

wrong, so we make it wrong. We make another one. (Koung Sisowath, rail department, Concordance Steps)

Over the course of my data collection at the woodworking company, work-related errors became cause for increased concern, and the topic eventually became an obvious point of contention among the employees. Jake Hansen, Koung's supervisor, told me:

We find out when the installers go out to the field that we often have to make modifications [on the finished stairs]. Some are minor, but some are major. We have to stop and backtrack. That puts them [the workers on the floor] in a bad mood. (Jake Hansen, rail department supervisor, Concordance Steps)

Hansen continued in a hushed tone that within the past year Concordance's owner had had two quality control teams in the building, and both had told him that the problems didn't stem from the workmen on the floor. Work orders had been written incorrectly; maybe the salesman hadn't measured from the first to the second floor properly, or maybe he had bent the tape measure when measuring so his calculations were slightly off. Recounting an anecdote about errors and modifications, Hansen explained,

We went out a few weeks ago to put a very expensive staircase into a house more than an hour from the shop. When we got there the contractor asked "where are the big blocks on which the staircase is to rest?" The installation team asked, "What blocks?" since they weren't told anything about blocks. The salesman responded, "Oh that's right, I forgot about that." (Jake Hansen, rail department, Concordance Steps)

There were also times when Hawks himself took an order or modification over the phone and either didn't pass it on to men in the shop floor or neglected to write it down. "He's everywhere. Things get lost in the process," Hansen explained. He continued that stairs were rarely delivered and installed in just one trip. Much more often they had to be returned to the shop, disassembled, and reassembled again. At times they had to be taken apart completely, and only a few small pieces could be reused. A year after my initial visit to Concordance, Chan began to keep a log in which he regularly documented these remakes, explaining that Pete, the shop foreman, had suggested the record keeping in order to determine the source of the mistakes.

But while this absorption with errors catalyzed grumbling (oppositional behavior at Concordance didn't seem to progress past mumbled complaints), managers focused on the process, rather than the individual woodworker. The attitude that *everybody makes mistakes* was part of the company's ethos. Not that mistakes were viewed as positive, they weren't. But they were seen as systematic within the company, rather than idiosyncratic to particular men or particular kinds of men.

YOU HAVE TO KNOW PEOPLE

At Concordance, the men's status within the company was also affirmed by supervisors' explicit attempts to foster a caring relationship with their thirty-five-man workforce. One example of these efforts was their rallying of support for Tang Preah during a personal crisis. As Jay Hawks described the circumstances, his eyes reddened in empathy for Tang's pain.

> I work with thirty-five people; you have to know people. We socialize with each other, have picnics. Another thing, another reason.... Remember Tang? He was robbed a few years ago; his wife was dropped from a second story window. The guys in the shop took up a collection, I went over, me personally with Chan, to the place they were staying. Had a cup of tea, gave him the envelope to hold him over for a week or so, buy some new things, a couple hundred bucks. I don't think I'll ever forget the look on his wife's face, tears were streaming down her face. (Jay Hawks, owner, Concordance Steps)

This sense of caring also extended to the men's co-workers. "These guys get along great," asserted shop's foreman. "If there's any bigotry, they [the co-workers] leave it at home." If in fact tension among employees existed on the shop floor, it was completely invisible to me as an observer. I saw no instances of what Frederick Erickson and Jeffrey Shultz (1982, 104) called "uncomfortable moments"[1] between the Cambodians and their colleagues. Instead I saw many instances of collegial joking and spontaneous instances of support and exchanges of information. The following, an excerpt from my field notes, illustrates two such interactions.

> During a morning visit to Concordance, the entire shop floor was hand sanding balusters. The sanding machine had broken, and in order to meet a contractual obligation to sand 120 balusters, all other work had been momentarily suspended. Everyone on the shop floor, including Pete Somelski, was sanding. Chan explained, "It would take one man an entire day to do them all."
> Some men were sanding by hand. Others devised ingenious

schemes using clamps and machines. Two Puerto Rican men, brothers who worked with Koung in the rail department, sanded with a drill bit they had covered with sandpaper. Koung walked toward the rail department with a piece of sandpaper rubbed bare in his hand. One of the brothers called him over, showed him the sanded balusters, and explained their sanding invention. "It's easier, man," he said.

Pete was at a machine a few work stations away. As Peang Sothearos passed, he gently poked Pete. Pete ran after Peang with a baluster, attempting to poke him back, and when he finally caught up with the Cambodian man, he jabbed him in jest with the wooden spindle. Like children playing tag, they both laughed at themselves and the interaction. (July 27, 1993, field notes, Concordance Steps)

"I was afraid that there might be some initial prejudice," Jay Hawks was quoted as saying in an interview for a professional newsletter. "But there has been absolutely none" (Hand 1989, B10).

Perhaps at least part of this camaraderie can be attributed to the company's equitable treatment of its employees. At Concordance, there was only one starting wage and one set of personnel policies. "We treat them like Americans," asserted Pete, implying that Chan and Koung were not singled out for treatment that was more or less than that received by the company's other employees. Equitable treatment included a livable wage, enough to "support my family," said Chan. Starting pay at the company was seven dollars an hour. "A guy like Chan is making eleven or twelve dollars an hour; without overtime that's twenty-four thousand dollars. With overtime it's over thirty thousand dollars," explained Jay Hawks. Chan's counterparts confirmed the competitiveness of Concordance's wages. Albert Medina, from the neighborhood and working next to Koung in the rail department, confided that, "Some of us are looking for other work. We look in the paper, when we go on the interview we find they're paying four dollars less than we get here. . . . Koung's been here seven years. Nowhere else can compete."

Equitable treatment also translated into an adequate benefit package. Moeun Daun, whom Chan supervised in straight stairs, had tested the benefit policy just before my arrival at Concordance. Moeun explained:

A piece of wood flew and hit my stomach, forty inches long and deep in my stomach. Pete took me [to the hospital]. I go to the hospital two times. They put in just a [colostomy] bag, two weeks, the second time after three weeks, then put my intestine back. I was out of work about four months together, and in the hospital for five weeks. (Moeun Daun, straight stairs, Concordance Steps)[5]

In and out of the hospital for two operations, Moeun contended that Concordance's benefit package was better than that of previous employers. He explained, "There they paid for hospital, not doctor. Here pay for doctor too." Jay Hawks added, "When Moeun was in the hospital, his worst fear was that he would lose his job. He didn't, and his operation didn't cost him a thing because of workman's comp. . . . We pay full benefits. A lot of guys don't realize that. Well, they realize that when they go out looking for another job."

APPRECIATING KINDLINESS

Chan's and Koung's stories involve taking on new identities. Refugee status has many liminal qualities; the men were neither completely American nor totally Cambodian. Ten years after immigrating to the United States, they were still negotiating what it meant to be part of two very different worlds. But while Chan and Koung were even farther from the mainstream than Henry and Ruth at Development or Dina and Joan at Church Hall, their difference was not made salient, problematic, or burdensome at Concordance. They recognized that they were treated fairly at work; Chan described his employers as "kindly" and supportive, and his workplace practice reflected these appraisals of equitable treatment. Literature on refugees and immigrants most often relates this conciliatory attitude to the immigrant experience, and to a combination of newcomers' high level of tolerance and hopeful buoyancy. (Bailey 1987; Gibson 1988; Ogbu 1974). According to anthropologist John Ogbu (1987, 271), "In general, whether in the past or among the more recent immigrants, the goal of self advancement is uppermost in the minds of the immigrants and acts as a strong incentive to exploit anticipated and unanticipated opportunities and to maintain pragmatic attitudes toward economic and other activities, even in the face of prejudice and discrimination." Ogbu's theories describe at least part of Chan's experiences. Chan recognized that power demarcated both his present and his future, and he was aware that his own powerlessness confined him to a position in the labor force that was not of his own choosing. At fifty-two, and the most senior of the Cambodian men in terms of age, education, community networks, and economic status, Chan had not planned to spend his adult years as a woodworker. As mentioned earlier, in Cambodia his family had been middle class. Had the country not imploded upon itself, Chan probably would have continued the family business. Since he had studied law at the university, he would have most likely also become a lawyer. But his aspirations were part of the life he had left behind. Now in the United States, he saw himself putting business aspirations on hold as well. Chan explained, "I want to do some business, but it cannot be. Because I want to learn computer. Everything is on computer. . . . I think I need more language, for communication. I think I will try to go to college. Two hours, two weeks, something like that. I will need more language because I want to be building up." Chan coped with the demands of an unforeseen future. With three children, ages twelve, eleven, and nine, to support, he was both wistful about the plans he was forced to put aside and frustrated by his lack of English.

However, Chan's practice at work related as much to the match between his beliefs about his own capabilities and the treatment he received as to his expectations as a refugee. Chan knew that he had been fortunate to find a workplace in which he was appreciated. "The boss was kindly," he asserted again and again. "The other people were kindly, and I was lucky to get another kindly boss and supervisor." As Chan and I talked during this initial interview, Pete Somelski passed through the reception area where we sat. Responsible for the smooth working of the shop, Pete supervised Chan and all the other department heads. Greeting me, Pete asked, "How's it going?" and added, "I see you got my boss down in here." As Pete left, Chan commented on the kind joking, with "See that, see what I mean?" Their familiarity was good-natured intimacy, indicative of the respect and mutual esteem engendered by the company's flattened managerial structure. Chan and the other men also talked about their colleagues on the shop floor with fondness and relative intimacy. Koung, for instance, commented,

> Tim [the computer programmer] is on the floor some of the time. He likes us. He says if we quit, he'll quit. Most supervisors in other companies don't work. Here Jake [Koung's supervisor] works harder than us. (Koung Sisowath, rail department, Concordance Steps)

Moeun Daun offered with some pleasure that Tim Brown learned the rules to and sometimes played their board game with them during lunch. Brown himself reflected that, "I learn as much from them as I try to teach. I've been interested in culture and religion of the East. I've been trying to improve my skills around here too."

At Concordance, the men were seen by supervisors in terms of an identity of motivated Asian, and as such, were given a position of respect and relative autonomy on the shop floor. The social organization of the workplace generally met expectations that had been mediated by the men's refugee experiences. This theoretical line modifies Ogbu's thesis by positioning the men within the same paradigm as Ruth, Henry, Joan, and Dina: not as individuals defined solely by their official identities, but as rational men and women engaging in interactions and making decisions based upon both their interests and constraints (Geertz 1973, 201).

ACCOMMODATION IN THE WORKPLACE

Most fundamental to Chan's story were the opportunities he was afforded at Concordance; his history with the company is testimony that cultural capital comes in all shapes and sizes. As already mentioned, after Chan's first six months with the company, he became foreman of the straight stair department, and when Concordance bought a CNC lathe, he was one of three men chosen to operate the new machine. These professional moves brought many learning opportunities. Working at the CNC with Tim Brown, the company's computer programmer, Chan was not only learning to use a keyboard and program the machine, but he also used a second computer in the drafting room to transpose salesmen's orders into measurements legible to the CNC. The transposition required a conceptual understanding of blueprints and a knowledge of both the programming language and numerical relationships that represented three-dimensional configurations. When video makers came to film the CNC for a trade show, they focused on Chan's operation of the large machine. Later, when Chan went to Atlanta with Tim and Jake Hansen for the two-day conference, the video was shown, and Chan became a local celebrity. He met people from a company in New Mexico that also used a CNC. They told him that in New Mexico an experienced CNC operator could earn sixteen to eighteen dollars an hour. "They didn't have this in Cambodia," Chan asserted. "[This is] good for the future." Difference didn't matter as long as Chan lived up to the hard-working Asian identity that had been imposed upon him. And difference didn't matter as long as Chan was treated equitably at work. He was able to balance the knowledge that his dream of "do[ing] some business . . . cannot be," with the opportunity to become computer literate. "Because I want to learn computer, everything is on computer," he explained.

Koung, however, had a different story, and the differences were reflected in the workplace practices of the two men. Koung had been a boy when the Khmer Rouge came to power, and he had spent the remainder of his youth in the Cambodian jungle. "I'm there for four years with men chasing me with guns," Koung explained. "My family was killed." "Koung was just a kid; he lived in the jungle in Cambodia," added Jay Hawks, the company's owner. "He was young when his parents died." When he arrived in the United States in his late teens, Koung had immediately enrolled in high school, where he became somewhat fluent in English and far more Americanized than his elder Cambodian colleagues. "I went to high school in the U.S.," Koung recounted. "In high school I still had all the training, hotel, motel, front desk, majoring in hotel services. " At least in part because of those early experiences as a teenager in the United States, Koung perceived himself as different from the other Cambodian men at Concordance. He explained,

> They all work with the straight stair. They're all Cambodians, they all speak Cambodian all the time. I work in the rail department by myself. Sometimes I work in the back, pulling out lumber and planks. There's always something there. When you need help you can just ask anybody. . . . Me, I speak Cambodian a very good little bit because I don't feel like talking Cambodian when American people are there. When I stand in front of American people I really don't like to speak Cambodian. They don't know what I say. (Koung Sisowath, rail department, Concordance)

Whether in fact Koung's self-imposed segregation from his compatriots stemmed from differences in age or marital status (he was the only unmarried Cambodian at the company), the psychological scars of long years hiding in the jungle, or a philosophical disagreement concerning interaction with English-language speakers, he clearly set himself apart from the other Cambodian employees. Working in the company's rail department, an area at the very front of the shop floor and separated from Chan's CNC and the straight stair area by about thirty-five feet, Koung socialized with his American counterparts. The other Cambodians, although genial with their non-Cambodian colleagues, spent their free time together talking or playing the handmade game they had enjoyed as children back home.

> During the morning break, Chan, Moeun, Tang and Peang played a game that looked like chess, but which Chan told me was like "checkers and chess." They played on teams, cheering partners as each moved small wooden pieces on the wooden board the men had made themselves. Moeun giggled when pieces were captured. (July 27, 1993, field notes, Concordance Steps)

Koung never played; he was rarely in the straight stair area during breaks or lunch. Instead he stayed near his own work station, sat in the lunchroom with the American workers, or opted for solo, and at times loner status.

Young, unattached, and according to Jay Hawks, the best English speaker of the Cambodian workers, Koung had not been able to access opportunities for advancement at Concordance that in any way rivaled Chan's workplace trajectory. As mentioned earlier, like the other men, Koung's first assignment at Concordance was operating the baluster machine. After six months he was moved to the rail department.

> The first time it's interesting, you change from one place to another. Just do straight rail, make the joint for straight rails. I do that job very fast, just sand and buff. The circle rail you do everything by hand. Lay out, bevel. It's really hard to do at first. But I don't think it's hard for me. I used to work when I was ten years old. I understand. It's easy. (Koung Sisowath, rail department, Concordance Steps)

More like many of Development's hourly workers, Koung's conception of self did not completely match his official identity at work. Tim Brown, the company's computer programmer, explained Koung's predicament most clearly. "Koung was the best rail maker before the CNC came," Brown asserted. "Now he doesn't have anything special." Although grateful for the salary he earned at Concordance, Koung talked frequently of his desire to return to school and of his affinity for the hospitality industry.

> After I graduated from high school, I decide I want to go to college. I could not afford by myself. I got job in a hotel, in front. Sheraton near the airport. But the money was low. I couldn't afford my rent. I went to VES for woodworking. It's good for me. After high school I want to do something. I go to school if it's free. Even now, they can help me get a job. You can learn if you're smart, can read, write.
>
> Last year I try to go back to school at night. The reason, my English is not well. If I work in front office, I need better English. If I can go back to school and probably find another job, like my first training. If you are really good, they probably pay you better. But if not I stay here. (Koung Sisowath, rail department, Concordance Steps)

This dissonance may also have been at the root of Koung's complaints about the shop's power tools. Koung confided:

> Because in here there's all the power tools. If you don't look you could lose your head. I was out two weeks. I cut my thumb. [He held out his thumb to show me the injury.] Before I hurt my shoulder, I was out of work about three months. I still get hurt sometimes. [He

stretched his shoulder and rubbed his upper back to reinforce his complaint.] I still get hurt sometimes, that's why I want to go back to school.

Just like Moeun, he just got kicked back from the table, just got punctured from his stomach from this side to this side. He got operation a couple of times. I get sorry about that. I get sad about that. (Koung Sisowath, rail department, Concordance Steps)

Koung's separateness and his complaints about the company may have been his own minimal opposition to a mismatch between his beliefs about himself and his limited opportunities at Concordance. But while Koung was the only member of this small cohort whose conception of self did not match his workplace profile, his relationship with work was more complex than his complaints appeared. He had worked in the United States before coming to Concordance, and so was aware of the company's relatively good benefits. He also appreciated Concordance's welcoming environment, and his excitement in talking about his work was an indication that on occasion he was even intrigued by the challenge of creating with wood.

Despite the obvious differences, then, in practice both Koung and Chan critiqued the end product of their investment in training in a similar light. They coped, negotiating internally over plans that had changed. Consistent with and yet amplifying John Ogbu's theories on immigrant minorities, most fundamentally, the men were pragmatic. Their experiences and practice suggest a slight modification in Bill Dougherty's statement about VES clients. Instead of, "They'll do what you want if it's what they want to do," they might argue, "We'll do what you want if it's what we want to do and what we need to do." The company's other Cambodian workers, Moeun Daun, Tang Preah, Peang Sothearos, and Sefan Ang, however, had very different origins, and for them, accommodating work was far easier. They had been farmers in rural Cambodia. After ten years in the United States, their English was still limited, and although we communicated adequately, they tended to respond in monosyllables, each choosing his words with great care. Their first exposure to English had been in the English as a Second Language (ESL) classes in which they found themselves upon arrival in the United States. "When I first came I study English, about two months," Moeun explained. "Just talk a little bit and understand together." Their perceptions about future possibilities reflected these past experiences and perceived futures. Content with his present circumstances, for instance, Moeun planned to stay at Concordance. "I try the same job," he stated, explaining that he was planning for the future of his two children. "If they can, I plan them to university."

With two teenage children to support, and already laid off from one carpentry shop in the past year, Moeun weighed his options wisely. His commitment to the company was even more striking given the serious injury he had sustained at work. The return to work had indeed been hard for Moeun. "The first time I don't feel happy. I still afraid," he told me. But Moeun chose to remain on the job, regardless of these initial trepidations. "Now it's okay. . . . I like the job." Moeun's choices were clear. As he asserted, "If nothing to do, I'm not happy."

LEARNING TO JUGGLE

The men's accommodation was made easier by the knowledge that their concerns were shared by their American colleagues. Everyone at the company, both the Cambodian men and the other woodworkers on the shop floor, voiced interest in taking a next professional step. But no orderly career path extended in or from Concordance. While the men talked of many possibilities, they perceived few real alternatives. Dave Somerton, a local guy working in circular stairs, was going to night school to be a card dealer in Atlantic City; he practiced his blackjack technique on the company's computer during lunch breaks. A few employees were actively looking for other work, but couldn't find anything that competed with Concordance's wages and benefits. George Stimpson, Koung's co-worker in the rail department, had difficulty even finding formal instruction to improve his woodworking skills.

> That's the thing, I've been looking for a school. The only one I found is at the community college. The classes are four hours a night, five days a week, September through June. More than I can do with this full time job. . . . I've seen schools in woodworking magazines. In the north and places like that. (George Stimpson, rail department, Concordance Steps)

Aware that few strategies for social mobility (not school, a better job, nor internal movement) existed, Chan, Koung, and the other Cambodian men at Concordance accommodated the demands of the workplace. While they had scaled down their expectations and narrowed their dreams, they were appreciative of the respect of supervisors and colleagues at Concordance, challenged by the demands of the work itself, and grateful for the company's wage and benefit package. The woodworking training had provided the vocabulary, math, and woodworking skills required to meet the demands of skilled work, and Concordance provided the opportunity to use those skills in an equitable workplace environment. They had learned along the way that life is a series of negotiations.

Concordance was a small, tightly knit shop, trying to remain afloat in an economic climate that wasn't necessarily kind to small businesses. Even in the best of times, in order to survive the company's products had to be both of high quality and competitively priced. Hard work and speed were required of the employees, and the Cambodians filled those requirements. Perceived as diligent and indefatigable workers, the men's work outweighed cultural differences and communication difficulties, and ensured them equitable status in the workplace, respectful acceptance, a sense of caring, and admiring co-workers and supervisors. Like the female clerical workers and the men and women in recovery at Development, the Cambodian men at Concordance had "learn[ed] to juggle the differential demands" of work and self in status positions that met their beliefs about their own potential and worth (Gibson 1988, 297). Respected, well liked, and challenged, they found that their social identities at work were a comfortable fit. While at times they worried that the style of this worker identity wasn't quite what they had envisioned, they had learned to appreciated its color and fabric.

Chapter 4
Jackson Hospital's Pharmacies and the Cream of the Unemployed

The technicians are counted on for everything here except for that last check. The pharmacists have to do, check it. And we go so far as to let technicians dispense things, which you'd never hear of in other pharmacies.

> —Cindy Peterson, pharmacist, Jackson Hospital

I find that the people that come through the program are exceptionally trained . . . the exposure to the medical industry, basically. The profession of medicine, medical terminology, exposure to disease, an understanding of the complexity of this kind of care and the severity of disease states, appreciation for the patients, an understanding of confidentiality, the technical skills that they learn compounding, calculations, pharmaceutical calculations. All those things combined really make them . . . very valuable individuals.

> —Dan Quick, manager, Outpatient Service, Jackson Hospital

Doctors, nurses, people respect pharmacy technicians. They really don't even differentiate you from a pharmacist. Sometimes we have to actually tell them, well I'm sorry, I'm not a pharmacist.

> —Tom Russo, pharmacy technician, Jackson Hospital

GETTING THERE

Jackson Hospital, a 707-bed teaching hospital in center city, was the most urban of all four sites, and its pharmacy technician training was the only training initiative that led to what were openly called "professional" jobs. Situated in the middle of the bustling downtown, the hospital was loud with visitors, patients, and staff, many dressed in green surgical scrubs. Outside, the pavements were crowded with shoppers carrying purchases in large shopping bags, office workers dressed in business suits, and an array of urban street dwellers begging for spare change and surveying passersby. The hospital had an affiliate university, and together, the campus stretched over eleven city blocks and occupied twenty separate buildings, including highrise dormitories, classroom buildings, and an affiliate eye hospital and hand center. The main and largest building had a bank, an apothecary, an information center, a gift shop, and a bank of elevators on the ground floor, with stairs leading to a large open atrium that housed a cafeteria and two connecting dining areas. Ten floors of patient rooms, diagnostic centers, and support areas overlooked the atrium.

In addition to all these services, the hospital complex ran its own in- and outpatient pharmacy. A pharmacy satellite serviced each floor of the main hospital, and Kay James and Tom Russo were among the fifty-five pharmacy technicians who staffed these satellites. Like thirty-four of their colleagues spread across Jackson's obstetrics and psychiatry departments, pediatrics floor, cardiac, chemo, and rehab wings, anesthesia and oncology programs, apothecary, and home infusion service, Kay and Tom were hired after participating in the hospital's six and a half month pharmacy technician training.[1] Theirs is a story markedly different from that of Henry and Rose, Joan and Dina, and even Chan and Koung. Theirs is a story told by voices that talked about respect and equity in the workplace.

Kay James was African American. At thirty-three and single with no children, Kay lived with her mother across the river from center city and commuted to the hospital every day by train. Sitting in the hospital's ninth-floor lounge and accompanied by sounds from the popular soap opera, *The Young and the Restless*, rising from the TV in the background, Kay told her story of leaving college one year shy of graduation.

> I had been to college, for biology. I was going to go to medical school to be an anesthesiologist. Believe it or not, I went three years. I was out there and I started workin', makin' money you know. And I said, oh, I can make money. So I didn't go back to school. (Kay James, pharmacy technician, Jackson Hospital)

But the "makin' money" plan didn't work out as well as Kay had expected, and at twenty-six, she found herself without a job or direction. She stumbled upon the hospital's pharmacy's technician training one Sunday morning in 1986 while paging through the local newspaper.

I opened up the Sunday paper, and it said do you want to be a pharmacy technician? So I called because I had been to college, I called up Jackson and asked them, can I, is it feasible for me to get this job without going through the training? They said yes, so I said, well, why do you think I need to go through this training. She said, well it's something new, you know it was six years ago. She was tellin' me a little bit about the program, and I always wanted to be in the medical field. So I said, I'll try it, and I did six months and I got hired before I was through training. And I'm glad I got into it.

I figure like this and of course this really came true. If they have a program, then sooner or later these other hospitals are gonna go, well why should I just hire you with no experience when I could get somebody who's been through the program and they know something about the pharmacy. (Kay James, pharmacy technician, Jackson Hospital)

Partnering with the local Union of Hospital and Health Care Employees and the city's Private Industry Council (PIC), Jackson's pharmacy department was able to provide tuition support to Kay with money from the Job Training Partnership Act (JTPA). Offered a position at the hospital right out of the program, she initially split a job with Kim Sherman, another technician. "We were working up on the psychiatric floor," Kay explained. "We came up with the idea to switch, three days on pediatrics one week, two the next week. Because we didn't want to stay on one floor." Kay and Kim circulated through pediatrics, oncology, and surgery each week. But after a few years, Kay left Jackson and found herself wandering from work in first one and then a second area hospital before returning to Jackson as a float technician. "When I came back, that was the only position open," she explained. "What's good about it is, I'm not like when you work on a certain floor, you know most of the things about pediatric floor. But if you went to five, which is cardiology, you know some medications. But you wouldn't know what to do with it or any special things to do. Since I float I know different things."

Like Kay, Tom Russo had also been restless. He had come to Jackson after an endless series of jobs, starting when he was a young boy selling pretzels on a street corner downtown. The same age as Kay, Tom was Italian from the city's south side, a world away from Kay's small town across the river. Medium build, with dark shagged hair, Tom wore his own urban uniform of T-shirt, jeans, and an Egyptian Isis earring when we first talked in the staff office on the hospital's thirteenth floor. We sat around the corner from the pharmacy satellite in which Tom worked straight evening shifts.

I've worked a good bit. In my family we're pretty much taught to work hard, not so much hard but to work. I mean I used to sell pret-

zels when I was like ten years old. I used to walk up and down the
street selling pretzels, little items here and there. I was always, so I
was pretty much always working. I had a job in a shoe store when I
was fourteen. Thirteen or fourteen. Stock boy. So I pretty much
worked all my life; I've had a wide variety of occupations. (Tom
Russo, pharmacy technician, Jackson Hospital)

Tom had had five jobs during his first year out of high school. He
tried each on for the fit, but like Goldilocks in the children's story, he
found each one wanting.

I worked in an industrial chemical plant as a maintenance mechanic,
until they went bankrupt. I got laid off. I worked in an insurance
company as a credit debit investigator. I worked as a waiter for RibIts,
I worked at Pep Boys. It was anything I could get that year. It was like
I hated this job and when I left, I got another one. And when I was
working there, this place called. (Tom Russo, pharmacy technician,
Jackson Hospital)

By sheer luck of applying, he found work at the hospital. "I worked
in the mailroom and the purchase department," he offered. After six
years there he took advantage of Jackson's pharmacy technician
training.

I went through the program with the union. It was really weird that
the union ran the program. Well, it was in conjunction with the city
and at that time the JTPA or CETA program. What it was was Jackson
ran the program, the union sponsored it, the union did the paperwork
on it, and the city paid for it. It worked well, I just couldn't understand why they were sponsoring something that wasn't unionized af-
terwards.
    I didn't like my job that I had at that time. I was real unsatisfied. I
wanted a career change. This was a good opportunity. It was a six
month program; I could get into the job market quick. Going through
the newspaper there was plenty of job opportunities at the time.
There was, I think, it had to do a lot with self-worth, rather than anything else because the pay, the pay is lower than what I was making.
(Tom Russo,pharmacy technician, Jackson Hospital)

Like Henry, Dina, and Chan, Tom and Kay attended government-
funded job training and moved from unemployment or underemployment to full-time, permanent jobs. But for Tom, Kay, and
their fellow technicians at Jackson, it was their capital, in the form of
social and cultural resources, and not a welfare categorization that
routed them to the hospital. Their capital allowed them to self-
select into training that provided technical skills and a professional

upgrade, it shaped the ways they were perceived and treated at work, and it changed the way they began to see themselves. They, like JTPA participants in other contexts, have been called "the cream of the unemployed," and that cream was an identity that brought them to a very different position in the marketplace.

THE COLLABORATION

This story began in 1981, ten years before I met Tom and Kay. During that year, two clinical pharmacists at the hospital (Phillips and Smith 1984) authored a market survey on the number and rate of turnover of pharmacy technicians in the area and reported a city-wide need for forty-two technicians each year. The labor demand, compounded by the department's ongoing reliance on on-the-job training, catalyzed arguments for more structured training for the technicians.

> We determined that there was clearly a need both internally at Jackson and externally for the market place for somebody to train these folks. It so happened that the administrator who was in charge of the pharmacy was also on the board of the Local's Training and Upgrade. And Jackson, as part of their contractual process, made a contribution to the Training and Upgrade fund. So when we discussed this with the administrator, how we thought we could make money doing this and also benefit the university and the health community in general, he said, "Boy, we could also get some money back that we've paid for the Training and Upgrading Fund."
>
> So that's where the focus on the Local, I guess we'd almost call it serendipity. We didn't go look for them, it was just the right people talking to the right people at the right time. That's my best recollection. (Donald Phillips, clinical pharmacist, Jackson Hospital)

The Health Care Local had much to offer the proposed initiative. Its Training and Upgrade Fund regularly hosted college and continuing-education courses at its midtown Learning Center. The bulletin boards in the Center's lobby were plastered with announcements for training programs that included health-related technical-training courses for medical records technician, psychiatric technician, medical recorder, EEG technician, central supply room manager, dental assistant, medical assistant, EKG technician, third party billing clerk, LPN, RN, and nurse assistant. Many of the programs were facilitated in conjunction with area hospitals and long-term care facilities; the tradition of partnering with large health care institutions enabled union members to learn skills in real work contexts. "Their size does that . . . you need equipment, autoclaves," explained Jim Howell, the Local's training director. The Local was also able to utilize these contacts with area hospitals to assist the trainees with job placement.

In addition to its experience and area networks, the Local's relationship with the local Private Industry Council (PIC) helped obtain government funding for the hospital/Local collaboration.[2] According to the Local's training director,

> What the hospital's motivation was, they were trying to get trained technicians. We put together the curriculum with them. They were looking to train ten people and take the best five. . . . We did the recruitment, screening, support services, which is key . . . and then the placement. The hospital helped with job leads, we did job placement supports. We did the paperwork with PIC, which is no small undertaking. (Jim Howell, training director, Health Care Local)

The hospital-based training of pharmacy technicians was formally initiated in 1982, with each partner in the collaboration assured a winning role. The hospital had a mechanism to ensure a pool of qualified technicians, the Local was involved in a training program that guaranteed training slots for its members, and PIC found a good investment for its training funds.

THE BEST FIVE

This was the context, this collaboration among hospital, union, and government, in which images of identity and ability were constructed at Jackson. Within multiple webs of social, economic, and political relationships, Tom, Kay, and their colleagues at Jackson Hospital came to tell a story of what it meant to embody Howell's notion of "the best five," and how that identity played out in their everyday practice of work. Theirs is a story of both cultural and social capital, a resounding mix of personal contacts, test taking abilities, and middle class norms. Over and over in interviews for example, men and women at Jackson made references to what Bourdieu (1990, 35) called their social capital as paving their way to Jackson. Like the salaried workers at Development, many of the pharmacy technicians had been connected to the hospital through social and professional affiliations Tom Russo, like Mary Russell in the fifth-floor cardiac satellite, had worked in a union job at Jackson. Tom had been in the hospital's mailroom, Mary in the laundry, and both had been linked to the training through the union's training upgrading fund. Their colleagues brought other kinds of social capital to the table. Samantha Wright, who worked with Tom in the psychiatric wing, had an ex-husband who worked as a pharmaceutical representative. He was her connection to the field. "Somebody I knew knew of the pharmacy training," she explained. Donna Watkins in obstetrics was referred to Jackson's training by her supervisor at the retail pharmacy in which she had spent the past year.

> Before Jackson I worked at Clover pharmacy. That work is retail work. You do mostly third party billing, deal with customers, give medicine to the customers. I helped the pharmacist count the drugs, put them in bottles. The pharmacist at Clover, she told me. She told me about Jackson and the Local. (Donna Watkins, pharmacy technician, Jackson Hospital)

Although the pharmacy's Afghani technicians, Ahmed Roashan and Namib Anwari, were far from the networks that had served them and their families at home, even they had social contacts that led them to Jackson. They had been referred to Jackson's training program by the nonprofit organization where they studied English. "So I heard through them, and also Ahmed's brother Farid who is working here also at night," Namib explained. Only Kay had been drawn to the pharmacy by a newspaper ad. But once on staff she began to expend the social capital she had accumulated at Jackson. "It's a pretty nice place to work," she explained. "I get my friends in here in this technician program all the time."

But being "the best five" also meant that Kay and Tom had the cultural capital necessary to navigate the rigorous screening process that the hospital and Health Care Local put in place to evaluate applicants. The program offered only ten slots per group (or twenty per year), but received an average of 150 applications for each training. A series of pencil and paper tests and face to face interviews pared the large number of applications to a manageable number, and ensured that the applicants who were invited to participate in the training had, as the novelist Tom Wolfe so poetically wrote, "the right stuff." Kay and Tom did. They had performed well on assessments and according to the hospital's director, showed "reliability . . . dependability . . . accuracy . . . and speed and dedication" in verbal and written testimony.

In order to be accepted into the Technician Training Program, Tom and Kay, like their colleagues in the hospital's nine pharmacy satellites, had to prove that they

- were residents of the county;
- met Job Training Partnership Act (JTPA) guidelines for income (usually translating to being eligible for public assistance) or were full-time members of the Health Care Local (applicable only if the training would result in a job upgrade);
- had high school diplomas or the equivalent;
- had no criminal records for larceny, burglary, or drug-related crimes;
- passed screening in basic math and verbal ability;
- had the physical ability to acquire the skills of pharmacy technician;
- and demonstrated motivation, intelligence, and verbal ability in a personal interview.

At least three of the seven entrance criteria and most of the screening instruments relied on academic certificates and test results, what Bourdieu called "objective mechanisms."

> It must suffice to point out that academic qualifications are to cultural capital what money is to economic capital. . . . Academic qualifications, like money, have a conventional, fixed value which, being guaranteed by law, is freed from local limitations (in contrast to scholastically uncertified cultural capital) and temporal fluctuations; the cultural capital which they in a sense guarantee once and for all does not constantly need to be proved. . . . The greater the extent to which the task of reproducing the relations of domination is taken over by objective mechanisms, which serve the interests of the dominant group without any conscious effort on the latter's part, the more indirect and, in a sense, impersonal, become the strategies objectively oriented towards reproduction: it is not by lavishing generosity, kindness, or politeness on his charwoman (or on any other "socially inferior" agent), but by choosing the best investment for his money, or the best school for his son, that the possessor of economic or cultural capital perpetrates the relationship of domination which objectively links him with his charwoman and even her descendants. . . . Once a system of mechanisms has been constituted capable of objectively ensuring the reproduction of the established order by its own motion (*apo tou automatou,* as the Greeks put it), the dominant class have only to *let the system they dominate take its own course* in order to exercise their domination. (Bourdieu 1977, 187–189)

At Jackson, "objective mechanisms" included a high school diploma, a school college and ability test (SCAT) and algebra exam, which measured math and verbal skills, and an essay and interview to "assess the applicant's motivation and communicative skills" (Phillips and Smith 1984, 2615).[3] Reliance on these "objective mechanisms" was clean, sanitized, and gave trainers rationale for screening in and keeping out that seemed almost scientific. Applicants were easily ranked, and those found deserving formed a pool of potential employees who looked dramatically different, in terms of both academics and economics, from the men and women employed at either Development or Church Hall.

The department's assessment of what sociologist Erving Goffman called an individual's "personal front" also ensured that Tom, Kay, and the other sanctioned applicants were different from Development's hourly workers or Church Hall's nurse assistants. Goffman (1959, 24) wrote, "As part of personal front we may include insignia of office or rank; clothing; sex; age, and racial characteristics; size and looks; posture; speech patterns; facial expressions; bodily gestures; and the like." Karen Miller, the pharmacy's training director during my visits to Jackson, was the official judge of applicants' "personal fronts." Each time the technician training was offered, the Local passed the names of thirty-five to forty individuals with the highest test scores and best essays to Miller for review, and she scheduled interviews with these best applicants to assess the appropriateness of their "personal fronts." According to Miller, her interviews were a "very good predictor" of who would be most successful in training. But in practice, her decisions were shaped more by her beliefs about culturally defined presentation styles than by any objective measure of worth. Relying on a "feeling" about the applicants' "maturity, motivation, intelligence, and verbal ability," Miller looked for work ethic and middle class values that were packaged in what was for her a culturally recognizable manner. Her decisions about applicants were grounded in a me/not me dichotomy reminiscent of what educational anthropologists Fred Erickson and Jeff Shultz (1982, 17) call "co-membership." Erickson and Shultz argued that co-membership, a sharing of status attributes such as "race and ethnicity, sex, interest in football, graduation from the same high school, acquaintance with the same individual," causes gatekeepers to notice particular attributes and disregard others, and ultimately affects their decisions about who obtains access to resources and opportunities. At Jackson, these me/like me distinctions were subtle, and most likely out of Miller's consciousness. They were much like the seemingly intuitive assessments made by police on their street beat, as documented by sociolinguist Harvey Sacks (1972). In his study, Sacks reported that police officers perceived their beat as a whole, with the street itself functioning as an actor in the scene. In order to detect potential trouble while on patrol, police added or subtracted items from a "cumulative set of values" that made up the beat. "What's missing here?" they intuitively asked themselves. "What seems out of place?"

In using interviews as a gatekeeping mechanism for Jackson's training, Miller incorporated a similar strategy of "cumulative" values. Contending that she recognized the right person for a particular job or training slot, Miller weighed applicants' relevant characteristics against this sense of rightness, adding traits she perceived as positive and subtracting those she believed to be negative. Punctuality, for instance, was an item Miller believed essential to her "cumulative set of values" of a successful applicant, and so she regularly noted an applicant's arrival time for interviews. "If they're late, they're not in the program," she asserted. "There are some exceptions. I have to use my judgment. What's their rationale for being late?"

This shared value on punctuality was just one piece of the cultural capital that Tom and Kay brought to this screening process. It was the sum total of their "language use, manners, and orientations/dispositions" that afforded them access to the training program's resources (Jenkins 1992, 85). As Miller explained, they showed "maturity, motivation, intelligence, and verbal ability," an amalgamation of qualities based upon prior experience, level of education, economic status, ethnicity, and gender. The blending of attributes into a positive profile was neither simple nor straightforward. It was not only membership in a preferred ethnic, racial, gender, or economic category that marked these men and women as worthy, but an elusive combination that included prior education and relevant work experience. Kay James, along with her colleagues Samantha Wright, Pauline Pierce, and Namib Anwari, for example, had all been to college. Like Chan and Koung at Concordance Steps, Namib had been forced to flee his native country, leaving part of himself behind. Nearly graduating from pharmacy school in his native Afghanistan, Namib suspended his studies when civil war broke out, and had been unable to bring either his university credits or documentation with him. Small, dark haired, and with a demeanor so serious that he seemed to reflect the disappointments of a lifetime, Namib explained, "I was back home in pharmacy school. I nearly finished school, pharmacy school. I was at the end of my graduation. Unfortunately, I left the country." Kay James hadn't finished college either. She had been was lured away in her third year by the opportunity to make money. Pauline Pierce also left college after three years as a biology major, but it was the birth of her son that disrupted her plans. Yet while incomplete college careers were the source of personal angst for Namib, Kay, and Pauline, having even some college provided the social and cultural capital that Miller valued. Donna Watkins in obstetrics possessed another resource. Watkins was neither a union member nor had she gone to college, but she had worked as a technician in both a retail and mail order pharmacy. Work, albeit at the margins of the profession, gave her access to a language that was recognizable in the department. In practice, this work experience, education, and network of social contacts were official stamps of approval, serving the same purpose as recommendation letters from respected institutions. Each served as a "certificate of reliability [that serves as] indication their holders have demonstrated the competence or persistence to complete a task and to get along with peers and superiors in the process" (Sewell 1971, 33).

BROAD-BASED FUNDING

At Development, Church Hall, and Concordance Steps, identity was constructed in large part by funding streams that named and marked particular categories of welfare recipients the hardest to serve, unmarried mothers, refugees. At Jackson, however, the source of funding for Tom's and Kay's training costs had far less to do with the ways they were perceived and treated by trainers and workplace supervisors. From the start, the training was supported by a broad funding base that was unrelated to any particular social identity. The first three classes of technician trainees blended both government-funded individuals and union members. After these initial cohorts, individuals ineligible for either JTPA funding or union support were encouraged to participate in the training at a personal cost of $1,500. In 1986, the pharmacy department convened the first training cohort composed solely of self-paid participants, and from 1986 through 1988 the training program hosted alternate cohorts of self-paid and government-funded participants.

Because the parameters for JTPA funding were broad, even this bifurcation between subsidized and self-paid provided no real markers of worth at Jackson. JTPA was a different kind of funding from state level TN and refugee streams, or from the federal government's AFDC program. Targeted not at the hard-core unemployed, but at unemployed workers in general, only 65 percent of the individuals funded by JTPA were required to fall under the rubric "hard to serve." In fact, 10 percent could access funds without qualifying as disadvantaged at all. Six of the technicians I came to know best were funded by JTPA, yet that support revealed little to nothing about their economic status. Kay James, for instance, had been unemployed when she applied for Jackson's training, but her colleague Donna Watkins had been working as a technician in a drug store discount chain and had been able to access government funds as part of JTPA's 10 percent window.

Also thrown into this mix were Tom Russo and Mary Russell, who used their union benefits to pay for training, and Johnny Michaels and Lisa Henry, who had financed the training themselves. Slightly younger than Tom Russo, Johnny worked as a pharmacy technician in the hospital's Home Infusion Service. Tall and clean cut in a light blue dress shirt and black pants, Johnny had his own unique form of cultural and social capital. His father was a pharmacist, and Johnny had been raised in the business.

> I had been out of high school for quite some time, I can't remember it's been that long . . . probably four years or five years. And I grew up around pharmacy all my life. My family owned pharmacies and I would always go in and help my father in his different hospitals. He was in home health care at one point with Baxter, who was, well, they were America Continued Care at the time, and so it was always in the back of my mind. And it came easily to me, just from everything throughout the years. So when he told me about it [the training] I went through it and did very well and enjoyed it. (Johnny Michaels, pharmacy technician, Jackson Hospital)

Finding money for the training had been harder for Lisa Henry, a technician in the third-floor chemo satellite. An African American woman from the city, Lisa had three years of college and two years of work experience in a mail order pharmacy when she applied to Jackson's training program. She talked about that experience as we sat in the third floor waiting area.

> I paid my way through. It was hard, that was hard too. I didn't pay up front, I think they let me pay in five hundred dollar installments or something like that. I saw in the paper like a month before I actually quit my job and started here. Before I worked here, I worked at a mail order pharmacy. I wasn't really making that much where I was. So I did pay, and I worked, I worked eight to four-thirty as a student, Monday through Friday, so you have an evening job or weekend job to supplement. So I went out and I got a job at Osteopathic and I worked as a clerk in the ER. (Lisa Henry, pharmacy technician, Jackson Hospital)

Regardless of funding source, JTPA, the union, family, or a part-time job in the evening and weekends, once they traversed the training's assessment and interview screens, Lisa, Johnny, Kay, and Tom blended into a cohort of trainees that the program's director labeled mature, motivated, intelligent, and articulate, and not, like the nurse assistants at Church Hall, into a mass of objectified other.

LEARNING SPECIFIC KNOWLEDGE

Jackson's pharmacy technician training was an introduction to a new world, with a new vocabulary and specialized math operations. As trainees, Tom and Kay's first six weeks were spent in one of the hospital's white tiled basement classrooms, where they attended lectures by hospital's pharmacists on medical terminology, aseptic technique, pharmacy math, pharmacy practice, and drug distribution. In postlecture classes with Karen Miller, their primary trainer, they talked of SVPs and LVPs (small and large volume parenterals), ampoules, hyper alimentation, red flags, and aseptic technique. They converted ounces to milliliters and changed concentrations from a D 10 to a D 7 in dextrose bags. And they engaged in endless exercises to commit the names, both generic and brand name, of more than six hundred medicines to memory. As Tom explained,

> Learning all the medications, to me that was the hardest part. Learning all the medications, the different names. It was memorization in the beginning, and then seeing them day in and day out. I think basically that's about the only way you can really learn them. You learn ten new words every day, I think we basically have about six hundred medications. We were quizzed each day. There was a test at the end of the week. We were asked to read a physician's order and to tell them what we would do. Everything, medication, what route it was going in, whether orally or injectable or whatever. The frequency it was given, once a day, twice a day. (Tom Russo, pharmacy technician, Jackson Hospital)

Barb Silver, an African American woman in training during my first few months at Jackson, had worked in a retail pharmacy before coming to Jackson. Six weeks of classroom instruction supplemented her prior on-the-job experience.

> In the beginning of the program we learned the drug names, generic and brand. I learned more than what I learned in retail. 'Cause in retail we just had to pick it up [the medication] and get used to it every

day. Here they give an explanation, the name of the disease or what
... in the respiratory system, the different systems in the body how
the drugs work for which system ... the aseptic technique to work
under the hood. Upstairs we were doing the chemotherapy, which are
sterile products. (Barb Silver, technician trainee, Jackson Hospital)

The didactic phase focused on knowledge specific to the profession; it also reinforced and was reinforced by the clerkship training
phase that followed. Like the woodworking program, training and
work were closely linked at Jackson. During their eighteen-week
clerkship, Kay and Tom rotated through five or more pharmacy
satellites in the hospital. They continued to attend pharmacology
and medical terminology lectures, and supervised by senior technicians, they applied their newly learned knowledge on-site, setting
patients' medicine boxes, delivering medicines on the floor, preparing intravenous products and chemotherapeutic agents under the
"hood," and stocking the pharmacy satellites. Kay explained that

the classroom was sort of abstract, but once we got into the practical
aspects of the fieldwork, floors and seeing how the floors are operating and really getting a feel for, that really really made a big difference. (Kay James, pharmacy technician, Jackson Hospital)

Introduced to the technical, social, and psychological aspects of the
job by senior technicians, they found that this clerkship phase complemented the didactic. Faith Hanson was a senior technician who
had been at Jackson for fifteen years, five years before the initiation
of the training program. She had been trained on the job, and talked
about the value of technicians' teaching technician trainees.

You know you really have to have somebody who thinks like a technician, and knows what it's like to deal with the pharmacist, and stuff
like that. ... And I can also teach them to be comfortable with that
(how it really is). That's good stuff, you know. Things like that they
really do, because a lot of times they come here, and they're really
frightened. They're scared they're going to make a mistake, kill
somebody. And that's for real [she laughs]. They could mistake a six
for a nine, and that's an easy thing to do. Things like that. (Faith
Hanson, pharmacy technician, Jackson Hospital)

Trainees, technicians, and the hospital's clinical pharmacists alike
praised Jackson's training and its melding of classroom and workplace. They all asserted that the technician training both ensured
that the right people had access to the training, and that the right

people were trained for the position. As Dan Quick, the manager of Jackson's pharmacy outpatient service, explained,

> I find that the people that come through the program are exceptionally trained . . . the exposure to the medical industry, basically. The profession of medicine, medical terminology, exposure to disease, an understanding of the complexity of this kind of care and the severity of disease states, appreciation for the patients, an understanding of confidentiality, the technical skills that they learn compounding, calculations, pharmaceutical calculations—all those things combined really make them very valuable individuals. (Dan Quick, manager, Outpatient Service, Jackson Hospital)

Much was expected of Tom and Kay during their twenty-four weeks of training, and they lived up to those expectations.

GETTING HIRED

During the seven-year hospital-union collaboration, Jackson hired approximately 40 percent of the training project graduates, JTPA-eligible, former union members, and self-paid alike. Both Tom and Kay had been fortunate to make the cut. Karen Miller, the training program coordinator, explained, "Grads are at other hospitals by default. Everyone wants to be at Jackson. They call me years after training asking if there are positions available."

The six-month training provided the opportunity for department staff to choose from an already select group to fill available technician positions. Prescreened for academic potential, Tom's and Kay's performance in training proved they were not only academically able, but dependable as well. "We require very careful, meticulous records," explained Miller. "Employers will take a B or C student with perfect attendance. Dependability is a must in the medical field."

> I mean, we've been hiring a lot of the people out of the training program, that's where the vast majority of them are. And if they successfully navigated that, they've been screened somewhat. We are coming up with people who are more motivated and more interested. (Bob Clay, clinical pharmacist, Jackson Hospital)

To be hired by the hospital, the trainees found that what Erickson (1987, 17) called "unofficial and emergent attributes that have to do with the quality of the students' interactional performance" were as important, if not more important, than their official, academic life. During training, Tom and Kay, like their more successful JTPA, union, and privately funded colleagues, had begun to look like technicians. According to Karen Miller, some of the less successful trainees had not. She explained that

> one African American woman, a trainee, carefully and proudly braided her hair, yet she had to take out the braids for work. Another woman, from Kenya, came to class with traditional clothes and an array of jewelry. She had not yet been placed. Students in job placement still encounter racism, ageism, sexism. White men are easy to place. The only ones not placed had problems indicating mental illness. One man was later homeless. He needed medication; couldn't get it without a job, but couldn't get a job without medication. (Karen Miller, Director, pharmacy technician training, Jackson Hospital)

Tom and Kay, unlike the African women and white men they left behind, were successful in obtaining jobs at Jackson not only because they performed well in training, but also because they were able to look and act the part of technician. They even began to internalize the me/not me dichotomy that had been embedded in the training's screening procedures, positioning themselves against these "others" in their own talk about JTPA applicants who had not been accepted into the training. I heard them contrast themselves with these less fortunate "people that they sent through the union." As Missy Brown, a technician in Home Infusion, asserted,

> I was also involved in some of the interviews of the people that they sent through from the union. And there were some people that, I mean, you didn't want to laugh at these people or anything when you sat and interviewed them. But there was just no way that they had enough of an education behind them to do this job. There were no requirements I don't think at the time. Or maybe some of them [the applicants] did have high school diplomas, but were those people that just got pushed along through the system and never made it. And just, they couldn't speak properly and there were just things that they, it was just, you would automatically just cross them off the list after talking to them for five or ten minutes because you just knew that they didn't have what you needed to have. But we had to interview everyone that the Local sent through. Or maybe there were people who had just been out of school, who had high school diplomas, just barely got a high school diploma and then got jobs and worked. And they did fine in their jobs but just never really used anything that they learned and they really lost a lot of that. (Missy Brown, pharmacy technician, Jackson Hospital)

Jackson's screening process, both formal and informal, did not filter out racial or ethnic difference. It did, however, identify and prioritize academically sanctioned knowledge and culturally appropriate practice, what Missy called "what you needed to have." So while Kay's and Tom's performance styles provided sufficient capital to purchase both training slots and subsequent job offers at the hospital, less successful applicants' nonstandard English, culturally different communication styles, and perceived lack of literacy and numeracy skills left them short. Unlike Development's inclusionary training, at Jackson, training was exclusionary. Difference perceived as dangerous or more simply as too different was screened out. At Jackson what remained post-training was difference disarmed.

AN OCCUPATION IN TRANSITION

Kay's college and Tom's union membership and work experience put them at least one rung up the economic ladder from Henry Thompson and Ruth Fallows even before they applied for Jackson's training. But after participating in the hospital's pharmacy technician training, they advanced so quickly it seemed as though they were ascending the ladder two rungs at a time. They had jumped through hoops to get to Jackson, and once in the role of hospital employee, they became professionals. In fact, within the hospital, the term professional was used routinely in referring to their technician role. "Professionalism is a word I use a lot with them," posited Khristin Carlson, one of three assistant directors in the pharmacy department.

Like the other companies, it wasn't the work in and of itself that defined this professional status at Jackson. In fact, technicians are traditionally seen as worker bees in a pharmacy. The hierarchy in Jackson's pharmacies followed suit: clinical pharmacist, staff pharmacist, and then technician. Clinical pharmacists were Doctors of Pharmacology (Pharm Ds), with five-year university degrees, two additional years of graduate school, and hospital internships. They taught at both the university and the hospital and consulted with other health care professionals on patients' cases. Staff pharmacists, satellite bound with a bachelor's degree from a five-year pharmacy program, supervised the satellites and the pharmacy technicians, processed physicians' orders, and answered questions about patients' drug orders. It was Kay, Tom, and their technician colleagues, however, who did the actual processing of patients' medication needs. In each satellite, often as small as seven by thirty-six feet, they filled prescriptions, drew up injectable medicines, set medication boxes, and maintained stock.

These basic routines remained constant across satellites. The mornings were hectic, afternoons more leisurely. Medicine distributions were scheduled across the day, once in the morning at 10:30, in the afternoon at 1:30, 3:00, 4:30, and 6:00, and several times during the evening. Filling medication orders stirred up a flurry of activity each morning.

The fifth-floor cardiac satellite was larger than many pharmacy workplaces on other hospital floors. Two large, windowless rooms connected by an open portal, the satellite most resembled two adjacent storage closets, their walls shelved, floor to ceiling in some places, and filled with boxes of medicine labeled by name and dosage in large black print. Two computers were in each room, and a large metal cart, nearly five feet tall, was parked to one side of the room. The pharmacy was alive with activity, a beehive of movement, with Mary Russell and Cathy Chambers, the technicians staffing the satellite, filling patients' pharmaceutical orders, and Cindy Peterson, the staff pharmacist, overseeing their work. Howard Stern's voice blared from the radio on one of the satellite's shelves as Mary filled medication orders from a computer mounted on a two-foot-wide shelf extending waist level from one of the satellite's walls. African American via Jamaica, Mary explained her work in the satellite with a lilt of the Caribbean in her voice. She pulled up a patient's order on the computer, which appeared on the screen as a form with spaces for the patient's name, pharmaceutical order, and the initials of the people who currently and previously filled the orders. Reading from the screen, she selected packets and small aluminum foil containers of pills from labeled boxes that were shelved in various places in the satellite. "We been here so long, we know where everything is," Mary explained. "We arranged this place." One by one she put items in a thin gray box, the "bin," that rested on the square table in the center of the satellite. When she finished filling the bin, she typed her initials in the space on the screen's order form. She filed the completed bin on a shelf on the tall aluminum cart, and took an empty bin from the cart. She pulled up another order on the computer screen and began filling the empty box with packets of pills. Each box took between five to ten minutes to complete.

Cathy Chambers was the satellite's second technician. A white woman in her early thirties, Cathy periodically brushed her long brown hair back from her face as she filled orders from a second computer across the room from Mary. Her accent was southern, Georgia to be exact. "This used to be the cardiac floor," she explained. "Now it's also general medicine. It's seasonal. Summer there's less people. There are fewer operations scheduled, there's less cardiac when the surgeons are on vacation."

Cindy Peterson, the staff pharmacist, also input patients' orders into a third computer at the other end of the room. By 9:30, Cindy changed activities, and began checking the filled boxes that Mary and Cathy had stacked on the delivery cart. Cindy, the youngest of the three women, was also the most senior. Thin, white, and well dressed in a khaki suit and silk blouse, she sat on a stool at the computer on which she had previously logged new orders. She selected a box, pulled up the patient's order on the screen, dumped the box's contents on the table in front of her, counted the items, and checked them against the order on the screen. Cindy typed her initials in a space on the screen's order form as she finished with each box. Although she occasionally removed an extra item from a box, most boxes required no modifications.

While the women worked, they also dealt with an endless series of interruptions. Pharmaceutical deliveries were made to the satellite, men in scrubs returned anesthesia bags, and nurses came to the door with requests for IV bags and small prescription orders. Both Mary and Cathy took care of these requests, at times individually, and at other times as a team. When a nurse called on the phone, for instance, Mary answered, saying, "Fifth floor pharmacy, Mary," "Procardilyn?" and "Okay. Do you want us to call you when it's finished?" Cathy then pulled the requested item from the shelf, and showed it to Cindy. Later, when the nurse came to pick up the medicine, Mary instructed her in its use. (July 20, 1993, field notes, Jackson Hospital)

According to Bob Clay, the clinical pharmacist who supervised Donna Watkins and Ahmed Roashan in the obstetrics wing pharmacy, the technicians' responsibilities were not completely unlike Henry and Ruth's at Development.

The technicians really are to be the manufacturers, the assembly-line workers I'll say. You know the ones that you have to do when it has to be done precisely, you have to have faith in them, but it's more materials-management type of thing. The pharmacists are in a sense responsible for the material management, but not necessarily the actually producing of the product. (Bob Clay, clinical pharmacist, Jackson Hospital)

Yet changes in the sociocultural organization of work in Jackson's pharmacies fundamentally altered both this definition of role and status of technicians in the satellites in the 1970s. An expansion of the responsibilities of hospital pharmacists in turn expanded the duties of the technicians. James Kelly, the department's first training director, described this shift in responsibilities as it unfolded across the department.

What pharmacists do was changing at the same time. You see, the pharmacists were traditionally involved with essentially dispensing of material, they were materials managers, if you want. And in the seventies that began to change, where the pharmacists became in essence consultants or sources of information about the appropriate use of product.

And for pharmacy to encourage that evolution to take place somebody had to be there . . . to handle the hands-on logistical aspects of drug delivery. So there was another force at work that had generated that need, and that is the changing role of pharmacists in the hospital, where hospitals were looking to pharmacists to assert more and more control over how doctors use drugs. But in order to get the pharmacist free to do that, you had to fill that vacuum and it was a lot less expensive to do that with a nonprofessional person. (James Kelly, former training director, pharmacy department, Jackson Hospital)

He added that a similar shift "happened in almost every health care profession."

If you look at nursing care or dental care or physician-generated care . . . well there's physician's assistants. And you have nurse practitioners moving into that, and nurse practitioners moving up and you have nurse aides, and supportive nurses coming underneath that. Dentists, you go to a dentist now, you first see an assistant. You may see a dentist for only five minutes.

And so it's not an unusual trend, and some people might say that's the reason why health care is getting so expensive. The trick is to use these people in the right way to provide more cost-effective care. And I think with pharmacy technicians that's the case. We don't need a pharmacist to sit there and do routine, mundane, repetitive kind of tasks, or just material transfer tasks. (James Kelly, former training director, pharmacy department, Jackson Hospital)

The Technician Training Program played an important role in this professional transformation. Addressing the hospital's own changing needs, the training program's stringent screening mechanisms and structured preparation ensured that Kay, Tom, and their colleagues were trained according to the hospital's specifications. Supervisors, who had become intimately aware of technicians' capabilities when they taught in and observed training sessions, felt increasingly comfortable ceding responsibility in the pharmacy satellites to them. And in practice, that is exactly what happened. As Donna Watkins in obstetrics stated, "They have a lot of trust in your work. They figure they trained you; you can do the work. Jackson gives us the opportunity to do our work." By the time I arrived at

Jackson, ten years after the initiation of the pharmacy technician training, the role of pharmacy technician was no longer that of "assembly-line worker." Kay and Tom had become professionals. Kay asserted,

> Even our administrators are really proud about this too. If they get a new pharmacist that comes in and comes on our floor, the technicians can run the floor. We can tell him, you know, what needs to be done. We know, you know, if this is too much to give a patient. If we don't know, we know where to look. (Kay James, pharmacy technician, Jackson Hospital)

Catalyzed by pharmacists' newly emerging role in the hospital and justified by training that familiarized technicians with workplace demands, the status distinctions in the satellites had blurred. Unlike Church Hall and Development, where the schism between Henry and Ruth or Dina and Joan and the next professional level was wide and institutionalized by personnel policies and workplace responsibilities, the lines separating responsibility in Jackson's pharmacy satellites had become indistinct. During my observations, for instance, I watched technicians perform tasks assigned to pharmacists. They input patients' medication orders into the computer, dispersed medications, advised nurses on their use, and answered questions both over the telephone and face to face. Pauline Pierce in anesthesiology explained,

> Of course every technician, if we can answer, if we feel confident answering a question, we answer it. If it's drug-related, those get, the pharmacist or whoever is qualified they take those calls. But for the most part, as far as equally answering the phone and taking care of the nurses, we all do it equally. (Pauline Pierce, pharmacy technician, Jackson Hospital)

I saw the lines blur in both directions. Technicians not only tackled the tasks of pharmacists, but staff pharmacists also filled medication orders and patients' medication bins when their help was needed. Bob Clay, a clinical pharmacist several levels above technician, confided that he often helped technicians in the pharmacy.

> I mean if it is a matter of, if the technicians are busy accomplishing whatever work they have to do. The staff pharmacists, they're busy and I'm the only one. And I feel strongly that the patient must get the meds rather than me sitting there waiting for something to free up, I'll make it up. I can make up an IV. I can draw up injections. I can do

whatever a technician or pharmacist would do. (Bob Clay, clinical pharmacist, Jackson Hospital)

Role differences between pharmacist and pharmacy technician were firmly grounded in legal distinctions. "It is illegal for anything to go from them [the technicians] to the patient," explained Karen Miller, the pharmacy's training director. "[Although] they can get to a pretty high level." Yet unlike the other worksites, at Jackson the differences were less clear in practice. Tom asserted,

> Doctors, nurses, people respect pharmacy technicians. They really don't even differentiate you from a pharmacist. Sometimes we have to actually tell them, well I'm sorry, I'm not a pharmacist. (Tom Russo, pharmacy technician, Jackson Hospital)

This expanded role commanded ample respect. "Everybody belongs; everybody has a job that's important," commented Missy Brown in Jackson's Home Infusion Service. "And your job, no matter what it is, is as important as mine."

A GOOD SALARY

Increased responsibilities manifested themselves in almost every facet of a technician's work, including both the salary and benefits. Technicians' wages ranged from $11.28 to $15.23 an hour. "Twenty-four thousand dollars for a high school grad is a good salary," commented Chas Hopewell, one of the first technicians I met at Jackson. Benefits included a choice of health plans, two weeks vacation per year, four personal days, seven paid holidays, and one sick day accrued per month. Tuition was waived for any internal university course, and an external tuition plan provided 100 percent reimbursement up to $2,000 a fiscal year for undergraduate studies and up to $7,500 per fiscal year for studies at the graduate level. All the technicians utilized the tuition benefits to take courses; during our conversations they offered a long list of subjects they had studied at Jackson after work:

> "I'm taking liberal arts classes, sociology, psychology . . . "

> "I took two courses in history, I've taken Western civilization . . . what else have I taken? I've taken an English course. . . . I just did it to, you know, continue my education. It's just that the hospital pays for it."

"I took my biology, biochemistry, microbiology, two chemistries, English."

Others had also taken courses at community colleges or universities closer to their homes, and received tuition reimbursement from the hospital. Everyone in the department was studying; everyone was thinking about career advancement. Khristin Carlson, one of the department's assistant directors, asserted,

> The other thing is that with the benefits package the opportunity is there for them to go to school. And you see a very high percentage, I don't know how many of my techs you've interviewed, but I'm sure a fair amount of them will tell you that they're in school. A number of them are doing their pre-pharmacy right now. And if you worked at Rite Aid or Thrift Drugs you wouldn't have that opportunity, you wouldn't be able to run over right after work and go to class. I think you'll find that people are able to support their families on that salary and they don't lose that dream of going, of finishing school or getting that degree, because you're constantly being stimulated and tweaked here. (Khristin Carlson, assistant director, Jackson Hospital)

The technicians confirmed Carlson's assertions. Of the ten I came to know best, four had applied to pharmacy school, three were taking pre-nursing courses, one was contemplating a physician's assistant track, and the two others were actively deliberating possibilities. Tom Russo had started a nursing program. He explained, "It's a nice benefit that I'm going to school now, and they're paying for that too, It's really helpful. Especially the way I spend money. . . . One less stressful situation where you don't have to worry about money."

The department's in-service workshops were also part of Tom's continuing education. In these sessions, he and his fellow technicians discussed topics based upon their own needs and interest. According to Donna Watkins, during these in-service sessions they learned "about the safety of the hospital, IV hood work, sterile compounding," and mastered new computer systems. Along with the workshops, the department also convened monthly technician meetings in which "we basically discuss any major business, hospital-wide," as Lisa Henry on third floor chemo explained. "Like about raises, or if there's a conflict on expiration dates on some particular drug or some procedure that we need training on, or if there's a new drug on the market or something. We'll discuss that." Both meetings and in-service workshops became opportunities for the men and women to explore their expanded roles in the hospital's operations.

ACTIVE MEMBERS

Unlike Henry and Ruth at Development, Dina and Joan at Church Hall, or even Chan and Moeun at Concordance Steps, Kay and Tom believed they played a substantive role in the actual organization of their own work at Jackson. Although the director and four assistant directors officially headed the hospital's department, "committee work," explained Sunny Morris, the department's operations coordinator, was "typical of our department. We work on group decision making, decision making in groups. The director would like input." (The department's committees are listed and described in Appendix E.) Khristin Carlson provided a historical overview of the pharmacy's management by committee.

It was before I came, I believe it was nineteen eighty-four. The department of pharmacy, apparently there was a feeling there was a problem with communication in the department. And they did a huge survey. One of the things they uncovered was that the employees felt that there was a bit of a dictatorship here and that decisions were not communicated or discussed with them. As a result of that, the department is now run pretty much by committees. And there's about eight to ten core committees. Some of them are working committees; some of them are information. A working committee would be the computer committee, the education committee. Then we have another layer which are task forces, and the task forces are developed on need, not ongoing needs but needs for a certain time period. That's a robot committee. The implementation on the robot is, we're not always gonna be implementing it. Once it's implemented they may go to the computer committee for maintenance.

What we try and do is get a representative from each area, from the seven satellites, from the back area, from the night shift. Then that representative from that committee is supposed to go back to their unit and tell them what goes on at the committee meeting and get a consensus and then come back. That's kind of how the structure works. Now, it's not a perfect world because we have patient care upstairs and if it's too busy or someone's scheduled off that day, you can't go to your meeting. But it's a lot better than it was. Things get into the minutes; there's documentation. You have more than one person's opinion and, for the most part unless it's like a research committee or residency advisory committee, there are technicians on almost all the committees in the department. I would say probably, on probably about seventy percent of them.

We have the technicians do reports at their own meeting. We have a staff meeting every month with the techs for all of our clinical area, and so the representative for the robot committee will say can one of you give a report to your fellow technicians. Having them do the committee reports, instead of the administrators doing it, gives the committee more credibility and gives those people more authority to come in and say, well look, I learned this. We're teaching each other rather than it just coming as an announcement from an administrator. (Khristin Carlson, assistant pharmacy director, Jackson Hospital)

Because participation was linked to performance evaluations and merit raises, technicians were not only allowed, but encouraged to join one or more of these committees. Nearly everyone was on at least one committee. Kay was on the robotics committee and the committee on nursing and pharmacy. Tom, who was the most active of technicians at least in terms of committee membership, was on the technician trainee selection committee, the program's standards committee, the committee on nursing and pharmacy, and the robot committee. Tom explained his participation.

Each year our raises are based on merit, so it looks good on paper. Some of them I'm interested in; I do like the pharmacy nursing one and I do like the program standards one. There's a few issues we've taken care of. When this robot committee came on, I jumped on that too because I thought that it's one of the ways the department's going to go.

Another reason I joined the technician training committee, 'cause I like what they did for me and I'd like to help them as much as possible. (Tom Russo, pharmacy technician, Jackson Hospital)

All but one of the technicians I came to know were active on at least one committee, and all had stories concerning the positive impact of the committees' work. Mary Russell, in the fifth-floor cardiac satellite, was firm in her insistence that the committees "do some projects. I wouldn't go if it was a waste of time." The drug distribution committee, for instance, standardized drug reconstitution, "so when patients are transferred from here to there the drugs will be the same all the time." While committees may have dealt with the little things, the quotidian tasks of work, the network of committees and task forces mediated a potentially hierarchical organizational structure. Through their membership, technicians participated in the process of organizing, managing, and improving the department. They had a voice in and sense of control over their own work.

Committee work can, of course, be complicated and frustrating, and according to Sunny Morris, it "takes a long time." One afternoon, while observing Mary Russell and Cathy Chambers in the cardiac satellite, I watched their intertwined feelings of validation and frustration unfold. Cathy, one of three technicians assigned to the satellite, had left to attend a robotics committee meeting, and upon her return, she discussed the meeting with Mary.

> Three-thirty in the afternoon, the pharmacy satellite on the cardiac wing had settled into a low hum. Teddy Stokes, the resident pharmacist, input orders on one of the satellite's four computers. Namib Anwari made up LVPs (large volume parenterals, injectables in laymen's terms) under the laminar flow hood, while Barb, a technician trainee, worked near Namib at another computer. Cathy had just returned from the robotics committee meeting and she talked with Mary in the outer of the two rooms. The pharmacy department was considering the introduction of robots into the system to take over responsibility for completion of standard medical prescriptions. Cathy related the logistical difficulties they had discussed in the meeting. "They don't know how much room is needed, who they're going to move and to where." She added, "I like having some input, but I never walk away feeling like we're doing anything. It's particularly true of this committee. Maybe we don't have enough statistics." Mary asked about other hospitals that had robotics systems and Cathy told her they have one in Pittsburgh, but not here. Mary asked, "Why not send someone out to visit a site that has one. Or videotape a working model?" Cathy replied, "That's a great idea. They want to track flags [i.e., specially prepared medications] since the robot will do that. Someone suggested going through the black binder for a year. Since we're on Millennium now [a new computer system] I told them we could trace through that." Mary asked, "What did they say?" Cathy responded, "They said that's great." "They should have all pharmacy techs on the committee," Mary commented to me. "Then we'd get things done." (July 20, 1993, field notes, Jackson Hospital)

While often frustrated by the slow pace of the group-based decision-making process, as active participants on committees and task forces, the women were regularly reminded of their worth. Accepted into the hospital's social and cultural order, Cathy, Mary, and the others were reinforced professionally by the knowledge that the hospital created space for the opinions and their voices.

BECOMING SUPERVISORS

At Jackson, the technicians' local knowledge was also validated through their own supervision of technician trainees. Mentored by senior technicians during their own training, they now assumed that role with incoming cohorts of trainees. Tom explained that he modeled the teaching part of his job after his own trainers.

I try not to tell anybody what to do. I mean even the trainees that come through anymore. I ask them. I guess it is a way of instructing, but I ask them what do you think should be done next. I think it's a better way of learning. It allows them to think for themselves; it encourages them to think for themselves rather than being told what to do. I mean it was what was done to me. The girls that taught me when I came through the program are still here too. It was the way they taught me and I was appreciative of it and it was how I learned. They made me think for myself. You know whenever I find mistakes with any new trainee's work, I'll give it back to them rather than tell them what's wrong. I just let them, if they're like, "well, I don't know," it's like, well, take it one step at a time. Just go through everything, is it the right name, is it the right medication, dose, right size, is it a solution, and so they find the problem themselves. This way the next time they make it [the solution] again they can go through that process themselves and everything will turn out right. (Tom Russo, pharmacy technician, Jackson Hospital)

During an observation in a satellite the following month, I watched the teaching interaction Tom described play out several times. Tom's "think for themselves" strategy seemed typical of the setting, not the personnel, since in the following vignette from my field notes, Cathy Chambers, rather than Tom Russo, was the supervising technician.

One-thirty, Cathy Chambers and Barb Silver were starting afternoon medication deliveries. Cathy, who had been at Jackson for twelve years, was supervising Barb, a trainee, during her clerkship on the cardiac floor. Pushing the cart that they had stocked with filled medication boxes that morning in the pharmacy satellite, Barb led the way. Cathy followed with me in tow. In the first hall, Barb took several boxes and bottles from the cart and disappeared behind a nursing station. As we continued walking, albeit more slowly, Cathy explained that Barb was putting the items in the refrigerator in the nursing station.

Barb returned in about two minutes, holding several bottles while announcing that one of the patients had been discharged. She asked Cathy, "What should I take out of the refrigerator?" "What do you think?" replied Cathy. Barb thought for a moment, and then answered "I guess about everything." "Why?" responded Cathy. Barb taking another moment before answering, looked down at the cart as though deep in thought. She then replied, "If the patient isn't there anymore, I don't need to leave anything in the refrigerator." "So what will you do with the supplies?" continued Cathy. Barb looked at her, gave herself thirty seconds, and then said, "I'll credit the patient's account when we get back." Cathy said okay, and we continued walking. (July 20, 1993, field notes, Jackson Hospital)

Cathy held back. Rather than supply answers to Barb's queries, she forced the trainee to reflect on the distribution process and come up with her own answers, in a manner like that described earlier by Tom. Cathy acknowledged Barb's problem-solving abilities and treated her with the same respect that she had received from senior technicians during her own training.

The professionalization of the technicians' role and the upgrading of their status at Jackson had not taken place overnight. The process had been long and slow. According to Khristin Carlson, she was at least in part responsible for pushing the upgrade forward.

> What I have been able to do is to get other people at the administrative level in this department to recognize the technicians. So I think if anything we've raised the level of consciousness and gotten the techs more involved in committee work and that sort of thing. It's pertinent because I think that you need the leadership to be able to recognize the technicians and I think traditionally the director and previous assistant directors have not really recognized technicians at Jackson. And it's been sort of a hard road to hoe but I think people are coming around finally, and if you keep. . . .
>
> Just overall by increasing their visibility, putting them on committees and sending them to conferences, they were never, they never went to conferences before. This will be the fourth year in a row we've been able to send them to conferences. All pharmacists can go to conferences at Jackson. I've gotten them [the technicians] dues. All pharmacists are eligible; they get three hundred dollars a year for dues for professional organizations, but techs never got anything. The techs now get money for professional dues.[4] (Khristin Carlson, Assistant Pharmacy Director, Jackson Hospital)

Hand-picked for their roles at Jackson, the department's policies helped Kay and Tom see themselves as different from people such as Henry and Ruth at Development, "people in an assembly line." The identity of professional that had been carefully nurtured at Jackson.

EMBRACING THE ROLE

I already knew quite a bit about Jackson's pharmacy system when I interviewed Pauline Pierce in the lounge outside her satellite. I had attended technician meetings, talked to managers and supervisors, and watched the everyday activities of the hospital's technicians. But listening to Pauline's story, I began to understand for the first time how the technician training and the status position to which

Pauline and her technician colleagues moved were shaped and re-shaped by each other. Pauline, an African American woman with her hair pulled back from her shiny face, had been a pharmacy techni-cian at Jackson for almost six years. She attended Jackson's phar-macy training as a JTPA-funded participant, worked at another hospital for a year, and was hired back at Jackson as an anesthesia technician, where she dispensed narcotics to the anesthesiologists on the hospital's third floor. Ten years ago, Pauline had been a col-lege student, majoring in biology. But she got pregnant in her junior year, left, and never went back.

> My son was two, I was at home, and I knew that I wouldn't be able to continue my college education so I needed to have some real tangible skills. I mean to say that you have three years of biology. That's not going to get you a job. I needed to work and knew that I needed skills. I coincidentally had a girlfriend who is now a pharmacist, at the time she said they have this program, why don't you try it. And so I did. And also coupled with that was also my desire to enter the health care profession.
>
> During training I was acclimatized to the environment and the system as far as dispensing the meds and using the computer. It just gave me a broad knowledge of the pharmacy technician field. I felt really confident that with that training that I could go anywhere and work pretty sufficiently. The classroom was sort of abstract, but once we got into the practical aspects of the fieldwork, seeing how the floors are operating and really getting a feel for that, that made a big difference. That was important, just knowing how to manipulate the syringe and how to put the needle in and in addition to that you can do it clumsily but then it's not going to be sterile and all. So the train-ing is good in that you get the opportunity to get rid of that clumsi-ness and to become more comfortable with it. And then in addition to that your time up on the floor is also spent doing those things. So by the time you got placed into a job you were fully, or you should have been at least, fully confident in that area.
>
> The program was funded by the Health Care Local so that was sort of the only way that you got into the program. They funded the program, so I didn't have to pay the tuition. And they also provided transportation fees at the end of the month, so that was really helpful. So I'm just really thankful that at the time that they were funding the program because otherwise I might not have been able to afford the training. (Pauline Pierce, pharmacy technician, Jackson Hospital)

With the help of Jackson's trainers, Pauline had found work post-training at Johnnes, another hospital in the area. She stayed there for one year.

Judging from the time I was here, in terms of the training program and in terms of the level of professionalism that I saw here [at Jackson], I didn't see that there at Johnnes Hospital. And the responsibilities of the technicians were much different; there the technicians really didn't have as much responsibility as they have here. Here technicians handle narcotics. Here the technicians do orders. Here the technicians, again if they feel confident answering, they could answer questions or follow through with things. Phone calls and those other things at the other hospital was primarily the pharmacist's responsibility. A technician was the basic manpower on jobs; that's the only thing they did in the other hospital. (Pauline Pierce, pharmacy technician, Jackson Hospital)

As the only technician at Johnnes who had been certified, Pauline asserted that, "being certified made a lot of difference. But in the same sense the reason I wanted to leave was that I felt that my skills I acquired here weren't being utilized there." With some effort, Pauline worked herself back into a job at Jackson.

I had been calling Jackson regularly and then they finally called me. The lady who I replaced left, so they needed someone. They asked me, I interviewed for the anesthesia program. Basically it was my performance in the technician program that opened it up to me, and the rest is history, I guess.

Now I dispense narcotics, account for all different pharmaceuticals as far as stock and those that are used. I have to double check and make sure that the doctors are accountable for what it is that they say they are using as far as narcotics with the patients. It's nice too because I'm involved with the doctors and I get to meet them, and as far as having them come to the door and say, "I want my meds, I want my meds." It's a little different so I do enjoy that aspect of the job. And then the second part of my job is the traditional technician duties, filling medication bins, preparing IVs, making deliveries, and checking the stock, making sure that the stock levels are maintained. We do some order entry in the computer, but at this point it's really limited. We do have pharmacists there who enter orders but we are capable of entering orders into the computer. Preparing medications extemporaneously, if something isn't available, let's say the doctor ordered a half a tab, we would have to prepare, we would have to package that half a tab. (Pauline Pierce, pharmacy technician, Jackson Hospital)

When I asked Pauline about her favorite part of the job, she quickly asserted, "definitely the anesthesia part of it."

Because number one I'm there by myself and in being there by myself I know that everyone who comes to the window is dependent on me, that gives me a higher level of responsibility. And for the most part the people who I have to interact with are pretty nice and they really don't want anything from me. They're not really nit picking or, it's a different, the needs are just different. They just come and ask for their box or if they might need something for a case, there's, with the nurses or whatever they have demands too. They come to the door, and they're like really picky and they want the stuff now. They don't realize that we're just one unit and that they might have four patients, but we have one hundred and twenty for the entire floor. You know, that we have to care for. So it's just different in that aspect. The level of responsibility, being in contact with the physicians, having the free time to myself, in the mornings just to be alone get my work done. (Pauline Pierce, pharmacy technician, Jackson Hospital)

Jackson's training had connected Pauline back onto a career track that was not so very different from the one on which she had set her eye during her university years, and to a job with a relatively high level of both autonomy and responsibility.

I think the training is really good, I would say that especially for someone who is unsure about the directions they want to take, they really don't want to consider college and especially in light of the economics, people with college degrees don't have jobs. And if they want to be involved in a health care environment I would recommend it. . . . Someone right out of high school, you get the training, and the pay is reasonable. You're not going to be a pauper. The level of respect that you can achieve is there. I just think it's great. (Pauline Pierce, pharmacy technician, Jackson Hospital)

In addition, Jackson's tuition benefits helped Pauline keep current and well positioned for a next professional step:

I took my biology, biochemistry, microbiology, two chemistries, English. I've just sort of reassessed goals and, being that I'd like to add to my family, I said, well, I don't really want to try medical school. So I was thinking about some other, above this, an upper-level way of continuing my education while at the same time being in health care. So I was thinking of enrolling as a physician's assistant, they have a program at Henry Hospital that I've been considering. So that is probably what I'll do, if not just going back and getting my degree and maybe teaching. (Pauline Pierce, pharmacy technician, Jackson Hospital)

By attending Jackson's training, Pauline had become a technician. But because the training also supported a shift in the way technicians were perceived and treated at Jackson, she had also become both a professional and an important member of the hospital's pharmacy department. She hadn't been a professional at Johnnes Hospital, where she was the only formally trained and certified technician. Pharmacy technicians had fewer responsibilities and less autonomy there, and Pauline complained that she had felt a growing sense of professional dissonance.

Kay James had experiences similar to Pauline's. Hired by Jackson Hospital right from training, she left to work first for a better-paying temporary service, and then for Doctors' Hospital. Unhappy with her limited responsibilities at Doctors' Hospital, she left and returned to Jackson four years previous to our meeting.

> When I went to Doctors' I found that they didn't let the technicians do as much as Jackson does. I felt like, I know I can do this, but they wouldn't let me. Here we dispense narcotics. If a nurse comes to the door with her narcotics sheet and needs a narcotic, we can sign it out and sign it into the nurse. But over at Doctors' we couldn't touch narcotics.
>
> And say there was a medication and you know what it's for, but the technicians over there had no clue. They're drawing up stuff all day in bulk but had no clue. I mean they knew the name, but had no clue what it's used for. Because they weren't trained. (Kay James, pharmacy technician, Jackson Hospital)

Moving back to Jackson, both Pauline and Kay found they occupied a role and affiliated status position which they could wholeheartedly embrace.

Erving Goffman first explored this notion of *role embracement* in his *Encounters: Two Studies in the Sociology of Interaction*: "To embrace a role is to disappear completely into the virtual self available in the situation, to be fully seen in terms of the image, and to confirm expressively one's acceptance of it" (1961, 106). Role embracement also described Tom Russo's experiences at Jackson. After countless jobs, Tom finally discovered home in Jackson's pharmacy department. It helped that "good money" and benefits also accompanied the respect and responsibility he received on the job. Tom compared his role as technician on the psychiatric floor with his previous union job in the mail room.

> If you want an indication when I was working in the mailroom, they'd give you twelve sick days and I'd use fourteen. I really was unsatisfied with my job. I didn't like my boss, not my immediate supervisor but the administrator above her. They were nit picky, and I guess because they had union personnel under them they had to be really

tough. I mean they were writing people up for buying a pack of Life Savers while working, making a delivery, walking, stopping to buy a pack of Life Savers. They wrote somebody up, who, as he was delivering something, had a cup of coffee in his hand. It's like, you're getting ridiculous here. Actually, pretty much of most of that department was that way. I mean there was some good people, the immediate supervisors were great people, I mean really nice and they went up to bat for you and really helped you. But the administrative end was really lousy.

The administration here is pretty good. Nice people, good people, fair, just. You want any indication, I haven't had one sick day yet this year. And I'd say tops I've had like maybe three. Three a year during the last eight years. I feel better about my job. I feel proud telling people what I do. I like what I do and I get a lot of self-worth out of it. (Tom Russo, pharmacy technician, Jackson Hospital)

SOMETHING'S KEEPING US HERE

But Pauline, Kay, and Tom were no more interested or focused than Henry and Ruth at Development, or Joan and Dina at Church Hall. In practice, all thirty-seven men and women across the four workplaces talked about a desire to do well in their newly earned role of employee. Yet as chapters 1 and 2 illustrate, men and women at both Development and Church Hall attributed their gradual "cooling out" not to their own lack of motivation but to the gap between their own expectations and perceptions of ability held by their employers. For some individuals, this space between local and official identities was manageable, and they were able to balance their continued perception of difference with opportunities they encountered in the workplace. This final section describes how the social organization of the hospital, unlike that of Development, Church Hall, or Concordance Steps, allowed Tom and Kay to assimilate almost completely into the hospital's culture. At Jackson, no gaps in perception of ability were evident, and assimilation, rather than resistance or even accommodation, most closely described relationships between the technicians and their work. Once again, to recall the metaphor of wearing an identity at work, these men and women wore their working identities well. Their coats were roomy, the color well suited, and the fabric of good quality.

Pauline's, Kay's, and Tom's assimilation into work at Jackson had more to do with the relative exclusivity of the technician training and the pharmacy department's management practices, than with any characteristic intrinsic to the men and women who found work in the department. The pharmacy technicians at Jackson had been hand-chosen. It wasn't that racial and ethnic differences no longer existed at the hospital. Pauline Pierce, Kay James, Mary Russell, Samantha Wright, and Donna Watkins were all African American women, Namib Anwari and Ahmed Roashan were Afghani refugees, while nearly all their supervisors, the department's clinical and staff pharmacists, were white. Kay James and Tom Russo, unlike Henry Thompson and Ruth Fallows however, did not fall under the *hardcore unemployed* nomenclature, nor were Pauline Pierce and Donna Watkins identified as single mothers on welfare. Many of the men and women were in fact, working parents, and their stories of the complexities of parenthood sounded very similar to those of Dina and Joan. Pauline's son was four when she began Jackson's training, and during our first conversation she talked openly about the difficulties inherent in balancing training and parenthood.

> It was difficult, it was difficult. Because in addition to coming here I was going to drop him off at day care to try to make it here by eight o'clock. So then I would pick him up and play mommy and then at the same time try and get my homework done because each day we were swamped with a certain amount of work. We were quizzed; we were quizzed, so we had to be on top of it and we had hundreds and hundreds of drug names to memorize and it was really a challenge. (Pauline Pierce, pharmacy technician, Jackson Hospital)

Namib's recent attempt to return to school was also indicative of the choices and concessions involved in caring for small children. He had enrolled in a local university in an attempt to complete his pharmacy degree. But even with a wife who was at home full time, the births of his two sons forced him once again to interrupt his pharmacy studies, this time after completing only three semesters of classes. Namib explained, "I had problems arise, and I couldn't continue. It's on hold. I have two small kids, so I always worry about them." Yet while both Namib and Pauline quickly discovered that children require a level and intensity of care that competes with the demands of school, at Jackson they were not defined by their role of parent. Unlike Development, Church Hall, or even Concordance Steps, where difference was equated with classifications of economic status and reinforced by race, language, residency, and lifestyle characteristics, at Jackson difference had been disarmed. The Local's academic ranking and the hospital's hiring procedures screened out anyone whose behavior or lifestyles did not meet workplace demands (i.e., trainees with frequent absences during training or women who looked and dressed too ethnic). The result was an absence of economic status as a variable of difference, and in turn, race and ethnicity had no "social meaning."

Yet passing through Jackson's multiple gates did not in and of itself ensure that the men and women would find what became a home at the hospital. As mentioned in the previous section, the upgrade of the technician position within the pharmacy system was also part of their story. In theory, the distinctions between pharmacist and pharmacy technician were clear and rooted in legalities. In practice, however, the changing role of the hospital's pharmacists and the institution of formal training for the technicians catalyzed a professional upgrade in their status and blurred distinctions in the pharmacies. Participation on committees was also part of their story. Through a network of core committees, working committees, and task forces, Tom and Kay felt their work and local knowledge were validated, and a potentially hierarchical organizational structure was mediated.

I heard supervisors link these same characteristics—pay, benefits, a positive sense of self on the job, and the perception of being respected—with the extended job tenure of most of the hospital's pharmacy technicians.

> My turnover rate was zero first year. It was about four percent the year before, which means I lost one technician. And it was zero the year before that. I know exactly why. They're the second highest paid technicians in the city. I see this on an annual survey that comes out. . . . It goes to our department of human resources and every year we do a salary survey ourselves to see where we are and we know that our techs anyway are the second highest in the city. So that's one reason. The second reason is I believe that we have a very solid benefits package.
>
> I think the size of the department gives them opportunity. If they get into a position that they aren't particularly happy with, they transfer to another floor. Since people don't leave that frequently, we don't have a lot of internal transfers, but I think that people would rather wait for something to open up, retain their benefits. They're up in the satellites, and they want to go to the central pharmacy; the opportunity exists within their own hospital without having to disrupt their life, without having to leave Jackson. And that does occur.
>
> And what really struck me, they know how well trained they are, and I know how comfortable I feel as a pharmacist leaving my satellite unattended. So I think that the tremendous amount of responsibility that they do have here, first of all, they're very busy. . . . They feel productive at the end of the day. They come home and it's not just, although it's task-oriented, I think they know that if they don't do that job that the patient's not going to get something. . . . I think

there is that sense that, which sounds corny in medicine, that you're doing something for sick people. But I think you feel that sense of accomplishment. (Khristin Carlson, assistant director, Jackson Hospital)

Virtually no technicians left Jackson, and a long list of training program graduates waited for an opening with the pharmacy department. "People who have been here awhile, stay." asserted Tom.

People leave, one woman moved, her boyfriend got a job in Florida, one was accepted to pharmacy school in South Carolina. But there's a lot of independence. They pretty much let you work on your own. I'm here second shift. It's just me and the resident. We know the process here. It's challenging to get things done on time. (Tom Russo, pharmacy technician, Jackson Hospital)

"I only know one technician who left," added Mary. "She moved to another state. Something's keeping us here." Technicians stayed at Jackson because they liked the work. They felt good about the professional identities they wore in the pharmacy and good about themselves. Coming to Jackson after years spent trying on options, college, work in the retail sector or in manual labor, Tom and Kay found a purpose, respect for a job well done, and room for their voices. At Jackson they found a role they could embrace and a place they belonged.

Part II
WHAT THE STORIES MEAN

Chapter 5
Analyzing the Circle

This book is about structure and practice: the practice of men and women who found themselves outside the economic mainstream in the United States and the practice of teachers and employers who helped connect them to the workplace. Their stories, of who gets what in the bureaucratic worlds that the poor inhabit in the United States, are the weaving of these practices into institutional structures and cultural manifestations of worth, success, and difference. They are pieces of a puzzle that together illustrate the ways in which everyday practice intersected with and reproduced an official system to deal with the poor, in a moment in time when moving from welfare to work still involved at least a minimal investment in human capital.

Despite the radical turn that welfare policy in the United States has taken, the meaning and message of these stories still ring clear. They present the human side of our conversation about the poor, and put faces and names to the stereotypes of welfare and welfare recipients. While each of the thirty-seven men and women actively participated in the move from unemployment or underemployment to employment, postwelfare they found themselves on divergent paths, in different jobs with inequitable work roles, workplace responsibilities, and wage packages. From pharmacy technician to woodworker to nurse assistant to assembler, they formed a continuum that spanned from high pay and professional to poorly paid and powerless.

Tom Russo and Kay James, along with a select group of men and women who were able to navigate Jackson Hospital's arduous screening process, received training in pharmacy theory and practice and certification through the American Society of Hospital Pharmacists. They found work that paid well, offered enviable benefits, valued their opinions and treated them as professionals. Chan Monivong, Koung Sisowath, and a few other men with refugee status accessed a program that integrated hands-on skills training with mathematics and language instruction. At work they were afforded opportunities to sharpen and refine their skills, paid a livable wage and benefits, offered job security, and as the shop foreman asserted, "treated . . . as Americans." But while the efforts of welfare case managers and contracted trainers "saved" other men and women, to paraphrase historian Linda Gordon (1994, 290), they "did not advance or foster them." Investments in employment training may have connected Joan Ford and Dina Haskell, Henry Thompson, and Ruth Fallows to unsubsidized employment at Church Hall and Development, but the work did not take them very far. They continued to live in dangerous neighborhoods, sharing apartments with family members, parents, and siblings, without enough money to live the middle-class norm that they had heard so much about in training seminars.

All four welfare-to-work initiatives "worked" because they linked unemployed individuals to jobs, but the policies on which they were based were misdirected. Grounded solely on categorical delineations, they minimized the talents and skills of many men and women who went unnoticed in cultural contexts in which only academically sanctioned knowledge was recognized. These stories of thirty-seven men and women, all successful by official definitions, illustrate that without an understanding of the construction and negotiation of identity in the daily practice of training and work, transition programs and other reform-oriented efforts designed to mediate poverty only reproduced and vilified cultural constructions of the poor.

THE PIECES OF CHOOSING

This organization of people into categories around the status of underemployed and unemployed was neither accidental nor coincidental; it reflected choices made by funders, gatekeepers, and former welfare recipients alike, choices calculated within a web of beliefs about ability, resources, worth, and possibilities. The men and women I came to know best, Henry Thompson and Ruth Fallows, Dina Haskell and Joan Ford, Chan Monivong and Koung Sisowath, Tom Russo and Kay James, among others, were actors in their own stories. They talked openly about the decisions they had made in coming to work. Dina Haskell, for example, like many of the nurse assistants at Church Hall, sought out the job based upon an image of herself as a caregiver. She explained, "If you look at it like this was your mother or your father or even yourself, one day I might need this help myself, that's the reason I do it. I look at it like I might get old and sick and be in a nursing home, and I would want somebody to give me the best care." Dina had been so insistent in her choice of a future profession that she refused placement in programs that offered training in food services or computer operations. "I said no, I don't want to do nothing else but be a certified nursing assistant." She waited three months for an opening in a nurse assistant training program. "Then I did get accepted." Although Mary Russell, technician in Jefferson's fifth-floor cardiac pharmacy, was far less deliberate about her pursuit, she also talked about the act of choosing:

> I was in the union. I used to work in the laundry here, and then I didn't like it because in the summertime it was too hot. The union had a training upgrading fund and that's how I got in. . . . They had nursing and all of that, but out of curiosity 'cause I remember going to the doctor and he would write a prescription and I couldn't read it, not a word on it. It was mostly out of curiosity I decided to check into the pharmacy training. (Mary Russell, pharmacy technician, Jackson Hospital)

Men and women across all four workplaces talked both about training preferences and desired workplaces. Despite their subsequent complaints, the assemblers at Development, for example, had been firm in their desire to find work with the agency after they completed their training. Maria Lopez explained that she not only chose to work at Development, but once hired she refused to consider jobs with other companies. "If you don't get a job here, you have to go outside, and that's a lot harder," she contended. "Ben [Spencer, her case manager at Development] comes up with jobs for me. I say no way."

These men and women had been agents in their moves from unemployment to employment, but they made choices from a predefined field of possibilities. They acted within prescribed universes, driven by personal histories and ideologies, politics, and economics. Their stories, as told in Part One, describe a cyclical relationship of beliefs, expectations, agency, and structure, in which men, women, their trainers and workplace supervisors, living within social and belief systems, actively co-created cultural images that in turn reproduced and reinforced the dominant ideology and social organization. This relationship of human action and structural constraints is central to their stories. Sociologist Anthony Giddens (1984, 26) named this cycle of production and reproduction structuration theory.

> According to structuration theory, the movement of the production of action is also one of reproduction in the contexts of the day to day enactment of social life. This is so even during the most violent upheavals, or most radical forms of social change. . . . In reproducing structural properties . . . agents also reproduce the conditions that make the action possible. Structure has no existence independent of the knowledge that agents have about what they do in their day to day activity.

Henry Thompson's path to Development provides a good example of this interaction between agency and structure. Like the other thirty-six men and women I came to know, Henry had charted a course for himself that he had assumed would lead him back into the labor market. But Henry's original plan had included a technological fix; he had wanted to enroll in a training program run by a local university. "I heard they had more hands-on electronics," he explained. Yet while Henry acted, his actions were constrained by material and political forces, all circumscribed by beliefs about poverty in America. He faced a predefined field of possibilities; he was bound by the choices at hand. The electronics program "didn't get funded," and so he found himself at Development, promised the job of warehouse manager and soon frustrated by his status as assembler in the kits department.

According to administrators of the local Private Industry Council (PIC), Henry's experience was not unusual. Money for employment training was insufficient to fund all training proposals and support all eligible applicants, and so proposed training was often not funded. "We can only serve two percent of the people who need help, maybe two to five percent," explained PIC's Director. But in addition to this financial shortfall, Henry's choices were narrowed even further by his status within the welfare population. At the time, four training-related funding streams existed for the poor. Title IIA of the Job Training Partnership Act (JTPA) funded training for unemployed youth and unskilled adults. As both a recipient of welfare and as an unemployed adult, Henry, like all welfare recipients and most unemployed individuals, was eligible for JTPA. But slots for JTPA-funded training were at a minimum; they were awarded competitively based upon an applicant's performance on formal assessments. Unlike his counterparts at Jackson Hospital, Henry wasn't good on tests, and without a high school diploma, he was low on JTPA's candidate list. The other three funding streams targeted specific groups of the unemployed. Federal moneys from the 1989 Family Support Act only funded training for AFDC recipients, while state moneys were reserved for TN and refugee training programs. As a single man, Henry had been grouped with other single adults under the state rubric of Transitionally Needy (TN), and as such, was also eligible for the state's TN programs. TN training was easy to access, but TN programs didn't offer a wide range of career choices. As Ruth conjectured, her choice, and that of many other welfare recipients, was from training options that led "to a poor-paying job."

En masse, these four tiers constituted a sizable list of possibilities; however, not all proposals for training were funded, not all individuals were eligible for every training program, and not every program had enough room for eligible applicants. Many had long waiting lists. Henry's first choice of "hands-on" electronics training hadn't been funded, while Dina Haskell had to wait three months for an opening in a program that offered nurse assistant training and certification. Henry chose, as did Dina, Mary, and all the others, but their choices were constrained by limited funding and exclusive eligibility requirements, as well, at times, by their own and others' imaginings.

TRAINING PROGRAMS

While the stories in Part One illustrate that the sorting of poor men and women was an inevitable outcome of welfare classifications, categorical funding for training, and too little money for job training across all categories, they also reveal that the matching of men and women to "suitable" work roles became an essential part of each training initiative. Across all funding streams, training, both in terms of pedagogy and future jobs, had been tailored for different participant groups. For Henry, Dina, Chan, and Kay, membership in a welfare category became the basis for matching them to particular training programs and subsequent roles in the labor force. They had been linked to "socially approved tasks" (Abrahamson et al. 1976, 295) based upon their identities as individuals with multiple barriers, as caregivers, as refugees, or as science-oriented high school graduates.

DPW and PIC staff, trainers, and employers all described choosing individuals for particular training programs and work roles. These gatekeepers, the DPW case managers who sent Ruth and Henry to Development, the DPW job developers and trainers who readied Dina and Joan for Church Hall, the trainers and managers at Vocational Employment Service who prepared Chan and Koung for Concordance Steps, the trainers at the Health Care Local who socialized Tom and Kay to their new roles as pharmacy technicians, as well as Development's owner and managers, the nurses at Church Hall, the supervisors at Concordance Steps, and the pharmacists at Jackson, all played an important part in this matching. At Jackson Hospital, for example, I was told that individuals with prior pharmacy experience made the best pharmacy technicians. Carol Sullivan, a clinical manager who assisted in screening applicants for the department's technician program, added that secretaries and waitresses also placed high on her list. She contended that the experience of prioritizing and dealing with people in a hectic environment translated well to the pharmacy setting. Sullivan continued that on the other hand,

> I had an applicant who's been in the automotive service field for years and years and years and years, and he is basically fed up with the dirtiness and the filth and he has developed some sinus problems. He's really looking for a career change. But he's a little bit of a shifty person, I really don't understand why pharmacy is his choice, and I don't really get great answers when I ask him. I have to admit it's more his personality than it is his coming from the automotive industry. But a lot of people who come are thinking about someday going back to pharmacy school or have interests in becoming pharmacists or have always been interested in pharmacy but want to find out if this is what they really want. And he doesn't mention any of that. (Carol Sullivan, clinical pharmacist, Jackson Hospital)

In describing her idea of appropriate, Sullivan did not confine herself to basic characteristics such as gender, racial, or ethnic identity. She talked instead about an applicant's work experience and far less quantifiable characteristics such as "sincerity," "interest," and "motivation." "I look for people who are motivated," she explained. "Who maybe have a sincere interest in making pharmacy a career." Complicated, unnamed, and subjective, across all four sites trainers' constructions of appropriate revolved around a combination of national and political status (e.g., a Cambodian or Afghani refugee is good, a U.S. citizen from Puerto Rico is less good), employment status (e.g., an employed or dislocated worker always outranks a welfare recipient), and behavior resembling that of the middle class (e.g., more education is better than less). The process became one of distillation (Burkhardt 1981). From the multiplicity of selves that Henry Thompson and Ruth Fallows brought to the welfare office, for instance, their case managers combined and subtracted until they fit into a cookie cutter image of the "hardest to serve." Case managers and trainers saw what fit and omitted what didn't, in Henry's and Ruth's case, enlarging the negative (e.g., the lack of high school diploma, or long-term unemployment) and minimizing the positive (e.g., being fast learners, having work experience). To quote sociologist Ruth Sidel (1996, 24), from her *Keeping Women and Children Last*, "When a community nominates someone to deviant class, then it is sifting a few important details out of the stream of behavior he has emitted and is in effect declaring that these details reflect the kind of person he 'really' is."

It wasn't that certain people deserved more than others. At least, no one packaged their decisions in that way. More like Carol Sullivan, the clinical pharmacist at Jackson Hospital, trainers and employers at all four sites talked about training prescriptions and workplace options in a language of need. They mused on what training was needed by whom and who was appropriate for a particular job. They grounded their assumptions in shared beliefs about men and women, about skills and potential, and about needs and concerns. DPW case managers were a good example of this well-intentioned paternalism. Most of the case managers I met were women in their mid-forties and early fifties who had attended universities in the 1960s when theories of cultural deficiency abounded. Schooled within a discourse that equated poverty to the breakdown of the black family, many of these women understood the role of job training to be one of compensating men and women more for their lack of work-appropriate behaviors than for a lack of technical skills. Writing about women such as these, historian Linda Gordon linked their beliefs back to the Progressive Era of the 1920s. Gordon (1994, 304) writes, "Continuing a Progressive Era moral-reform legacy, they never entirely shed the belief that something more than lack of money was wrong with the poor, especially poor single mothers. They were convinced that the poor needed casework—counseling and rehabilitation—and they designed ADC (Aid to Dependent Children) to regulate morals and housekeeping." The best intentions of case managers and social workers, in the form of their referrals to Development, Church Hall, VES, or Jackson Hospital, stemmed from their own learned beliefs about poverty, merit, and deficiency. Educational psychologist Valerie Polakow (1993, 146) complemented this analysis when she wrote, "Teachers [and in this case, social workers and trainers] do not live above their culture; they too are participants in the pervasive poverty discourse that conceals economic and educational inequalities, state-induced destitution."

SORTING THE POOR

Sorting men and women such as Henry Thompson and Kay James, Dina Haskell and Chan Monivong into categories based upon gender, age, biography, and social class is a long tradition in this country, a history that generally reflects a societal differentiation between the deserving and undeserving poor. In his *The Undeserving Poor*, historian Michael Katz (1989, 12) traced this division between deserving and nondeserving to the poor laws of Great Britain and the colonial United States, when distinctions between able and impotent poor were first drawn. Stemming from the desire to differentiate "neighbors and strangers," and later, "the genuinely needy from rogues, vagabonds, and sturdy beggers," the concept of pauperism became not only an administrative but a "moral category" as well. The first series of stratification studies conducted in the United States continued to use these judgments of worth. In their classic study of economic status in a New England community, W. Lloyd Warner and Paul Lunt (1941) divided the poor into upper-lower and lower, positioning individuals with minimal skills and some work experience in local factories as superior to a bottom stratum of "disreputable poor." Following suit in his *Plainville USA*, James West (1945, 134) dissected the economic layers of a small town in the United States into five categories, three of which he labeled lower class. These lower classes, the "good lower class," "lower element," and "people who live like animals, [who] can't be judged by conventional standards of respectable people," were clearly differentiated across moral lines, sustaining the divide between deserving and undeserving.

These categories of worth are not only externally constructed; they have also been internalized by members of poor urban communities. When the sociologist Ulf Hannerz (1969) borrowed community members' own classification system to provide an insider (or in anthropological terms, an *emic*) portrayal of ghetto lifestyles, the categories differed little from those coined by Warner, Lunt, and West. Various neighborhood residents identified themselves and their neighbors as "mainstreamers," "swingers," "street families," and "street-corner men," and described a range of lifestyles that were bookended on one side by "respectable" and on the other by "no good." Not surprisingly, both the "street families" and the "street-corner men," (variously labeled as "tricksters" and "badmen") hovered around the "no good" pole. In a more recent article, urban sociologist Elijah Anderson (1994, 82) also used community members' labels to describe residents in an east coast inner-city neighborhood. He argued that while they associated "decent" families with a commitment to middle-class values, "street families, that is, those deemed less than decent, were often consciously opposed to those of mainstream society."

Over time, these value-laden divisions have crept into the public policy arena, where we hear welfare theorists and policy makers argue that the poor have different histories and problems, and therefore require dissimilar levels and kinds of support. The typical rationale offered is that categorizing the poor allows assistance to be tailored to each group's distinct needs, and therefore creates a more efficient system (Danziger and Weinberg 1986; Ellwood 1988). Writing within this ideological framework, David Ellwood, an architect of President Clinton's plans to reform welfare, suggested the following three needs-based categories:

- families in which the adults are already doing a great deal for themselves;
- those individuals who are suffering temporary difficulties because of a job loss, a change in their family circumstances, or some personal problem;
- and the few who are healthy but who seem unable to find work on their own and need some form of long-term support. (Ellwood 1988, 11)

The bifurcation between deserving and undeserving poor has been sanitized in Ellwood's writing. But in practice, it still looms large. Policies for the poor have not only categorized people around beliefs about problems and worth, but they also name, define, and relegate the poor into an us/them dichotomy that then legitimizes a way to think about and deal with poverty. Michael Katz calls this process one of socially constructed difference.

> Because the language of poverty is a vocabulary of invidious distinction, poverty discourse highlights the social construction of difference. Some ways of classifying people, such as undeserving or even poor are so old we use them unreflexively; others, such as homeless or underclass, though much more recent, quickly become unexamined parts of discourse. The problem with this language of difference is both philosophic and practical. We assume that verbal distinctions reflect natural or inherent qualities of people. By mirroring natural divisions, we think the language of difference represents objective distinctions. In fact, it does not. For reasons of convenience, power, or

moral judgment, we select from among a myriad of traits and then sort people, objects, and situations into categories which we then treat as real. (Katz 1989, 5-6)

The categories we treat as real are institutionalized by agencies designed to assist the very men and women who have been categorized. Development targeted the hardcore unemployed, DPW's Job Development Unit focused on single mothers on welfare, the VES woodworking training worked with welfare-eligible émigrés, and Jackson Hospital's technician training, while accepting applicants from the welfare rolls, privileged the un- and underemployed. Through this process, individuals were neatly organized by age, ethnicity, gender, education, and work experience. Across the four work-sites, this organization reflected the following:

- Henry, Ruth, and their co-workers at Development had the least formal academic experience, with most work experience in temporary agencies and the manufacturing sector. They proportionately faced more barriers in terms of substance abuse and prior legal offenses. In addition, Development employed the most African American graduates and was the only work site that employed Puerto Ricans;
- Joan, Dina, and the other former welfare recipients working at Church Hall all had prior work experience as nurse assistants. They represented both the highest proportion of women and the highest proportion of unmarried women with small children;
- Chan, Koung, and the other individuals referred from VES to Concordance Steps were all men and all Cambodian refugees. They all spoke English as a second language, and most had prior experience working with wood;
- Kay, Tom, and their fellow technicians at Jackson Hospital had the most formal academic experience. Two-thirds attended college, most with a background in science.

THE UNDERCLASS

Much to their dismay, when Ruth Fallows and Henry Thompson applied for welfare they found themselves grouped in a category that sociologists have named the underclass, a term that has gained importance in public discourse about the poor. The sociologist William Julius Wilson (1987, 8) described this group by their marginality to the "mainstream of the American occupational system." He writes that men and women who fall within the category were

> individuals who lack training and skills and either experience long-term unemployment or are not members of the labor force, individuals who are engaged in street crime and other forms of aberrant behavior, and families that experience long term spells of poverty and/or welfare dependency.

Ken Auletta, in his 1983 book *The Underclass*, named four distinct subgroups within this group of the poorest of the poor, each with its own problems, history, behavior, and pathology.

> First are the hostile street and career criminals who openly reject society's dominant values, a surprisingly small number of whom are responsible for the majority of crimes in most cities. The second group consists of the hustlers, those who out of choice or necessity operate in the underground economy, peddling hot goods, reefers, or hard drugs, gambling and pimping. Although their activities are illegal, unlike the hostile individual they are usually not violent, frequently they are skilled entrepreneurs. Third are the passive, those who have become dependent over the years on welfare and government support. The fourth group is made up of the traumatized—those whose minds have snapped and who have turned to drink or drugs or roam city streets as helpless shopping bag ladies, derelicts—or sadistic slashers. (Auletta 1983, 4)

Ruth and Henry didn't really fit into any of Auletta's categories. They were not criminals or hustlers; they were neither passive dependents nor traumatized derelicts. Some of their colleagues, however, were a slightly better fit. Edith Jenkins, Will Chandler, and the other men in recovery, for example, or even women such as Donna Hastings or Enid Castro, who had found themselves getting too comfortable on welfare, more closely matched Auletta's descriptions. But while the hourly workers at Development all had their problems, for the vast majority, being unemployed in a city that had lost 64 percent of its manufacturing jobs in the twenty-year period between 1967 to 1987 was the worst (Wilson 1996, 29). Ruth and Henry were victims of what Wilson (1996) called "the disappearance of work"; they were left behind when local factories moved to places where labor costs were cheaper, or when new companies chose to locate in the suburban fringe rather than the inner city. Despite these structural changes, however, a category catering to the underclass has been created within a web of beliefs about the poor, and as single adults, unskilled and poorly educated, Henry and Ruth were placed there. In coming to the welfare office for help, they had become what the state called the Transitionally Needy, and what poverty theorists called the underclass.

Without ever really knowing or at least articulating it, Dina Haskell and Joan Ford had also been grouped under this rubric. They were poor women with children, they received AFDC benefits, and they were part of a status group that has long been held suspect in the United States. According to historian Linda Gordon, the rationale for identifying single motherhood as a social problem has long been contested. During the early part of this century, feminists positioned single mothers as victims of abusive men. Other Progressive Era reformers however blamed the women themselves. They were seen as part of the influx of immigrants from southern and eastern Europe who were overcrowding the country's urban centers and contributing to not only their own, but also the country's decay. Gordon draws a thread from these earlier reformers to our current portrayals of single mothers. "One important ideological division in the discussion of single mothers resembled that in the debate about the welfare poor today: liberals tended to present them as victims of structural forces, like unemployment, while conservatives positioned them as responsible agents, their poverty due to lack of character" (Gordon 1994, 32). Over time, unmarried motherhood, intensified by a combination of race and the concentration of poverty in the inner cities, has become a symbol of the aberrant behavior we associate with the poor. "When many people think of welfare, they think of young unmarried black mothers having babies. This image persists even though almost as many whites as blacks were AFDC recipients in 1995, and there were also a good many Hispanics on the welfare rolls. Nevertheless, blacks were disproportionately represented" (Wilson 1996, 171). The sociologist Ruth Sidel (1996, 167) adds, "Over the past several years, but particularly since the 1994 congressional election, we have witnessed the systematic stereotyping, stigmatizing, and demonizing of the poor, particularly of poor women. They have been pictured as the embodiment of the characteristics Americans abhor—laziness, willful dependence on government, wanton sexuality, and imprudent excessive reproduction." AFDC, as well as recent official efforts to reform, and unofficially to eliminate AFDC, have in turn functioned as yet another explanation for the structural inequalities we have named the underclass.

The antidote prescribed for these poorest of the poor, these hardest to serve men and women, has always been more psychological than vocational. Immersed in a social work tradition based upon theories of cultural deprivation, Development's administrators, counselors, and business managers, DPW's trainers, and Church Hall's LPNs and RNs were convinced that their inner-city trainees and employees were devious, weak, and inexperienced. Both their beliefs and the actual components of Development's supported work and the DPW/Church Hall collaboration were deeply rooted in poverty theories developed over the past forty years by anthropologists and sociologists in the United States. As political scientist Michael Harrington wrote in his classic treatise, *The Other America: Poverty in the U.S.* (1962, 168–169)

> Perhaps the most important analytic point to have emerged in this description of the other America is the fact that poverty in America forms a culture, a way of life and feeling, that it makes a whole. It is crucial to generalize this idea, for it profoundly affects how one moves to destroy poverty. . . . They are people in the affluent society who are poor because they are poor; and who stay poor because they are poor.

Both Development's Work Support program and DPW's five day orientation to work attempted to compensate for what was perceived as lacking in poor individuals, poor families, and poor communities. According to official description, Henry Thompson and Ruth Fallows lacked work experience, decision-making capability, and the ability to work in a team; Development's supported work aimed to plug these holes. Dina Haskell and Joan Ford, on the other hand, were said to lack an understanding of the employer's world. They didn't know how to get a job, and once at Church Hall, they still didn't know how to act. The job of trainers at both DPW and Church Hall, then, became the shaping of men and women, filling them with the knowledge they lacked and the sensibilities they required.

REFUGEES

Identified by their refugee status rather than by chronic poverty, Chan Monivong, Koung Sisowath, and the other Cambodian men I met at Concordance had been separated out from this group of indistinguishable poor. In applying for welfare, they were clustered not with TNs or AFDC mothers, but instead, in a category that had been constructed around the influx of Southeast Asian refugees following the Vietnam War. For the men, this institutionalized identity of refugee generated training and workplace experiences that were substantively different from those of the Puerto Rican men and women at Development or the African American women at Church Hall.

The Nigerian anthropologist, John Ogbu, has written extensively on the negotiation of immigrant identity in educational settings, and his theories are relevant here. Examining why members of certain ethnic groups succeed in school while others do not, Ogbu has developed a theory that links ethnic identity with a cultural frame of reference. According to Ogbu, each group's history and relationship with the dominant culture shapes its "folk models of schooling" and its members' subsequent experiences in schools.

> The nonimmigrant minorities tend to equate schooling with one-way acculturation or assimilation into the dominant group which they consciously and unconsciously resist. Consequently they do not behave in a manner that maximizes academic success. In fact, they are generally characterized by what may be called low-effort syndrome or lack of persevering academic effort. The immigrant minorities, on the other hand, do not equate schooling with acculturation or assimilation and feel freer to adopt behaviors that enhance school success. Unlike the nonimmigrants who see schooling as one-way acculturation, the immigrants adopt what may be called an alternation model which permits them to behave one way in the school setting and another when they are at home or in the community. (Ogbu 1987, 258)

Although this was not written as a description of adults' interactions with educational or professional settings, Chan Monivong and Koung Sisowath would nonetheless fall under Ogbu's grouping of immigrant minority. As such, they should have felt "freer" than nonimmigrant minorities "to adopt behaviors that enhance" success. But in practice, the identity of refugee was more than a cultural frame of reference for Chan and Koung. It was not something they alone had internalized. Instead, it was an identity imposed upon them by policy makers and employers—a stamp of approval that the men came to the workplace complete with a Protestant work ethic and malleable personality. Sociologist William Julius Wilson (1996) and his colleagues on the Urban Poverty and Family Life Study (UPFLS) provide an compelling description of how these official beliefs unfold reflexively in the marketplace. In 1987 and 1988, UPFLS researchers surveyed 2,500 community residents and conducted participant observation and life history interviews in several poor neighborhoods in Chicago. Comparing the opportunities and experiences of African American men to those of recently immigrated Mexican Americans, the study's authors describe a scenario less about immigrants' ability to withstand discrimination and prejudice in the workplace and more about the relationships between structural change and belief systems. The researchers contend that

> [t]he loss of traditional manufacturing and other blue-collar jobs in Chicago resulted in increased joblessness among inner-city black males and a concentration in low-wage, high-turnover laborer and service-sector jobs. Embedded in ghetto neighborhoods, social networks, and households that are not conducive to employment, inner city black males fall further behind their white and Hispanic counterparts, especially when the labor market is slack. Hispanics "continue to funnel into manufacturing because employers prefer Hispanics over black and they like to hire by referrals from current employees, which Hispanics can readily furnish, being already embedded in migration networks."[1] Inner-city black men grow bitter and resentful in the face of their employment prospects and often manifest or express these feelings in their harsh, often dehumanizing, low-wage work settings.
>
> Their attitudes and actions, combined with erratic work histories in high-turnover jobs, create the widely shared perception that they are undesirable workers. The perception in turn becomes the basis for employers' negative hiring decisions, which sharply increase when the economy is weak. (Wilson 1996, 144)

Exchange *Hispanic* for *Cambodian refugee* and Wilson and his colleagues describe the experiences of Chan and Koung. As mentioned in chapter 3, VES staff argued that they would have had more difficulties had their clients been African American men. Their argument was not about characteristics inherent in members of a particular ethnic group, but instead about employers' beliefs. Individuals spoke to these interwoven relationships among beliefs, imposed and assumed identities, and market place, labor force, and workplace structures. As Bill Dougherty, the program's training director claimed, "We talked to employers and they weren't necessarily interested in African Americans as woodworkers. Because of the labor market I don't know if it would have really worked." Koung Siswath voiced a similar hypothesis about a reflexive relationship between work and workers in his own talk.

> We have some trouble. They, the blacks, Spanish, they think we take their jobs. Blacks, Spanish can't get good jobs. But we know if you work hard here, and if your boss likes you, you can do good. (Koung Sisowath, woodworker, Concordance Steps)

Koung's sentiment was reinforced in the workplace, when Concordance's owner, Jay Hawks, addressed the absence of African Americans on the shop floor. According to Hawks, he had tried to hire a few blacks, but only six or seven had ever applied, and none were as qualified as the other men in the applicant pool.

> And anyway, there aren't a lot of blacks in the industry. In construction sites blacks only compose five percent of the workforce. The VES training program has a very different study body. In another world the Cambodians were almost middle class. We can deal with their problems. I don't know if we can handle drug abuse, low skills, no work ethic. A lot of things we can't handle, a lot of grief all the time. (Jay Hawks, owner, Concordance Steps)

Chan and Koung assumed many socially defined identities. They were fathers, husbands, sons, customers, friends, and so much more, and they played a range of roles related to each. But the institutionalized identity of Southeast Asian refugee had become their definitive persona in training and at work. That social persona, combined with the synchronicity of people and policies described in chapter 3, took the men a step forward on their long journey.

ASSESSMENT AND THE CREAM OF THE UNEMPLOYED

In response to their requests for training, Kay James and Tom Russo, on the other hand, had become part of a select group for which the lines between unemployed and employed had blurred. Program participants in Jackson Hospital's pharmacy technician training were a mix of men and women from the city and the suburbs, some of whom had used JTPA money to subsidize the costs of training, others of whom had paid for the training themselves. Kay had been on welfare when she applied to the hospital's training program. Tom had had a job in the hospital's mailroom, and had participated in the training in order to upgrade his position in the hospital. At Jackson it wasn't a shared ideology about the poor, or even the government's response to a looming crisis through which Kay's and Tom's identities were constructed. Instead, it was their ability to surmount the hurdles that had been erected by hospital and union staff that proved most important to Kay's and Tom's stories. Officially constructed as a means of determining who could best take advantage of the technician training, unofficially, Jackson's screening determined who was most worthy of the opportunities that the hospital's training would afford. Prior education and work experience were essential to Kay and Tom's entry into the hospital's training program; formal and informal assessment mechanisms played an exaggerated role in ranking them and the cultural and social capital they had brought with them. Over the past twenty years, this relationship between assessment and the sorting of students in school settings has intrigued social theorists (Oakes 1985; Mehan et al. 1996 Varenne et al. 1998). The writing of economist Lester Thurow extends the conversation about testing into the realm of the workplace.

> Because of the ease of measurement, education and IQ probably have been overemphasized as sources of economic ability. Physical dexterity, personality or a host of other characteristics may eventually prove to be more important personal background variables than those we typically consider. (Thurow 1975, 128)

Watching all thirty-seven individuals successfully accomplish assigned tasks, solve problems, and create new ways of doing work across four very different workplaces forced me to question the validity of screening based only on paper and pencil tests and a series of interviews. The tasks involved in kit assembly at Development—organizing materials, coordinating tasks, filling orders, maintaining inventory, and working in a team for instance—were not so very different from the skills required in Jackson's pharmacy setting. Yet Jackson's reliance on formal assessments and its prioritization of academic experience and the social norms associated with the middle class ensured the availability of an employee pool that was dramatically different from that at Development. Employees' status, rather than a difference in the actual activities of work, then justified inequitable employee packages (i.e., wages, benefits, professional status, and working environment). Again according to Thurow,

> [I]n many cases there is no relation, or a weak relation, between test scores and the capacity to earn income. Education creates income earning capacities, but the particular facets of education which create income earning capacities are not yet isolated. Perhaps education creates skills; perhaps it creates industrial discipline; perhaps it is a convenient screening device to select labor. (Thurow 1970, 46-47)

Testing and academic experience neither encompassed nor ensured the negotiation of workplace demands. What it did do, however, was determine levels of appropriateness. It invited in and screened out, creating a group identity at Jackson that defined Kay, Tom, and their colleagues by their formal academic experience, backgrounds in science, and middle-class norms rather than a perceived level of need.

RANKING INDIVIDUALS

Through these classifications, former welfare recipients were perceived not as unique individuals but as members of particular welfare categories. The categorical identities provided trainers and employers with a relatively simple way of organizing the un- and underemployed, and fast became what Ashforth and Humphrey (1997, 48) called "reified as objective and normative accounts of social reality." The labels became "mirrors of reality," defining both trainees and training prescriptions, and workers and work in a reflexive cycle of identity formation and validation. What seemed to be best intentions look different in hindsight. In hindsight, it becomes clearer that these four government-funded training initiatives assumed the multiple functions of identifying and informing men and women of their place within the labor market queue, convincing them of their appropriateness for those tasks, teaching the knowledge and skills required to accomplish those tasks, and instructing them on job-appropriate demeanor and behavior. This socialization played out differently across the training sites.

- At Development, men and women designated as having multiple barriers were taught to accept authority, follow directions, and work as part of a team.
- In DPW's orientation and Church Hall's subsequent training sessions, women were taught to "present themselves" to employers as neat, positive, and organized, to provide care for elderly residents, and to assume a subordinate position in the facility's hierarchy of care providers.
- At VES and later at Concordance Steps, Southeast Asian refugee men were taught to speak the language and do the math involved in woodworking, to solve construction-related problems, and to work independently on projects involving design and fabrication.
- At Jackson, college-educated, work-tested men and women were introduced to medications in a hospital setting, guided through the math of manipulating those medications, and mentored to assume the role of quasi-professional.

Cumulatively the programs resulted in a ranking and distribution of individuals along lines drawn by academic levels, work experience, co-membership, ethnicity, race, and gender. In all four welfare to work transitions, more and the right kind of cultural capital, evidenced in a variety of ways (i.e., a high school education or more, performance on paper and pencil tasks, the right ethnicity and language group membership), served as map and key to additional resources and capital.

Within this context, Henry's hourly position at Development begins to make more sense, at least from a management perspective. Although Henry had come to Development after more than twenty years of factory work, his lack of a high school diploma and his adamant refusal to return to school obstructed his mobility and solidified his marginal stance. Henry summarized his feelings about school when he talked about his last job:

> They wanted me to go, but I said no way. 'Cause I hated school. I learned on the way up. The guys from college knew the theory, but I knew the on the job stuff. (Henry Thompson, assembler, Development)

Henry's reaction to school may have been based upon real and still vivid experiences, but it left him poor in terms of institutionally valued capital. He wasn't encouraged to increase his capital during training, because at Development, the focus was on workplace socialization rather than skills enhancement. Across the sites, men and women such as Henry who came in with the least and the wrong kind of cultural capital remained capital poor. They continued to be marginal. In the end, rather than assisting all individuals in "overcoming barriers to economic self sufficiency" (Department of Public Welfare 1992, 50) the four welfare-to-work transitions sorted in and sorted out. Consistent with social scientist Gosta Esping Anderson's arguments in his *The Three Worlds of Welfare Capitalism* (1990, 23),

> the welfare state is not just a mechanism that intervenes in, and possibly corrects, the structure of inequality; it is in its own right a system of stratification. It is an active force in the ordering of social relations. [Social programs] help determine the articulation of social solidarity, divisions of class and status differentiation.

JTPA AND JOB TRAINING

Funding and employment training go hand in hand; across all four transitions to work, the tailoring of training to particular subgroups of the un- and underemployed was closely related to the ways funding streams were designed and funding was dispersed. The Job Training Partnership Act (JTPA), which funded Kay Thomas's participation in Jackson's pharmacy technician training, is a good example of this linking of funding, beliefs about poverty, and training prescription. JTPA has been a point of controversy to men and women who work with welfare recipients since the act's inception almost twenty years ago. But their concerns stem not so much from the act's substance as from the way funds have been disbursed and programmed locally. The history and mechanics of the act are important here. JTPA, sponsored by Senators Ted Kennedy and Dan Quayle and passed by Congress in 1982, was a radical attempt to change the way that employment training was delivered in the United States. JTPA's predecessor, the Comprehensive Employment and Training Act (CETA) of 1973, was a large-scale subsidized-work program designed to decrease unemployment through Public Service Employment. Part of the Reagan Administration's efforts to privatize government services, JTPA was a direct and deliberate move away from CETA's reliance on the public sector. It prohibited job placement of participants in public sector positions, and instead emphasized skills training and an increased role for the private sector. Federal job-training money, dispersed by the Department of Labor to local service delivery areas (SDAs), was filtered through Private Industry Councils (PICs), 51 percent of whose members were local business leaders. According to workforce specialists Thomas Smith and Carolyn Trist (1988, 21), under JTPA "business leaders work together with other representatives from education, labor, and the general community to develop training programs that will provide low income, unemployed, disadvantaged, and dislocated workers with skills that match local employment demands." Through contracts with service providers such as "public schools, community colleges, proprietary schools, and community based organizations" (Abt Associates 1993, 4), or through the work of their own staff, PICs have provided classroom training in occupational skills, on-the-job training, job-search assistance, basic education, work experience, and miscellaneous support services to prescribed groups of the "disadvantaged." The Act's Title II A has been directed to training services for disadvantaged youth and adults, Title IIB to summer employment and training programs for disadvantaged youth, Title IIC to year-round programs for youth, and Title III to assist dislocated workers (Smith and Trist 1988, 22).

Yet despite its explicit focus on the disadvantaged, JTPA has often been criticized for "discourage[ing] SDAs from serving clients who are most in need" (Abt Associates 1993, 7). This criticism stems in large part from the Department of Labor's (DOL) reliance on performance standards to ascertain "if that investment [in human capital through training] has been productive" (JTPA section 106 (a) as quoted in Abt 1993). Performance standards, preset "employment and wage rates" for adults and "employment and attainment of one or more measures of skills enhancement" for youth, must be met by training programs in order to receive the full amount for their services. But because JTPA is what Judith Gueron and Edward Pauly (1991, 80) called a "Selective-Voluntary program," in which "eligible people can select whether or not to enroll, and program operators can select among eligible applicants," training program personnel have been able to develop mechanisms to invite in and screen out. In an attempt to ensure total payment for their services, training program staff have been accused of selecting individuals from the unemployment rolls who would be most likely to meet the standards. According to Gueron and Pauly (1991, 100), "these programs serve a group of people who are motivated to seek out services and, sometimes, screened to meet program eligibility and other standards."

The Job Training Reform Amendments of 1992 addressed these concerns about "serving clients who are most in need" (Abt Associates 1993, 7) by requiring that a minimum of 65 percent of JTPA adult and youth participants have "identifiable barriers to employment." Yet statistics on JTPA funded programs continue to reflect a clientele that looks different from Development's "hardest to serve." As Chart 5.1 illustrates, the barriers to work identified by JTPA and TN have created two very different client populations. While the numbers show a higher percentage of unemployed JTPA participants and a slightly greater percent who read below a seventh grade level upon application to a training program, ex-offenders, substance abusers, and the homeless are noticeably absent from the JTPA list of barriers. This variance in the types of barriers identified by the two funding streams reflects a fundamental difference in the way being poor was defined. Kay James and Henry Thompson, for example, may have both been out of work when they applied for training; however, they were relegated to categories and cohorts that defined them in dissimilar ways. Henry, with his minimal education and blue-collar roots, was clustered in a group that was perceived as "hardest to serve." Kay, with three years of college and funding

Chart 5.1. JTPA and TN Client Populations

JTPA Intake across Ten Identified Barriers to Work, 1987 to 1989
- 67% were employed 15 or fewer weeks during the
  26 weeks before application to JTPA
- 35% lacked a high school diploma
- 22% read below the 7th grade level
- 9% were ex-offenders
- 9% were physically handicapped
- 9% were war veterans
- 9% were long term AFDC recipients
- 6% were over 55 years old
- 4% had limited English ability
- 3% were displaced homemakers

(Abt Associates 1993, 5)

TN Clients from 1987 to 1993

- 32% had no recent work history
- 20% scored below 7th grade on literacy assessments
- 27% were ex-offenders
- 35% of TN program clients throughout the state were
  recovering substance abusers
- 21% were homeless
- 4% were limited in their knowledge of English

(Bureau of Employment Training Programs, 1993)

through JTPA, found herself in a group in which members were defined by their un- or underemployment, rather than by their personal deficiencies.

DOWNSCALING TRAINING

The tailoring of training can also be seen in the ways the Private Industry Council (PIC) funded training after the passage of the 1989 Family Support Act. PIC, the local representative of area businesses, had been the mechanism put in place to program federal JTPA funds into local communities. Traditionally funding what was considered to be high-level training, bookkeeping training for instance, or emergency medical technician training, or photocopier repair training, PIC was often criticized for its "creaming" of the most academically able of unemployed applicants for its participant pool. But with the passage of the Family Support Act in 1989, local PICs merged money from JTPA with that from the Family Support Act to tailor efforts to AFDC recipients, the new priority of welfare reform. To better accommodate this new target population, PIC simultaneously scaled down its training menu. In their evaluation of PIC's new training focus, Irene Lurie and Jan Hagen (1993, 104) wrote, "Over the past three years, it [PIC] shifted the emphasis of its programs and management style away from advanced training and performance-based contracting to facilitate serving greater numbers of welfare participants, a pool of individuals who are more difficult to place in jobs than the JTPA's traditional clients." Gone were high-end JTPA training programs such as Jackson's pharmacy-technician training. Downgrading its skills training to serve this new population of single female welfare recipients with children, PIC "spent nearly three fourths of its $6.3 million on skills contracts to train clerks, nurse aides, food service workers, and security guards," all low-paying, low-end jobs (Stark 1994, C1). This refocus embodied a belief that high-level training and subsequent employment opportunities such as those associated with the pharmacy technician training were most appropriate for unemployed and underemployed individuals with some college education. Welfare mothers, on the other hand, were more suitable, or, in official terms, would better benefit from initiatives such as Church Hall's nurse assistant training. In her *Lives on the Edge: Single Mothers and their Children*, Valerie Polakow explains this pattern by positing a relationship between gender and ideology.

> Welfare expenditure funneled to AFDC has not transcended the norm of a stay-at-home, unskilled, untrained mother to be supported by her husband. But those norms represent an ideology of domesticity and motherhood which are themselves a product of a gendered system. This ideology continues to see women as citizen-mothers, not citizen-workers, thereby perpetuating low-wage temporary employment, low-status pink-collar jobs, and the unavailability of public child care and maternity leave provisions, all of which leave poor women with few options other than welfare when they have young children. (1993, 51–52)

Polakow's writing is as applicable to Joan and Dina's placement at Church Hall as it is to Barbara's experience at Development. In both

cases, the identity of what Polakow has called "citizen-mother" provided justification for low wages, low-status jobs, and in Barbara's
case, a return to welfare. Inherent in PIC's re-tooled training options
were culturally embedded assumptions about individuals' potential,
once again reflecting divisions of "like us" and "not like us," able
and deficient, deserving and undeserving, that mapped over the social organization of training programs and work sites.

DEFINING WORK

Within this paradigm of sorting and stratification, matching men and
women to work roles became alarmingly simple. Individuals were
sorted by their category of unemployment, characteristics were ascribed to these categories and subsequently to men and women as
members of the categories, and people were matched to employment roles that were perceived, within our shared belief system, as
appropriate to those ascribed attributes. This sorting, grounded in
welfare categories and embodied in training-program pedagogy, led
to a stratification of individuals across four workplaces. But it was not
the professional roles of assembler, nurse assistant, woodworker, or
pharmacy technician in and of themselves, that determined the reception of Henry Thompson, Dina Haskell, Chan Monivong, or Kay
James at work. Instead it was the "social positions" imposed upon
these work roles that was salient. Sociologist Anthony Giddens's
writing on "social positions" is helpful to this discussion.

> Social positions are constituted structurally as specific intersections
> of signification, domination, and legitimization which relates to the
> typification of agents. A social position involves the specification of a
> definite "identity" within a network of social relations, that identify,
> however, being a category to which a particular range of normative
> sanctions is relevant.
>   A social position can be regarded as "a social identity" that carries
> with it a certain range (however diffusely specified) of prerogatives
> and obligations that an actor who is accorded that identity (or is an
> "incumbent" of that position) may activate or carry out and these pre-
> rogatives and obligations constitute the role-prescriptions associated
> with that position. (Giddens 1984, 83-84)

Across sites, men and women not only functioned in different capacities, but they also occupied distinct social positions and were
assigned corresponding social identities. Assignment to these posi-

tions and their requisite "prerogatives and obligations" were by no means accidental. They were instead the translation and codification of trainers' and employers' beliefs about Henry Thompson, Dina Haskell, Chan Monivong, and Kay James, as seen through their welfare assignments. Assessments of identity and potential were reflected in each company's workplace policies, management structures, and social organization. At Development, for example, authoritarian managers had come to believe that Henry Thompson and Ruth Fallows were members of the hard-core unemployed, and as such, were less reliable, less responsible, and less resilient than their professional colleagues. These attributions of "lesser than" required a system of extrinsic rewards and punishments designed to reinforce their attendance at work and justified lower salaries and thinner benefit packages. At suburban Church Hall, the administrative team and supervisory nurses saw Joan Ford and Dina Haskell as their skin color and inner-city residence. Reduced to an image of black woman as suspect, angry, and even deviant, the women were worked hard, paid little, and silenced in the workplace. And since women of that ilk, like Henry Thompson and Ruth Fallows at Development, could not be trusted to control themselves, here too, a system was instituted to reward perseverance and loyalty to the workplace. On Concordance's small shop floor, self-proclaimed low-pressure foremen also saw the new arrivals from Southeast Asia through their ethnicity. But while these managers believed the men's foreignness required sorting around skill levels, abilities, and inclinations, prior conceptions of Asians as hard working, diligent, and sharply focused warranted a shop organized around autonomous work teams, and justified competitive pay and benefits. At Jackson, hospital supervisors relied on an array of screening mechanisms to restrict the technician training to the most educated and culturally similar of applicants. The screening assured them that the pharmacy technicians were worthy to enter the ranks of professionals, with all of their requisite "prerogatives and obligations."

Employers' and trainers' assessments translated ultimately into the "social positions" that not only defined the differences among Henry's and Tom's, Ruth's and Kay's places in the labor market, but also replicated preexisting economic and political disparities that had long defined their lives. The men's and women's resultant job status, responsibilities, and wage packages were messages, loud and clear, about each man and woman's potential and worth. But while many individuals internalized these notions of self and appropriateness, others did not, and their subsequent assimilation, accommodation, or resistance in the workplace, were rooted in their acceptance or rejection of the ways in which they had been defined and treated by trainers and employers.

MAKING SENSE

The focus now shifts back to Henry Thompson and Ruth Fallows, Dina Haskell and Joan Ford, Chan Monivong and Moeun Daun, and Kay James and Samantha Wright, and to the ways in which they made sense of their access to the labor market. As Ruth suggested, power paved her path to Development, leading her to the inner city rather than downtown to Jackson Hospital. Power and her own feelings of powerlessness defined the status position in which she found herself at work, and catalyzed the disequilibrium she felt. That power and the ways in which Ruth and the other men and women dealt with it provides a background for their practice at work. For some, part of that background was the futility that hovered around their actions, a futility that rose from frustrated ambitions, disappointed dreams, and from the knowledge that, for many, life held few better options. For the men and women who found themselves, postwelfare, as hourly employees at Development or as nurse assistants at Church Hall, dealing with their situation became a struggle between the pride of a job well done and the perception that their jobs, and hence they themselves, were not respected.

The first half of this book described this negotiation, focusing on what anthropologist Sherry Ortner (1984, 154) calls the men and women's "practice of everyday living . . . the little routines [they] enact, again and again, in working, eating, sleeping and relaxing, as well as the little scenarios of etiquette they play out again and again in social interaction." For it was in Ruth's and Henry's "little routines" and "everyday practices" at work that their lives postwelfare were revealed, and it was in Joan's and Dina's conversations and "little scenarios of etiquette" that their negotiation of these social identities was made visible at work. This section looks at this negotiation across all four sites. The work of sociolinguist Erving Goffman on what he called "situated activity systems" provides one frame of reference for this conversation. According to Goffman (1961, 133), "[I]t is argued that the individual must be seen as someone who organizes his expressive situational behavior *in relation* to situated activity roles, but that in doing this he uses whatever means are at hand to introduce a margin of freedom and maneuverability, of pointed disidentification, between himself and the self virtually available for

him in the situation." Goffman conceptualized an individual's negotiation of self and imposed role as one of *role distancing*, a process of
identity formation and validation that is neither mechanical nor passive. According to Goffman (1961,133–134), "Surely in every case,
however, there will be *some* discrepancy between the self emerging
from a situated activity role and the self associated with the role title
in the name of which activity is carried on. Role distance attests to
this discrepancy." Role distancing can unfold on two levels. On the
superordinate level, role distancing may express "a willingness to
relax the status quo," which is often evidenced as "charm and color-
ful little informalities" on the part of the superior to make subordinates feel more comfortable and less distant. However, on the
subordinate level, individuals who "must take orders or suggestions
and must go along with the situation as defined by superordinates"
often distance themselves by their sullenness, sarcasm, mutterings,
and jokes, as though to say, "I want you to know that you haven't
fully contained me in the state of affairs."

DISTANCING FROM AN IMPERFECT FIT

As Henry Thompson discovered, "the self virtually available for
him in the situation" was not a perfect fit. One year after he was
hired from Development's training to assume the role of department supervisor, Henry was not only still waiting to be made supervisor, but he began to feel more like a "messenger" or a "stock boy"
than a part of Development's management team. Excited, motivated, and enthusiastic when he first came to work, after a few
months on the job his demeanor soured, his willingness to suggest
innovations decreased, and his grumbling increased. Although he
continued to perceive himself as capable, motivated, and hard working, he felt slighted, undervalued, and at times, invisible in the
workplace. Unable to access livable wages and benefits, he was
given neither voice in decisions about work in which he was a hands-
on expert, nor support that encouraged or enabled his professional
growth. He experienced what Erving Goffman (1961, 42) called
"dysphoria," a growing state of tension between the two worlds, work
and outside work, that he inhabited, and his attitudes about and
practices at work reflected this discontinuity. Henry's grumbling and
giving supervisors the cold shoulder were ways of distancing himself
from the role that he had been assigned. But what made his predicament even more frustrating was that Henry believed he played at
least some small part in its construction. Coming to Development

for training, after all, had ultimately been his decision. And despite repeated warnings to the contrary, obtaining work with the agency had also been his idea. "Everyone told us not to work here during training," Henry reflected. "I thought different, but we learned soon. Now we're stuck."

As the previous chapters illustrated, Henry wasn't alone in either his feelings or his actions. They were shared by many of the men and women at both Development and Church Hall, those hourly workers and nurse assistants who found their work roles confining, their skills unappreciated, but who felt powerless to improve their condition. For many of these men and women, however, Goffman's description of subordinates distancing themselves from the self to which they were relegated at work does not fully account for their actions in the workplace. For them it was not only a matter of not fitting an identity imposed upon them, but of actively resisting what they perceived as the unequal conditions and inequitable treatment that accompanied the bad fit. They not only distanced themselves, but to draw upon the work of Frederick Erickson (1987, 345), they withheld assent. Not able to go along with the "prevailing definition of the situation," they engaged in oppositional behavior, appeared hostile toward supervisors and other managers, and in some cases, "blatantly rejected" the positions in which they found themselves (Goffman 1961, 133). Nurse assistants at Church Hall, acting out of their own discontent over low wages, overburdened work loads, and a lack of voice in the workplace, grumbled and were confrontational with supervisors. In the hope that their newly earned certification was worth more elsewhere, most abandoned the work altogether. Some, like Joan Ford, walked off the job after public disagreements with supervisors. Others just stopped coming. They didn't call; they didn't give formal notification of their departure; they just stopped coming to work.

Henry's co-workers at Development also complained about low wages, limited benefits, and physical conditions at work. They felt stifled and stuck at Development, relegated to the bottom of the employee pool and salary scale, and disconnected from either internal or external labor markets. They saw few opportunities for advancement in or outside the agency; the time they spent in factories or in temporary jobs, their minimal education, and their poor test-taking abilities left them vulnerable in a city with a rapidly shrinking manufacturing base. Their opposition to this quandary took the form of grumbling, gossip, work slowdowns, petty theft, and withdrawal from social activities at the agency. Like a coat that was too small and made of material too thin, at both Church Hall and Development men and women saw almost everything about their identity and role at work as unsatisfactory. But they dealt with this poor fit in different ways. The nurse assistants cast off their roles, believing that they would be able to purchase a better-sized identity, a coat cut of finer cloth, elsewhere. Hourly workers at Development, however, knew they had no cultural or social capital with which to purchase a more respected identity at another workplace. They grumbled at the tight fit of their poor-paying jobs, pulling at the sleeves and patching the torn seams. But they feared the cold more than anything and knew that their jobs at Development were their only protection against the city's winter chill.

This is certainly not the first time resistance theory has been applied to the study of education, work, and the poor in Western societies. Sociologists Elliot Liebow (1967), Paul Willis (1977), and Lois Weis (1990) have all described the construction of identities in contexts in which an individual's sense of self is fashioned against, or in resistance to the contexts of school and work. Written within that tradition, the stories of Henry, Ruth, Dina, and Joan illustrate the construction of oppositional identities through unorganized and often passive resistance to power in the face of powerlessness. But their experiences also reveal that this taking back of one's voice had unintended consequences. While Henry's actions, for instance, may have been the only way he could maintain his sense of self in a context in which he felt misjudged and even scorned, they did not result in increased job satisfaction, expanded power, or an improved status. His attempts to appear aloof to management resulted in little more than a chill that lingered in the spaces between himself and his supervisors. Henry's and Ruth's oppositional behavior may have emboldened their own sense of self-worth, but it did little to improve their circumstances. In fact, the opposite was true; their sullenness, anger, and indignation only reinforced supervisors' strongly held beliefs that Ruth and Henry, like their inner-city colleagues at both Development and Church Hall, were strange and estranged; that they were "other." When Joan Ford and Lynn Brown began to assert their own knowledge at Church Hall, they appeared to supervisors to be acting with defiance. When they later abandoned the job out of anger or frustration, they only confirmed their supervisors' image of them as dangerous and irresponsible. As the sociologist Michel Foucault so elegantly wrote, "People know what they do; they frequently know why they do what they do; but what they don't know is what what they do does" (personal communication, as quoted in Dreyfus and Rabinow 1982, 187). Through his own opposition, Henry played an active, yet often unwitting role in creating meaning, identity, and in establishing his relationship to work. In that process, he contributed to the construction of his own identity as marginal and poor.

A BETTER FIT

Not all the men and women who had moved from welfare to work, however, voiced dissatisfaction with the outcome of their investment in training. Many found themselves treated well by those in power. For these men and women, it was a desire to accommodate or at times even assimilate into the social organization of work that was located in their conversations with one another and their supervisors, and in their relationship to the work. At Jackson, Tom Russo and Kay James were pleased with the roles in which they found themselves. They praised their salaries, the responsive supervisors, their high level of responsibility and autonomy, the collegiality in the pharmacy satellites, their interactions with patients, and most importantly, their feelings of self-worth. Respected and welcomed into the hospital, they claimed ownership of their work. They defined themselves as technicians and identified themselves as important members of hospital's pharmacy department. The professional identities in which Kay James and Tom Russo found themselves matched, and at times, even exceeded their own expectations. They walked proudly in their newly garbed selves.

Chan Monivong, Moeun Daun, and their compatriots at Concordance also found that the roles they came to occupy at work fit comfortably. Although language, ethnic, and class differences precluded their assimilation into the company's corporate structure and culture, their experiences at work were positive. They voiced satisfaction with their pay and benefits, their job security, the amity on the shop floor, and their responsive and good-hearted managers. Like these men, Enid Castro and Donna Hastings, Development's clerical workers, were also grateful for what they considered to be their good fortune. Arriving at Development with neither direction nor high school diploma, they found support, guidance, hope, and job-specific skills inside the building's brick walls. Content with both the work roles to which they were assigned and the ways they were perceived at work, they felt challenged, respected, and well liked. Theirs was also a comfortable fit.

There was a circular quality to expectations and practice here as well. Men and women who were perceived as capable, hardworking, and dedicated were treated with fairness and respect. They found real, supported, and accessible opportunities for growth; quickly became productive, invested employees; and proved their reputation as capable, hard working, and dedicated. Men and women who were (or who perceived themselves to be) undervalued at work, on the other hand, believed they were disrespected and unsupported. Unable to access opportunities for professional growth or advancement, they quickly began to complain about being stifled and unchallenged. Within this self-fulfilling paradigm, supervisors perceived their resultant dissatisfaction and resentment as laziness, a lack of motivation, and deviousness. Across these four welfare-to-work transitions, welfare categories and employment training initiatives propelled, rather than disrupted a cycle of identity and expectation. Through this coupling of structure and agency, our dominant ideology concerning the poor played out in the actions of individuals, employers, trainers, employees, and former welfare recipients alike. To quote Nelly Stromquist, "Thus, a cohesive vicious circle is created" (1993, 205).

Chapter 6
Other Possibilities

Political winds change, and between the conception of this book and its completion efforts to reform welfare have altered the context of these stories. "Presumptions of a national budget crises, . . . cynicism about what government can do, and . . . extreme pessimism about the intractability of the problems of the inner-city poor" have translated to "end welfare as we know it" (Skocpol 1991, 411). Since 1996, both welfare-training programs and entire welfare categories have been de-funded, and supports that seemed essential to a move off poverty just a few years ago are now perceived as pandering to the poor. Essentially, PRWORA removed poverty from public discourse. Welfare as we knew it no longer exists, so dependency on welfare must no longer be a problem. It remains unclear, however, whether the cutbacks have addressed the fundamental problem of poverty in the United States or if instead, an upswing in the economy has absorbed former welfare recipients into low wage jobs. The economic boom of the last eight years, for example, has spurred employment rates of young African American men, who have been "perhaps the most economically disadvantaged, socially alienated group in America." (Nasar and Mitchell 1999, 1). Employment figures for men such as those typically classified within the state's now defunct Transitionally Needy welfare category have risen from 52 percent to 64 percent in the fourteen areas where unemployment has been below four percent each year since 1992. But as *New York Times* reporter Jason DeParle (1997, 34) wrote, "No state has faced the economic downturn that will test its safety-net commitments."

PRIORITIZING WORK

This positioning of work in and of itself as ameliorative for social ills has been long been compelling to policy makers and the general public alike. Job matching and job training have long been prescribed to reduce unemployment rates, alleviate the problems of the economically disadvantaged, and maintain a competitive international edge. The array of initiatives designed to move individuals into work include programs stemming from the Comprehensive Employment and Training Act (CETA), the Job Training Partnership Act (JTPA), the Family Support Act's JOBS legislation, individual state programs for single adults, and most recently, the Personal Responsibility and Work Opportunity Reconciliation Act (PRWORA). All place such a high value on work that they measure programmatic success by tracking job placement rates of the participants. Like existing strategies, the newly positioned welfare reform package continues to assume this supply-side stance, wrapped in rhetoric about the role of work in transforming both poor communities and the lives of unemployed men and women.

> The first time I met Bill Perkins, Development's architect, director, and self-described grandfather, was in his office, its walls plastered with certificates and awards for his community work and his activities as a golf coach at a local university. We sat surrounded by photographs of Bill and Donald Trump, Bill and the mayor, Bill and the vice president, Bill and the governor, and a sketch of the former YMCA that Development had recently rehabbed into low-income housing.
>
> Bill steered the conversation; he was accustomed to taking the upper hand, and I let him. He preached on about job development and community development, asserting that community-development corporations place too much focus on housing and not enough attention on jobs. A proposal budgeting $65 million for a housing development was circulating at the state and federal government levels. Instead of housing money, he advocated for the construction of a shopping center in the area. "The best housing project is a job," he insisted. "A shopping center would create at least two hundred jobs." (May 4, 1992, field notes, Development)

Perkins's proposal that "the best housing project is a job" is not atypical either in debates about the legions of American workers still on the lowest rungs of the income ladder or in conversations about reforming the welfare system. In public rhetoric, work itself has become a social prescriptive. "Work is the best social program. . . . It gives hope and structure and meaning to our lives," as President

Clinton asserted in a speech in Kansas City (Rankin and Hess 1994, A1). Sociologists and psychologists agree. William Julius Wilson, in his 1996 *When Work Disappears*, makes several powerful arguments about the debilitating effects of long-term joblessness.

> As Pierre Bourdieu demonstrated, work is not simply a way to make a living and support one's family. It also constitutes a framework for daily behavior and patterns of interaction because it imposes disciplines and regularities. Thus, in the absence of regular employment, a person lacks not only a place in which to work and the receipt of regular income but also a coherent organization of the present—that is, a system of concrete expectations and goals. Regular employment provides an anchor for the spatial and temporal aspects of daily life. It determines where you are going to be and when you are going to be there. In the absence of regular employment, life, including family life, becomes less coherent. Persistent unemployment and irregular employment hinder rational planning in daily life, the necessary condition of adaptation to an industrial economy. (Wilson 1996, 73)

Because of their rare coupling with jobs at the end of the training, even if jobs were offered only to the most perseverant and fortunate of the trainees who completed all four training programs, the welfare-to-work linkages in this research deserve inspection. Catalyzed by and in answer to different needs, training philosophies, histories, politics, and funding availability, each welfare-to-work link took a different shape. Yet by attending to the demand side of the equation, each turned the classic supply-side model of job training on its head. Through its small business incubator, staff members at Development offered jobs to selected training program graduates. DPW's screening initiative was designed specifically to funnel women into jobs at Church Hall as nurse assistants. VES staff consulted with employers in the design of the training, and Jackson Hospital initiated the pharmacy technician training to meet its own employment needs. Each link provided welfare recipients with important networks to the private sector, each training initiative afforded learners with valuable situated learning experiences (Lave 1993; Rubenson and Schütze 1993; Sticht et al. 1987), and each program offered employers a relatively inexpensive and efficient hiring network and screening filter (Bailey 1987). Workforce specialists Smith and Trist assert that this linking of private and public sectors, albeit across an array of manifestations, is essential to effective job-training programs. They wrote that

> a principal lesson of the CETA era is that training not directly related to actual jobs is ineffective and has little overall impact on the level of

unemployment. In fact, the record over the last decade has shown that job training alone will do very little to improve local employment conditions. Even though the availability of skills to some extent co-determines labor market demand (by enabling industries requiring those skills to grow), jobs create the demand for skills and not the other way around. Therefore, it is essential that specific employers and job opportunities be linked to specific training programs so that the content of those programs is as responsive as possible to local labor markets. Links between institutions can make use of the occupational information that would be made available through networks, such as a Community Occupational Information Coordinating Committee.

Job training and educational preparation for work have a greater chance for success when conceived with reference to the local economic environment. Context-based planning for training cannot be accomplished by individual institutions in isolation but must at least be informed by, and at best be jointly undertaken by, the relevant stakeholders in that environment. (Smith and Trist 1988, 29)

These authors and others have compiled lists of "cooperative" training-to-work relationships that include both open-ended and project-specific collaborations between industry-education councils, quasi-public skills corporations, state-funded employer-based training, contracted training, joint labor-union management programs, and private sector representatives.

Although descriptions have been published on models of successful workplace literacy and training programs (Mikulecky 1993; Kutner et al. 1991; Seitchik et al. 1990; Hudson Institute 1988; Carnevale et al. 1988), on the design of high performance workplaces (Hirschhorn 1984; Marsick 1990), on favorable adult-learning contexts in developing and developed countries (Puchner 1993; Cross 1981; Freire 1970), and on incentives for learners (Kahler 1982; Ryan 1993), far less has been documented on the catalyst to hire welfare recipients. The motivation of managers at Development, Church Hall, Concordance Steps, and Jackson Hospital offer something to this conversation. At each worksite, supervisors were prompted to hire welfare recipients by the need for employees, the convenience of hiring already filtered, prepared applicants, and at Concordance, a bit of social activism. The literature is limited, but what is available talks to two different kinds of business leaders: forward-looking company officials such as Jay Hawks at Concordance Steps, or even Bill Perkins at Development, and employers such as Donald Phillips at Jackson Hospital or Ron Driver at Church Hall, who confront a tightening labor market and perceive training program graduates as an available and potentially productive labor force (U.S. Department of Labor 1989).

But their experiences offer far fewer lessons on improving work-place conditions for workers on the lowest rungs of the employment ladder. The cry for livable wages resounds not only from Henry, Ruth, Dina, and Joan, but from a myriad of studies examining welfare-to-work programs. Yet no one knows how to transform those appeals into practice. The relationships among welfare recipiency, training, and the organization of work are still rarely discussed. Instead, the marketplace remains relatively unbridled by labor's demands or cries for economic restructuring, and the question of jobs remains obscured. Work may be "the best social program," but it has still only been a spectator in the drama of welfare reform. As these stories of thirty-seven men and women reveal, whenever the context of work does get introduced into the formula, the scenario becomes far more complicated, and the casting of blame and responsibility becomes far more complex.

COOLING OUT AT WORK

Almost ironically, this research was conducted at a time when talk about increasing worker productivity, and as a corollary, improving the organization of work, appeared throughout trade journals, local newspapers, national magazines, TV talk shows, and in conferences and seminars. Couched in the discourse surrounding W. Edward Demming's Total Quality Management (TQM), slogans about customer satisfaction and worker involvement became part of the public discourse. In the quest for increased worker productivity and more efficient corporate organization, Robert Reich (1991b), the secretary of labor for the first four years of the Clinton administration, advocated increased worker training and supportive private sector policies. Motorola Inc., Xerox Corporation, and Federal Express were positioned as models, and Demming and his disciplines facilitated workshops across the globe applying his principles of management, quality, and training to real life. Yet of the four work sites described in Part One, only Jackson Hospital, with its committee-based management, hospital-wide focus on professional development, and generous tuition benefits, adopted anything that even closely resembled either Reich's call or Demming's TQM. While Concordance Steps positioned itself somewhere in between an authoritarian-management structure and a worker-run shop, management practices at Development and Church Hall were unabashedly authoritarian. Both companies reflected a top-down hierarchy that resulted in the distancing of many lower-level employees from their work. Men and women at both sites had little voice in the organization of their own workplace practice, and equally little access to avenues for advancement or opportunities for growth within the companies. Silenced at work, their initial motivation, interest, excitement, and energy were also stifled.

According to the Commission on the Skills of the American Workforce, a research team of twenty-three private sector executives given the task of examining the country's workforce, the situations in which Henry, Ruth, Dina, and Joan, found themselves were far from rare. The commission's 1990 report, entitled *America's Choice: High Skills or Low Wages*, speaks to a national culture that is defined by low expectations. While the following passage refers specifically to students in school settings, the commission's argument could easily be applied to individuals in the workplace.

> More than any other country in the world, the United States believes that natural ability, rather than effort, explains achievement. The tragedy is that we communicate to millions of students every year, especially low income and minority students, that we do not believe that they have what it takes to learn. They then live up to our expectations, despite the evidence that they can meet very high performance standards under the right conditions. (The Commission on the Skills of the American Workforce 1990, 4)

Over the course of my observations I quickly realized that what I was seeing was exactly what the commission described. Rather than being challenged or motivated, many men and women were in fact "cooled out" at work (Clark 1960). Soon aware that their employers' demands were lower than their own potential, they found themselves living down, rather than up to these external expectations, adjusting their relationship to work to their supervisors' beliefs.

While many of the commission's recommendations focus on the formal educational system, the report also references the workplace to make a point that's relevant to this discussion.

> The vast majority of American employers are not moving to high performance work organizations, nor are they investing to train their nonmanagerial employees for these new work organizations. The movement to high performance work organizations is more widespread in other nations, and training of front-line workers, funded in part by national assessments on employers or general public revenues, is commonplace. (The Commission on the Skills of the American Workforce 1990, 7)

Managers at Development, Concordance, Church Hall, and Jackson Hospital all made choices between high performance and low wages. Jackson Hospital's pharmacy department, for example, was on a clear path toward high performance. Pharmacy technicians there were viewed as front-line professionals. Their participation in task forces, committees, and quality-control groups was encouraged by performance evaluations and salary increases, and ultimately involved them in decisions about the operation of the pharmacy and the organization of their own work. This management model translated to Kay's and Tom's productivity on the job, and their clearly articulated satisfaction with the work. Managers at Church Hall and Development, however, took a very different path, one the Commission (1990, 4) described as "the low-wage choice." Power in each of these companies was organized hierarchically; work roles were narrowly defined and segmented. As a result of this management hierarchy, Dina Haskell and Joan Ford at Church Hall and Henry Thompson and Ruth Fallows at Development were made to feel overworked and undervalued, and they dealt with their dissatisfaction by grumbling, slowing down at work, and at Church Hall, abandoning the job. Jobs at Development and Church Hall were a way off welfare, but as Valerie Polakow (1993) writes, not a route out of poverty. For these men and women, it was not lack of motivation or ambition, laziness or disinterest that kept them poor. Instead, it was managers' decisions about the organization of work, wages, benefits, and job security that kept men and women marginalized and economically fragile.

Concordance's owner and supervisors chose a path somewhere in between. Since work was organized at Concordance around projects, Chan Monivong and Koung Sisowath felt that they contributed in important ways to the work as a whole. Competitive salaries and equitable benefit packages added to their feelings of comfort. Yet the company's management structure was essentially top down, so while the men felt responsible for their work, they were not involved in decisions about the organization or administration of the workplace. Unlike Tom Russo and Kay James at Jackson Hospital, the men had no way to become involved in management's conversations or to make their voices heard. In practice, many of the woodworkers were torn. Content with their work, Koung and many of his more assertive, non-Cambodian co-workers felt frustrated nonetheless with their lack of power and authority.

A FOOT IN THE DOOR

Jobs were indeed an important part of the move from welfare for Henry, Dina, Chan, Mary, and their un- and underemployed colleagues in training. They wanted jobs and they begged and cajoled, smiled and performed to get them. Diligent during training, they tap-danced in interviews in the hope of obtaining work. But while securing a job was crucial, they were also aware that the availability of good jobs was equally important. And as Ruth Fallows reminded me, good jobs for people like her were rare. "I think they only pay for training when it leads to a poor paying job. Any training that leads to well paying jobs you have to pay for yourself." Development's job wall confirmed Ruth's assertion. The job wall was actually the four walls of the agency's lunch room, an open passageway from the redistribution center to the main offices. The area, lined with chairs and tables in both booth and free-standing configurations, served as a place to relax or eat lunch on cold days. It was also a source of inspiration for Development's trainees, who were in constant job search. Job signs, large pieces of white cardboard delineating jobs, dates, and names of successful job seekers, covered the area's yellow walls like wallpaper. They reminded men and women that they too might find work. The signs, arranged both horizontally and vertically, listed assembly worker, warehouse supervisor at Development, receptionist at Development, general laborer, production worker, secretary at Development, utility worker, general helper, custodian, machine operator, health care aide, communications, housekeeper, building maintenance, presser, chef, data entry, mental health aide, and shipping and receiving. They reflected an array of job outcomes, but as Ruth suggested, they were all low-paying, low-rung jobs.

Public officials outside Development also confirmed Ruth's assertion about training. As a local PIC representative explained:

> PIC is the organization that trains you to get basic entry level jobs. If you're smart, as soon as you get your first job, you'll enroll in courses at the Community College. It is on you at that point. We need to get people to accept that responsibility. They have to internalize that message. (Administrator, Private Industry Council)

According to the rhetoric about welfare and jobs, the objective of transition programs for the poor has been to move men and women from welfare to entry-level employment. The assumption is that once in the door, they will be able to access career ladders on their own. Yet regardless of an individual's ability to budget time and money, surviving on minimum wage in the United States even for a few years is not easy. Recent research on low-wage jobs such as those listed on Development's job wall reveal that they provide even less than the salaries suggest. Quoting an article that appeared in a June 1998 issue of The *New York Times* (Passell 1998, 23), "More than 80% of workers received paid holidays and vacations in 1996, but less than 10% of those in the bottom tenth received paid leave of any kind. Similarly, about 70% of workers have pension plans, while less than 10% of those in the bottom can count on any employer-financed retirement benefits. Access to health insurance follows a similar pattern." The lack of benefits meant Noreen Diaz was unable to access sick leave when she developed asthma from packing and unpacking kits in Development's dusty warehouse. At Church Hall, it translated to the $133 deducted from Dina Haskell's bi-weekly pay checks for the health care that was so important to her three daughters.

In addition, the career ladders that had been offered as the putative answer to low-wage jobs were inaccessible at best. At worst, they were nonexistent. At Church Hall, for instance, women who had tested the waters of health care as nurse assistants were able to gain a valuable credential, their state certification, through DPW's initiative. DPW job developers served as transition, helping Donna Dixson, Nil Harper, and Joan Ford return to the workforce and obtain this now-essential government requirement. Their newly earned certification, however, did not allow them to advance in the labor queue as much as it secured their current status. And while its possession did prod many women to search out better-paying work, they soon found themselves stuck in a revolving door of low-paying, low-level jobs in other care facilities or temporary agencies. Aware of this professional treadmill, more than half of the nurse assistants at Church Hall voiced the desire to return to school; they believed that with support they could manage the demands of both Licensed Practical Nurse (LPN) training and workplace responsibilities. Yet school remained inaccessible for nearly all of them. Outstanding loans to proprietary schools, a disinclination to once again become indebted to an educational institution, and lack of time, energy, and disposable income, rather than interest, motivation, or ability, impeded the women's real mobility. This next step was obscured not by personal deficit, but by structural barriers.

Even men and women employed as pharmacy technicians at Jackson, by far the best case scenario of the four, voiced frustration at their difficulties in accessing a career ladder. The wider context of the marketplace was fragmented and enigmatic. Although their cultural capital afforded them positions of respect in the workplace, abundant aspirations, the hospital's challenging professional environment, and a relatively generous tuition benefit package weren't enough to support more than a few technicians' climb to the next professional rung. The difficulty was that for the technicians the next step up was a large one. Thanks to Jackson's tuition reimbursements, for example, Lisa Henry had completed all the prerequisites and was contemplating enrolling in pharmacy school. Yet she continued to insist that, "As a technician there really isn't a career ladder for us to go higher. The next level from pharmacy technician is pharmacist, and it's as simple as that. It's not like nursing where you can go to pediatrics or cardiac, you know what I mean. It's not that, it's not that varied." For Lisa, with a full-time job and a new baby at home, the logistics of taking that next step were complicated. "It's hard because you need to go to pharmacy school full time and you also need to work full time to get tuition reimbursements. There's not many who have done it. There's only one technician who has done it, and she quit to go to pharmacy school." Karen Miller, Jackson's training program coordinator, agreed. She explained, "Only one student of mine graduated as a pharmacist. A couple are planning to go on. Not all of them understand the demands of future education." At Jackson, where employment training functioned as it should, providing a good job with a livable wage, Tom and Kay may not have had much in common with Henry and Ruth. Yet without a more inclusive, cohesive, and continuous system of education and training for adults, one thing they shared was a lack of upward mobility.

Of course, not everyone wanted to return to school. But even those men and women who were not academically focused were not all interested in remaining in their current workplace position. While individuals were pleased to access their first job post-training, most soon voiced interest in learning more, in becoming more invested in their work and in moving up. Discussions about welfare reform are short-sighted when, embedded in the belief that the poor should be satisfied to join the ranks of working poor, they are confined to a goal of getting people off welfare rolls and into jobs. In policy conversations, the next professional step is either outside the parameters of the discussion or delegated to the rhetoric of "pulling oneself up by the bootstraps." Yet the old adage is only that, a truism stemming from an ideology that allows us to blame those for whom the system doesn't work. If we are interested in successful transitions to work and real worker productivity, continuous opportunities must be made available to all individuals, not only those perceived to have the appropriate cultural capital or who have informal support systems on which they can draw.

IMAGININGS

If indeed our preoccupation with reforming the welfare system rises from a concern about those individuals most marginalized from the economic mainstream, then we must begin to imagine other visions of moving from poverty to economic self-sufficiency. The welfare-to-work initiatives described here are not the only possibilities. Training worked for men and women at Concordance and Jackson Hospital. But other men and women might have told very different stories had they been given opportunities to participate in challeng-ing training programs and assume positions of respect in the work-place, or had they been encouraged and rewarded with a work upgrade for a continued investment in accessible training. Our current wel-fare reform strategy, cutting the welfare rolls and rejecting a shared commitment to the poor, is also not the only alternative. The prob-lems that Henry, Ruth, Dina, and Joan encountered may be best ad-dressed not by the dismantling of welfare policy, whatever that policy is at any given moment, but by addressing real issues of poverty and social mobility in the United States.

These are difficult issues for a country that is simultaneously grounded in a liberal ideology, beliefs about community responsibil-ity, and the remnants of Progressive Era reforms. As political analyst Anne Marie Cammisa wrote in her *From Rhetoric to Reform* (1998, 137),

> We are torn between our desire to help the poor out of a feeling of community with them, and our faith in individualism, capitalism, and hard work as the keys for people helping themselves. We are not sure whether the poor are worthy or unworthy of our assistance. And we have a great deal of difficulty determining the difference.

History, both personal and societal, has shown us that opportunities for social mobility have been structural, not personal. Structural op-portunity has meant both the availability of economic opportunities through economic growth and the opening of new, previously un-charted areas for development. Ruth Sidel writes in *Keeping Women and Children Last* (1996, 31–32):

> The central problem American society must deal with is not the char-acter of poor women and the structure of the welfare system; the cen-tral problem is poverty, the multiplicity of ways that it is embedded in the structure of American society, and the need to find real ways of al-tering that fundamental structure in order to truly help people move out into mainstream society. We must recognize that people are not

poor due to character defects but rather that the poverty that plagues so many Americans has been socially constructed and therefore must be dealt with by fundamental economic and social change.

Moving off welfare requires policies that help the poor take advantage of economic opportunities, and not curing what we perceive to be their psychological ailments. In an era in which the economy has shifted its focus from manufacturing to service, and the world has changed from one of national boundaries to an integrated global marketplace, addressing poverty within a framework of structural constraints is essential.

FLEXIBLE TRAINING MODELS

Models of flexible training dispute the "foot in the door" premise that guides the placement of welfare recipients into bottom-rung jobs. Assuming that moving onto the job ladder requires not just a first step, but second and third steps as well, programs such as Chicago's Project Match have supported individuals through a combination of idiosyncratic routes from welfare to work over a period of three to five years. Most immediately and importantly, the program was designed around the belief that participants come to the program with their own needs, concerns, and objectives. Nearly all on public assistance, participants at Project Match took idiosyncratic routes from welfare to work. Some started with an entry-level job and then returned to school full or part time; others worked through a series of jobs; others attended college classes and worked part time; and yet others volunteered, obtained a GED, worked, and then attended college. Staff members wrote about this process based upon the data from their tracking system (Herr et al. 1991, 10).

> Two interrelated findings from the tracking system data framed our initial analyses. *The first is that leaving welfare is a process, not an event.* This finding becomes self evident with a longitudinal perspective. But very little research or program activity in the welfare-to-work field has taken such a perspective. The second is *that people take many different routes out of long-term dependence.* By route we mean the particular set of activities in which a person participates (e.g. vocational training, GED, employment), the order in which they are sequenced (i.e. GED leading to employment or vice versa), and the time frame for making progress toward achievement of milestones (e.g. how long it takes before one is ineligible for AFDC).

Project Match was unusual in its construction. Instead of bounding welfare recipients by relief categories, it looked different for different individuals, and treated participants as adults, who like the rest of us

> progress from one educational level or career activity to the next . . . supported and facilitated by other people, as well as by the norms and expectations, in the social world [we] inhabit. . . . They get feedback from family, friends, teachers, and employers, telling them they are on track, helping them feel good about themselves, and providing motivation to take the risk of trying next steps. They meet new people who provide new role models and sources of identity, information about next steps such as job openings or interesting educational or training programs, and assistance with transitions from one activity to the next. (Herr et al. 1991, 26–27)

Given this difference in ideology about the poor, the program also positioned assessment in a different place than any of the welfare-to-work transitions examined in this research. Again, staff members wrote,

> Project Match operates on the principle that assessment and goal setting are an on-going process rather than a one-shot event that occurs at the time of enrollment in a program. Project Match staff has learned that easily measured characteristics of people such as age, educational attainment and work history do not directly predict success in school and on the job. (Herr et al. 1991, 9)

Competency-based training, on the other hand, presents a different set of assumptions about job training. The Center for Employment Training (CET) in San Jose, California, has been a statistically successful example of open entrance/open exit, competency-based training. Funded through multiple and mixed sources, CET impressed federal government officials and propelled the Department of Labor (DOL) to fund replication efforts throughout the country. While DOL's reliance on quantitative measures to determine project success may have overstated the impact of project outcomes in the lives of the participants, CET's theoretical underpinnings and competency-based training paradigm merit consideration. CET did not require applicants to take entry exams or to possess a particular educational level upon entry into one of its eleven skill components (each based upon area employment needs). These vocational areas included building maintenance, child care, commercial food services, CAD drafting, automated office skills/data entry/computer operation, electronic testing, machine tool operation, medical assistant work, printing and graphics, sheet metal fabrication, and shipping and receiving. The program's tenets, as delineated in Gordon and Burghardt's evaluation (1990, 9), are listed below:

- Anyone can improve his or her employment skills and go to work; access to occupational skill training need not be predicated on aptitude (as measured through formal tests) or prior mastery of specific basic educational skills;
- Practical skill training in demand occupations is the activity that responds best to the goals and motivations of persons who face employment problems;
- The benefits of practical skill training are accessible to all applicants, even though many need to improve their basic literacy, math and English language skills, while pursuing job training;
- Trainees learn and master skills at different speeds and thus require the flexibility of courses structured to permit "open entry" and "open exit";
- Support services and a supportive "family" environment at the program are essential to help trainees overcome logistical, emotional, and motivational problems that could undermine their success in training and at finding and retaining employment.

During the program's two-week orientation, participants attended classes and met with instructors to determine the vocational area in which they would focus. Program staff assessed an applicant's "remediation needs," and together, staff member and participant developed a training plan that combined hands-on skills training with GED, ESL, or reading and math remediation. Individuals advanced at their own pace, success was measured by meeting skill-based competencies, and graduation occurred when the participant obtained training-related employment. Competency-based models such as CET, with broad-based funding and multiple-target groups, can offer training in skill areas that include high and low technologies, and accommodate choices based upon interests and skills rather than on categorical-group membership and academically sanctioned knowledge. The comparative success[1] of CET and its fundamental belief in human potential is even more striking given a target population composed primarily of Mexican American migrant farm workers. A report by the U.S. Department of Labor's Secretary's Commission on Achieving Necessary Skills (SCANS) supported CET's competency-based training focus. Arguing against "an excess of testing in our nation's schools (U.S. Department of

Labor 1992, 60), the SCANS report advocated instead for the development of performance standards that will better assist workers, students, trainers and employers to understand and meet the demands of particular jobs. SCAN's prominence in discussions about employment training has strengthened the place of models such as CET in debates on welfare-to-work policy.

Both CET and Project Match embody beliefs about the poor and a corresponding pedagogy that are fundamentally different from the welfare-to-work initiatives that Henry, Joan, Chan, and Kay encountered. Competency-based training, as embodied at CET, disputes the assumptions that funneled Henry and Ruth to Development's training and Pauline and Donna to Jackson. And flexible training, such as Project Match, questions the "foot in the door" premise that moves welfare recipients into bottom-rung jobs. Both alternatives assumed instead that like our own experiences, moving onto the job ladder requires the trial and error that is not just a first step, but supported second and third steps as well.

EDUCATIONAL NETWORKS AND SUPPORTS

In postindustrial America, connections to work have become tenuous not only for welfare recipients but for all men and women. After years of downsizing, right sizing, and re-engineering, rethinking the connection between education and work is a discussion that has not been confined to the poor. Linking individuals to the workplace has become a broader conversation, and the transition from school to work has emerged both as a topic in policy discussions and as a new focus for government funding. Catalyzed by beliefs that workers in other countries are better trained and more productive than the U.S. labor force, and that non-college-bound students in the United States are inadequately prepared for work, existing vocational programs have been examined and critiqued and new school-based vocational training programs have been funded. As a 1993 GAO publication asserted, "Change is reported to have begun." Articulated agreements between secondary and postsecondary educational institutions called tech-prep programs have created a context in which high school students can continue their technical training in a college setting through a sequenced course of study. "Tech prep programs formally link high school and post secondary education in a coordinated 4-year curriculum leading to an associate degree or in a program completion certificate" (General Accounting Office 1993, 22). These combined secondary/postsecondary programs focus on a range of technical areas, all linking rigorous academics and vocational skills training with tertiary education. The popularity of these programs was evident in the increase in the number of two-year colleges reporting tech-prep programs, from 21 percent in 1990–1991 to 36 percent in 1991–1992, with 58 percent of the colleges surveyed in the process of developing programs.

This emphasis on easing the transition from school to work was institutionalized in 1994 by the School to Work Opportunities Act (PL 103-239). Funded by the federal government and administered jointly by the Departments of Labor and Education, the act has a three-tiered focus that includes school-based learning, work-based learning, and connecting activities. The three components emphasize career exploration, academic and occupational preparation, the development of work-based learning opportunities, and the connection of high school and postsecondary schooling. Together they exhibit a clear orientation toward work across grade levels and disciplines. To quote Pennsylvania State University professors Kenneth Gray and Edwin Herr (1998, 254),

> Perhaps the most significant implication of the School-to-Work Opportunities Act was a change in emphasis from workforce education that called for formal preparation, particularly of occupational skills in classroom/instructional lab settings, to an emphasis on initial general preparation including academic skills, and on transition accomplished through on-the-job-learning. This focus was on placement in the workforce, and the rationale was that this would be best accomplished if a majority of the skills development took place at the work site as was the tradition in the apprenticeship system in Europe.

These incipient school-to-work initiatives, with their high expectations and supports for non-college-bound students, however, have been set apart from welfare-to-work initiatives by both design and implementation. This separation of welfare-related training from other forms of adult education is a reflection of the historical fragmentation of funding in the United States across levels (i.e., K through 12, adult education, higher education), kinds of education (vocational education, literacy education, bilingual education), and economic status (welfare recipients, dislocated workers, unemployed, tuition assistance for the lower and middle class). Bounded funding streams have resulted most visibly in training initiatives such as those at Development, Church Hall, and JEVS positioned as part of the larger welfare-transfer system rather than as components of labor market policies or of higher education (Osterman 1980). This separation of training frameworks minimizes the potential of an entire stratum of the workforce, contributes to a reduction in the country's labor productivity, and creates a powerful dilemma for the working poor. Making a successful first move from welfare, Henry and his colleagues in Development's kits department and Dina and her co-workers at Church Hall soon realized that they remained economically precarious. They began to feel undervalued at work, and without access to continued professional growth, they became frustrated and angry. They were overlooked by a system that supported their transition from welfare, but offered no training or educational assistance once they were working.

An advancement strategy for low-wage workers has been a topic of on-going conversation between economists and politicians in hallowed corridors of power. And it has been a conversation with more questions than answers.

> The need to retrain low-skilled workers is generally recognized by policymakers and informed observers in both Europe and the United States. However, the most serious discussions about training for the new economy have focused on young people and their transition from school to work, or from school to post secondary training. The cost of retraining adult workers is considerable, and none of the industrial democracies has advanced convincing proposals indicating how to implement such a program effectively. Moreover a heavy emphasis on skill development and job retraining is likely to end up mainly benefiting those who already have a good many skills that only need to be upgraded. (Wilson 1996, 234)

We need to imagine possibilities; we need to reframe the debate about welfare reform from a discussion about moving welfare recipients from the welfare rolls to a conversation about a well-integrated, universal system of adult education that is inclusive rather than exclusionary, provides continued rather than discrete and fragmentary access, and draws welfare recipients into the mainstream rather than segmenting, marginalizing, and stigmatizing them. Training must be positioned not as an entry condition but as a continuous process, not as the movement of individuals into work, but as a transformative experience that involves negotiating work and outside work. This strategy, of embedding welfare-targeted initiatives within universal programs is no longer atypical. William Julius Wilson, in his *The Truly Disadvantaged*, advocated a similar philosophy as far back as 1987.

> The important goal is to construct an economic social reform program in such a way that the universal programs are seen as the dominant and most visible aspects by the general public. As the universal pro-

grams draw support from a wider population, the targeted programs included in the comprehensive reform package would be indirectly supported and protected. Accordingly, the hidden agenda for liberal policy makers is to improve the life chances of truly disadvantaged groups such as the ghetto underclass by emphasizing programs to which the more advantaged groups of all races and class backgrounds can positively relate. (Wilson 1987, 154–155)

What is suggested here, however, is not only a political strategy to increase public support for targeted-manpower programs, but an educational system that supports a flexible, competitive, and productive workforce and affords professional growth and incremental mobility. This exhortation is consistent with former Secretary of Labor Robert Reich's thesis (1991a, 42) on the value and need to support and nurture "the problem solving, problem identifying, and strategic brokering skills of a nation's citizens." Yet while Reich consistently asserted the need to support the "future productivity of *all* Americans" (ibid., 52), he emphasized increased funding of present programs rather than an analysis and redesign of the status quo.

A cohesively organized, accessible, and open-ended network of education and training is needed to combine literacy and adult education, job training, community college, and higher education and to integrate life-long education and the local economy. This network would take the place of the present nonsystem, a fragmented array of differentially funded programs and institutions that are difficult to understand and access, and that departmentalize individuals into positions "their social order deems appropriate" (Zwerling 1976). The Work Force Investment Act of 1998 is a proposal to do just that. Through the development of "individual Training Accounts" and accessible career counseling and placement assistance, "[the Act] empowers workers, not government programs, by offering training grants directly to them, so they can choose for themselves what kind of training they want and where they can get it. . . . The law streamlines and consolidates a tangle of training programs, therefore, into a single common sense system" (Clinton 1998). But the Act will only be successful if it transforms the jumble of disparate adult education and training programs into a cohesive, open system, accessed at work and other central locations (as well as via the Internet). It will only be successful if it encourages individuals to enter when and where appropriate, and if it supports them over a lifetime of a voluntary moves from one professional step to the next. Education can be combined with work, simultaneously, consecutively, or in any number of configurations to create an essential interspersion of work and learning. Work allows individuals to apply newly acquired skills in context, to see results, encounter problems, and ask the questions that a subsequent investment in training will answer. Building a continuum of professional growth possibilities will allow individuals who successfully maneuver from the underclass to the bottom of the workforce to continue their investment at their own pace, as well as provide opportunities for professional growth that are now relatively inaccessible to many segments of the larger populace.

Although the focus on an inclusive training system may seem excessive and extravagant, a series of reports released by the General Accounting Office (GAO) in 1994 foreshadowed these policy recommendations. The reports analyzed 154 employment training programs that targeted four groups of individuals, the economically disadvantaged, dislocated workers, older workers, and youth, with a combined FY 1994 budget of $25 billion (General Accounting Office 1994a; General Accounting Office 1994b; General Accounting Office 1994c; General Accounting Office 1994d; General Accounting Office 1994e; General Accounting Office 1994f). The reports called for a consolidation of these training programs in order to avoid an "overlap" in program services, client groups, and service delivery approaches. Quoting from just one of the reports, *Multiple Employment Training Programs: Overlap Among Programs Raises Questions about Efficiency* (General Accounting Office 1994d, 26),

> Problems with the multitude of employment training programs have prompted the administration and Members of Congress to suggest a major overhaul and consolidation of employment training programs. We found programs targeting the economically disadvantaged, dislocated workers, older workers, and youth overlap considerably in their goals, clients, services, and service delivery mechanisms. These redundancies foster inefficiencies and make it difficult to determine the effectiveness of individual programs or the system as a whole.

The goal must be multifaceted: connecting individuals to work, enhancing the existing skills and job responsibilities of employed individuals, and integrating all the diverse strands of education and training for adults. Education as we now know it, its appearance, purposes, and relationship to learners, must be reconfigured into a system that is accessible, inclusive, and life long. As the Work Force Investment Act suggests, universally targeted skill and job enhancement will require upgrading current training initiatives. Models exist to help us imagine what these enhancements might look like. Educational Opportunity Centers, funded by the U.S. Department of Education to provide financial and academic assistance to low-income individuals interested in pursuing postsecondary education, offer one such model. In existence since 1975, the centers are located and operated by colleges, universities, nonprofit organizations throughout the United States. They embody a one-stop integrated approach, with the mission of assisting adults in their entry or return to school. While research on the centers has been limited, and record keeping on program performance has been inconsistent across sites, the concept of integrated assistance and support around tertiary education warrants another look. In a similar fashion, programs associated with the Carl D. Perkins Vocational and Applied Technology Education Act provide a model for linking secondary with both postsecondary vocational education and the workplace. Although the Perkins Act currently funds local vocational education initiatives, in the form of equipment, curriculum, learning labs, staff development, career counseling, remedial classes, and the expansion of tech prep programs, the activities are primarily geared toward in-school populations. Programs associated with the Perkins Act could be opened to adults interested in upgrading their skills, with training made accessible before or after work or on the weekends. In addition, supportive services could be made available to learners to ensure on-site child care and accessible transpiration. Other initiatives have made community college more accessible to individuals who may not fit the typical college student profile. *Step-Up*, an innovative local program funded through the JOBS program, provided financial and material supports to economically eligible community-college students. It modified tuition payments, the manner of payment (i.e., loan repayment in terms of work), curriculum requirements, and the scheduling of classes.

GOOD JOBS, GOOD PAY, GOOD BENEFITS

We have become accustomed to thinking about welfare and welfare reform in a vacuum, as though questions concerning work and its organization are tangential to the real conversation. But the stories in Part One illustrate that the opposite is true. The availability of both jobs and jobs within "high performance work organizations" is not only an essential part of the welfare-to-work equation, but should also be the starting point of any public dialogue concerning welfare and welfare reform. The discussion must extend beyond the question of jobs for welfare recipients to one of good jobs. Without links to good jobs, welfare-funded training fails to provide a "favorable"

context for adult learning, the "existence of an opportunity or benefit structure linked to the knowledge to be acquired" (Puchner 1993,
191).

Without an emphasis on good jobs, success in moving off welfare
becomes a hollow phrase. Although Henry Thompson and Dina
Haskell were both considered successful because they obtained
work and remained on the job, their "success" at work was skewed
by the realities of the workplace. Official indicators, that is, job-
placement rates, pre-and postprogram earnings and job retention,
gave a measure of only relative success. They defined the success of
Development's training only as it compared with other TN programs. But meeting men and women at Development, Concordance, Church Hall, and Jackson Hospital, I quickly learned that I
could not measure their success postwelfare solely by their staying
at or leaving a workplace. I found instead that they saw their own
success as embedded in both their engagement (or lack of engagement) with work and in their level of financial self-sufficiency. Yet
engagement and economic independence are vastly different from
the criteria commonly used to measure performance. According to a
government report on labor issues (General Accounting Office 1992,
17), this is certainly not a new argument.

> JTPA is viewed as a relatively successful program because most of
> those who enroll in the program get jobs. However, we do not know
> how well these individuals would have done without JTPA assis-
> tance, or the long-term benefits of such training. Initial results from a
> study of JTPA's effectiveness suggest that, on a short-term basis, the
> program may not be effective for youth and may be only marginally
> effective for adults.

Without a lens wide enough to encompass longer-term benefits of
training and other supports in the lives of real men and women, we
will continue to find that the impact of moving off welfare remains
obscured and policy makers, training-program staff, participants,
and the general public alike will continue to be misled about the
move from welfare to financial independence. Without good jobs,
defined in terms of livable salaries and benefit packages and opportunities for continued professional growth, former welfare recipients
such as Henry, Ruth, Dina, and Joan, stay poor, and their best efforts
to advance result in a revolving door of low-wage jobs, in frustration
and anger, and perhaps worse, in giving up.[2] Yet the means and
methods for encouraging businesses to collaborate with training programs, to hire welfare recipients, and, equally important, to treat
them and their co-workers with equity, respect, and fairness are still

debated. According to the American Management Association (Welfare to Work Partnership 1998), 62.8 percent of employers surveyed do not hire welfare recipients because they lack information on relevant programs and practices. The Targeted Jobs Tax Credit (TJTC) was designed in 1978 as an attempt to encourage these very employers to buy into welfare-funded training programs. Policy analysts Anthony Carnevale, Leila Gainer, and Janice Villet (1990, 135–136) described this incentive in *Training in America: The Organization and Strategic Role of Training*:

> The Targeted Jobs Tax Credit (TJTC) is made available to employers that hire workers who are in certain targeted categories—usually those who fall below the federally determined poverty level. Employers receive a federal tax credit up to a specified amount when they hire employees who meet certain criteria. While the TJTC does not in fact have any training provisions, in effect it often results in training. Because training of the economically disadvantaged can be financed by other public job-training funds, TJTC can effectively lengthen the period of on the job training when another funding source expires.

The TJTC translates to a tax credit of up to $3,000 for the first year and $1,500 for the second year to employers who hire disadvantaged individuals, as defined by the following seven categories: recipients of social security, the handicapped, Vietnam veterans, disadvantaged youth between the ages of eighteen and twenty-four, ex-convicts, general assistance recipients, and youth in cooperative education programs. But even this best effort has not in any way ensured the adoption of responsive management strategies or the movement toward a high-production workplace. All four companies took advantage of targeted tax credits when they hired training program graduates, yet when asked, managers identified motivated workers and training-related supports as the most valuable dividends of their cooperation with DPW and Private Industry Council (PIC) offices. Consistent with previous research on employer incentives and subsidies (Bassie 1994; Roberts and Padden 1998), in these four cases tax credits offered a nice dividend for what employers would have done anyway.[3]

While examples exist of "forward looking company officials" who recognize labor shortages and "make significant changes in corporate attitudes, structures, and programs to anticipate it" (Hudson Institute 1988, 176), they tend to be idiosyncratic, a few altruistic individuals out of a city of small and large businesses. For far too many men and women however, dependency upon these hit-or-miss efforts has not been enough to support their move off welfare. We need to move beyond a reliance on the good will of a few humanitarian employers for the health of our communities and ourselves, and instead foster a cultural climate that values the creativity, productivity, imagination, and motivation of all citizens, in their rainbow of hues, genders, preferences, languages, and ethnicities. We need to construct visions of workplaces as transformative learning environments (Erickson, private correspondence), and to participate in the long-overdue task of reinventing work as a context in which human resources are valued and nurtured. Government can play many roles in this process. It can provide "national political leadership" by setting the tone and using the administration as the ever-popular "bully pulpit." It can establish a government-level office to coordinate and guide training efforts, support and accredit work-based training programs, coordinate with other government departments in human resource training and management, and fund demonstration efforts. It can fund local information centers, similar to but more proactive and visible than the currently funded Small Business Centers. In these centers businesses could obtain information on best practices (i.e., in the form of brochures, videos, computer networking, etc., seminar participation, exchange site visits), human resource models could be highlighted and honored, field-level supports could encourage small and medium businesses' adoption of work-based training programs, and technical assistance could be provided in the form of the training designs and trainers who work with employers on site-based training for employees at all levels. Government can expand financial support (i.e., in the form of wage supplements or similar to customized job training, etc.) for employers' on-the-job training efforts. It can fund accessible adult education and skills centers and subsidize center-based support services, including the provision of child care (U.S. Department of Labor 1989). It can encourage employer payroll set asides for employee training, through the provision of tax credits, public training and employment schemes, renewal funds, or taxes, similar to various OECD country models (Mikulecky 1993, 57). And finally, it can provide tax exemptions for expenses incurred by individuals who continue their education.

This reorientation is a tall order in a society that is ruled by vested interests. As illustrated by the Clinton administration's unsuccessful attempt to reorganize the country's health care system, we have a great deal of difficulty reframing issues. We don't reconfigure well, but we should not dismiss the obvious simply because necessary changes are difficult. The new welfare-reform legislation has further obscured this issue of good jobs. By confining public discourse to reducing the welfare rolls, work has once again been relegated to the role of spectator. After two years, articles on the aftermath of leaving welfare still only rarely appear in the mainstream press. The effect of moving massive numbers of the poor off the welfare roles on extended family members, on grandmothers, other surrogate caregivers, and social service agencies is still relegated to an occasional article in the local newspaper (DeParle 1999b). The early returns, measured by enormous reductions in the welfare rolls, are enough for most of us. The more complicated issues of moving from poverty, on or off welfare, has been relegated to a conversation we are not yet ready to have.

BUCKING THE NATURAL TREND

If our preoccupation with reforming the welfare system rises from a concern about individuals most marginalized from the economic mainstream, then we can imagine other possibilities. But if the current attack on welfare instead masks a move toward government downsizing, then this ideological shift in assigning responsibility for economic inequities from the federal to state governments, and from states to the poor themselves, functions as a diversion, obfuscating the real budgetary choices the country is making. In that event, the men and women's stories presented here are best-case scenarios of what is to come. But for far too many of the individuals most affected, the stories portend a future of frustrated dreams and prolonged poverty. For the larger society, they augur an increasing marginalization of an entire stratum of the workforce, an inevitable reduction in the country's labor productivity, and the intensifying alienation and hostility of the poor. While cutting welfare may be a "natural trend," the assumption that work in and of itself, even in the form of high-turnover, low-end jobs, is the only possible, or even the most expedient solution to the "welfare problem" denies both the agency of the poor and the implications of their actions (Maynard 1995). The backlash may have already started. A small-scale demonstration against low-wage jobs was staged recently by representatives of the Kensington Welfare Rights Union in Philadelphia. According to a reporter from the *Philadelphia Daily News* (Dean 1999, 16), the protestors, wearing hats and shirts from a nationwide fast food restaurant chain and carrying signs stating "Stop Killing the Poor" and "Time's Up: Living Wage Jobs Now," objected to the low-wage jobs in which former welfare recipients now find themselves. As long as the economy remains strong, this more formal resistance may remain isolated for some time to come. But without a thoughtful examination of the relationships between education and work, not only for the poor but for ourselves, our neighbors, and our children, the resistance will surely grow. The ensuing opposition of the working poor may not improve their own plight, but multiplied by ranks far more numerous than represented in these stories, it will surely amplify the growing divisions in the United States between the rich and the poor, the haves and the have-nots, the inner city and the suburbs. Civil unrest can be very expensive. We had best be clear about what we choose to afford.

Appendix A:
Ethnographic Methodology
and Methods

Although ethnographic research has gained acceptance in disciplines outside the field of anthropology, it continues to confuse many readers who have problems with the size of an ethnography's sample or the validity of making generalizations from a study of one site. In this section I attempt to speak to those concerns, and in the process, to make the ethnographic research on which this book is based more comprehensible to the reader. I describe decisions made during the course of the research, highlight the strengths, and address the limitations of the ethnographic method as it was used to examine the unfolding of four welfare-to-work transitions. The section also provides a window into the connections and lack of connections between welfare, training, and work, to help the reader gain a better understanding of the mechanics behind the four transitions on which this book is based.

RESEARCH ON GOVERNMENT-FUNDED
EMPLOYMENT TRAINING

Government-funded job training had been a basic strategy for moving individuals into the economic mainstream long before Lyndon Johnson declared War on Poverty in the 1960s. Research on these government-funded programs has traditionally been in three forms: descriptive narratives of program components or graduates' success stories, telephone followup to randomly selected training program graduates, and econometric evaluations that measure program impacts on earnings and welfare dependency. Each has its strengths and weaknesses. Narrative accounts, for instance, typically take the form of a press release about a successful client or a case study of a training project and its components. The images of the role of training in transiting welfare recipients into work or of the motivation of particular individuals are generally positive, but provide limited information about program efficacy. Given both their form and lack of context, the accounts appear to be written more for mass consumption and public advocacy than for systematic analysis.

Telephone surveys, on the other hand, are most often conducted by training-program personnel in response to funding mandates. In order to assess program success, they collect and compare information on the activities of former welfare recipients with preset performance standards. Although federal and state guidelines generally allow local areas to specify these standards, they typically include a minimum percent of participants completing program activities, working in jobs at a wage set above the legislated minimum wage, and working ninety days after completion of training. A consultant, contracted by the local Private Industry Council (PIC) to conduct this type of telephone followup on the activities of training program graduates, described his work:

> We contact clients thirteen weeks after termination. Our followup is based upon sampling, to determine if a program meets the standards. You can only speak with the participants, you have to make contact with the participants by telephone. What this state does, it selects individuals to come up during the tenth week after they've been terminated. They send the individual a letter informing them that we will contact them.
>
> We call, ask where the person is working, for how long and about wages for any given time, for any given period. It does not have to be in the same job. Some of those who come up in the survey not having worked, those individuals have every reason not to cooperate. Some are receiving assistance. (Consultant, Private Industry Council)

While collecting important details on life postwelfare, PIC's followup was the tracking of bodies at particular points in time. It did not typically include communication with employers, followup on an individual's employment status after three months, nor measures of his or her quality of life. As the chief executive officer of the local PIC asserted, "I want to do longer followup, but there's not enough money." Equally important, collected information was neither been relayed to caseworkers to improve supports for men and women moving off welfare, nor was it forwarded to training vendors to make programs more responsive to clients' needs.

Because of their reliance on control and treatment groups, cost-benefit analyses—a third type of research on employment training initiatives—are considered to be the most rigorous of evaluations (Hollister 1984). Ranging in size and complexity from evaluations of single projects within one city to multisite projects and multicity demonstrations, these analyses are embedded in a larger program design. Upon application to a training program, individuals are randomly assigned to either a treatment or a control group. Comparisons are then made between postprogram earnings, fringe benefits, transfer payments, allowances, criminal activity, and arrests of program graduates and members of the control group. The breadth of these analyses, however, has caused some concern. Comparing costs to benefits across training programs or training sites has been problematic when programs share goals of increasing earnings and improving participants' labor market status, but describe improved labor market status in various and not always compatible ways (i.e., as increased job placement, increased ability to secure future employment, or improved life cycle employability). Programs also target a wide range of divergent groups including unemployed and underemployed workers in depressed areas, dislocated workers, the structurally unemployed, disadvantaged youth, refugees, immigrants, single, economically disadvantaged heads of households, and pregnant and parenting youth, and offer very different combinations of training, counseling, job development, and job-search related supports. Like comparing apples and oranges, these differences in definitions, target groups, and treatments skew comparisons. To quote a group of researchers who employed cost-benefit analysis to evaluate a range of Supported-Work programs (Kemper et al. 1980, 239), given the "inevitable differences among target groups served, prevailing economic conditions, and analytical approaches used in the evaluations, comparisons among programs are difficult to make and when made are susceptible to misinterpretation."

But putting aside this methodological critique for a moment, an overview of cost-benefit analyses conducted on employment training programs by the General Accounting Office (GAO) (1993:3), also revealed troubling information about program efficacy. While stating that particular employment training programs successfully increased earnings, the GAO report showed that the increases were actually quite modest, neither sufficient to lift an individual or family out of poverty nor adequate for a family to become economically independent of all housing and public assistance support. The problem here is that in the reality of people's lives, an increase in earnings is not always enough. Numbers by themselves can obscure prolonged suffering. As sociologist Ruth Sidel asserted in her *Keeping Women and Children Last* (1996, 150), "Statistics, it has been said, are people with the tears washed off." A good example of this discrepancy between numbers and faces is the case of San Jose's Center for Employment Training Program (CET), one of the most commonly noted success stories in the employment and training field. A cost-benefit analysis of CET and three other employment training programs for minority female single parents, all utilizing random assignment procedures, found that during the fourth quarter after enrollment CET's participants averaged monthly employment rates that were 10 percent higher than the control group's (46 percent to 36 percent), and monthly earnings that were 133 percent higher than those of the control group (Gordon and Burghardt 1990). The program's sponsor, the Rockefeller Foundation, and contracted evaluators attributed the program's success both to its integration of basic education and work experience and to its simulation of actual workplace conditions. According to Schwarz and Volgy (1992, 104), however, even this success left the San Jose participants with average incomes of $4,992, a figure that falls far below the official poverty rate. "The result [was] that the public assistance the participants received, $291 a month, was only marginally lower than the $306 a month assistance the control group received." CET, with its innovative competency-based design and integration of skills training and individualized academic remediation, was effective in raising the income levels of the participants. Yet the increases in earnings were not sufficient to pull families out of poverty (General Accounting Office 1993; Gueron and Pauly 1991; Couch 1992; LaLonde 1986).

Schwarz and Volgy's analysis illuminates the essential paradox of employment training for the poor. Even the most successful welfare-related training efforts have not been able to move welfare recipients from poverty. What the research has not revealed, however, is why welfare recipients have not enjoyed more than modest salary increases, or how their participation in training has affected their advancement in the workplace. These omissions can be tied to the very nature of both cost-benefit analyses and performance standards. Reliant on preset, decontextualized measures and "reductive" in their effort to translate benefits and outcomes into dollars and cents, these quantitative evaluations have been unable to encompass a range of factors, including the length of time an individual remains at a particular company or position, the relationships between training experience and life at work, decisions involved in staying on or leaving a job, or the effect of increased postprogram earnings, fringe benefits, allowances, and decreased transfer payments, criminal activity, and arrests in the lives of former welfare recipients (Hollister 1984, 29).

In spite of the historical dependence on numerically based criteria of success, official rhetoric around welfare and training talks to quality of life issues that are far less easily translated into dollars and cents. Take the mission statement of the Private Industry Council (PIC), the city agency that dispensed government moneys for job training, for example.

> PIC's mission is to establish a training philosophy that will satisfy employers and provide clients with the necessary support services and life skills training to make the successful transition to permanent employment. Our goal will be to help each individual gain marketable and lasting employment skills, ultimately providing them with quality jobs leading to economic self-sufficiency. (Private Industry Council 1992)

Putting the mission statement into practice demands the operationalizing of outcomes as they unfold in individuals' lives. Do increased postprogram earnings, fringe benefits, and allowances, and decreased transfer payments, criminal activity, and arrests translate to "successful transition[s] to permanent employment, marketable and lasting employment skills, . . . ultimately providing them with quality jobs leading to economic self-sufficiency?" And if not, why not?

Opportunity exists then, for another kind of research on employment training as an antipoverty strategy, research that incorporates individuals' workplace experiences, relationships, interactions, and negotiation of postwelfare contingencies into an analysis of program and policy efficacy. For even if we recognize that the objective of job-training initiatives may be more closely associated with moving recipients from the welfare rolls than empowering them to become self-sufficient in the labor market, without an analysis that contextualizes program outcomes in the lives and circumstances of real men and women, the real impact of welfare reform and the efficacy of employment training strategies can neither be understood, appreciated, or heeded in policy decisions (D'Andrade 1991; Roseberry 1989).

A DIFFERENT PLACE

By posing questions about transitions from welfare to work that could not be asked by cost-benefit analyses, random sample telephone followups, or anecdotal narratives, I positioned myself in a place that was radically different, both in terms of epistemology and social theory, from previous poverty-related research. With a focus on the role employment training played in supporting welfare recipients' transition to work, the challenges and choices individuals encountered in the workplace, and their negotiation of multiple dimensions of work, this ethnography attended to problem posing and solving, to meaning making, and to the negotiation of sociocultural constructs. These moments of interaction could not be explored through a positivist design, which is best employed for the purposes of meta-analysis or for programmatic evaluations using predefined criteria. They could also not be understood by case studies, which tell a story about an intervention or a situation in context, but do not necessarily probe for participants' implicit cultural knowledge and meanings. Ethnography, however, is a social science research methodology traditionally used by anthropologists to study culture and social organization. Through systematic participant observation, in-depth interviews, and archival analysis conducted over a period of a year or more, the ethnographer collects the data necessary to develop a description and interpretation of local practices that incorporates both insider and outsider perspectives. Deep rather than broad, ethnography captures what anthropologist Clifford Geertz called "rich description" of both action and meaning. It reveals particulars of a bounded context and generates hypotheses that move from the specific to the general. These are ethnography's strengths, its capturing of implicit cultural meanings, its examination of what people do and what those doings mean to them, and its situating those practices within a larger theoretical context. To quote from Geertz's *The Interpretation of Culture* (1973, 14), "the aim . . . is the enlargement of the universe of human discourse."

My research focus was on the workplace and my research questions concerned both knowledge and skills required at work and the ways in which former welfare recipients and their co-workers acquired that knowledge. Given our ideological prioritizing of supply-side issues in discussions of education and training, the inclusion of the workplace in an analysis of employment training was somewhat atypical. However, in order to understand how a "successful transition to permanent employment, marketable and lasting employment skills, and . . . quality jobs leading to economic self-sufficiency" translated to men and women's daily practices of work, an analysis of employment-training programs had to include the context of work. Employment-training programs and workplaces are cultures with their own sets of rules, beliefs, practices, and measures of appropriateness, and the four worksites were culturally diverse places where rules, beliefs, practices, and measures of appropriateness differed across race, language group, class, and gender. I looked at these cultural beliefs and practices in each of the training initiatives and worksites, and examined the ways in which men and women entered and participated in the social organization of those cultures.

Ethnography, however, is particular by nature. Conducting an ethnographic inquiry would allow me to examine how a particular set of individuals negotiated their particular transitions from welfare to work and their own change in social identity from welfare recipient to worker. But while the data would reveal much about particular individuals, these data could not encompass every individual, every welfare recipient, or every workplace. I was able to widen this playing field by utilizing a multisited model advanced by William Firestone and Robert Herriott (1984). Their model employs similar, mixed method data collection and analysis strategies across different settings varied by size and type of business. Conducting ethnographic research across four workplaces allowed me to make both tentative comparisons between and among sites and conjectures about systematic relationships across sites.

PRACTICALITIES

My first challenge was locating businesses that were considered successful in hiring and retaining former welfare recipients. This initial step was arduous and, in hindsight, clearly reflected a lack of firm connections between government-funded, means-tested employment training programs and the market place. My first stop was the Chamber of Commerce, the organization that represents area businesses. A Chamber representative explained that although the Chamber had had close ties with job training in the past, she was now the only person in the organization who had any ties with "workforce issues." "PIC is the one that funds money and does the bulk of placement. I'd stick with PIC," she suggested. But while the Private Industry Council, or PIC as it is called, was the organization through which federal job-training money was funneled in the state, its employees also lacked information on possible sites. PIC's (PIC 1992) mission was "to serve as the primary training-based bridge connecting [the city's] unemployed, at risk youth and adult, and dislocated worker populations with area employers," yet staff members of PICs in the city and in two neighboring counties could not identify any potential employers for my research. They did not keep records on the number of individuals hired at specific worksites, nor did they identify model employers. A PIC staff member described the agency's followup on job placements:

> The agency is very targeted. It doesn't give you any of that kind of information [on employers]. I wish we did have more quality information, but we don't have the money. The problem is, area companies may be hiring, but they don't know that PICs trained the people.
>
> I think that's a big problem. I bet if we printed up a list of job placements, we'd have CYRUS [a large insurance company] twenty-five times, but from twenty-five programs. (PIC staff member)

In his article "New Directions for Employment Training," Paul Osterman (1989, 511) asserted, "We lack a good way of thinking about how employment and training policy fits into the labor market, and hence programs tend to be marginalized and irrelevant. [The] tenuous relationship of the employment and training system to the private sector makes involving companies difficult." Osterman had "not found firms to be an eager customer for trainees," a phenomenon confirmed both by my own investigation and an earlier Bureau of National Affairs survey. According to the survey, only 9 percent of businesses collaborated with government job-training programs, and when companies were involved, "there is usually the aura of public service and charity" (Bureau of National Affairs 1986, 22). Describing training programs as "floating in air," Osterman (1989, 518) contended that the private sector does not expect the employment training system to be of "significant assistance in meeting human resource needs." My experience supported Osterman's claim. Government-funded training for the poor did indeed "float in air." As PIC representatives explained, their planning was based upon state-level labor market analyses, and not on the needs of local businesses. PIC's marketing director described his planning:

> It's a big process, with a lot of actors. It starts with the feds, who mandate jobs paying six dollars an hour with fringe benefits, thirteen-week retention. That automatically slices out a lot of jobs. The second factor is the state. In this state they calculate their own statistics based upon job growth on an annual basis. You need to put together an annual plan. They tell us the areas they want us to focus on. Their projections show areas of decline. In general we don't train in declining areas. That really drives us.
>
> A while ago we'd release an RFP [Request for Proposals] in March. When proposals came back, we'd evaluate proposal by proposal for a good track record. We'd tell them what we wanted to see in

terms of academics. Now we only RFP for new providers. If a training provider is successful, we're going to continue, automatically continue. (PIC marketing director)

A planner with a suburban PIC added,

> You get planning instructions from the capital. I take a look at what comes out, what's happening with the labor market. The Department of Labor puts out statistics. They give us a range, which tells you for instance how many people are unemployed, how many are disadvantaged, dropouts, AFDC, which is the welfare population. How many are dislocated workers. You want to look at what your picture is. We have a five to ten year situation garnered from the latest census. And we get local labor market reports.
>
> One of the other things is information from the capital. Participant Completion, of those that terminated what did they do, where were they placed, how many placements were training related. With performance standards they really want to know are they getting training related jobs. Are they becoming dishwashers?
>
> Then there's information from the Department of Labor; it will give you one hundred and fifty occupations that are hot. It also might give you one hundred occupations in the country. That's the kind of thing I would look to. Now obviously if there are only one hundred and seventy-seven openings [the state] will ask you to justify a course if they feel it's not viable. (Planner, suburban PIC)

As long as a potential training provider both proposed a training focus that fit within the Department of Labor's market projections and illustrated the capacity to facilitate training, PIC funding was likely. A more localized fit, targeting specific local businesses or researching local job markets for instance, was neither necessary nor encouraged. And training providers were automatically renewed unless problems arose with existing agreements. Driven by pragmatism and logistical concerns, the "floating" system was self-perpetuating.

Lack of information about employment sites may have also stemmed from the way PICs fund job training. "PIC subcontracts [training]; we don't do placement," a PIC staff member explained. So while PIC representatives could not refer me to specific workplaces, they did provide a list of what they called their "proven" subcontracted trainers. I had somewhat better luck here. PIC-contracted trainers were well aware of the emphasis placed upon employment because PIC funds were performance-based; they were disbursed in a series of steps built around performance standards that included a minimum percentage of individuals enrolled,

completing training, and placed in jobs. Yet even with these payment schedules looming, of the fourteen training programs I visited,
only two program directors or job developers could name more than
two area employers with whom they had a consistent and dependable relationship. Although flimsy training to job links played a part
here, other factors also proved important. Trainers provided an array
of convincing explanations for their inability to name names, including job placements with temporary employment agencies or in small
companies in which only one graduate was employed, graduates'
unwillingness to remain in contact after finding employment, and
individualized job routines to which an observer could not gain
access.

My search for possible research sites continued. I met with the
deputy executive director of the city's welfare office and with the supervisor of the office's Job Development Unit (JDU) to inform them
of the research and obtain names of training providers they found effective and area businesses they believed were responsive in hiring
welfare recipients.[1] They referred me to eight "quality" training
providers and six local businesses with whom they had worked.
Added together, my efforts resulted in a list of thirty-nine area businesses. Because the food-service sector frequently lacks avenues for
upward mobility, I excluded the twenty-four fast food restaurants on
my list, and contacted the directors of the remaining fifteen companies by letter and then by phone. Although only one bank refused
access during the first telephone conversation, arranging site visits
with three other organizations, an insurance company, a university,
and a health care facility, also proved logistically impossible. I visited the remaining eleven companies and talked with individuals
occupying a range of management positions.

I hadn't anticipated how long, slow, and arduous the process of locating possible sites and gaining permission for access would be,
commencing in February 1992 and proceeding through November
of that year. I made what seemed to be endless phone calls and
spoke to many answering machines. My journal entries reflected my
growing frustration:

> I am trying to keep in mind that this difficulty in obtaining access is
> part of the research process, particularly in a project that requires per-
> mission from the private sector to enter secret domains. (October 9,
> 1992)

> This waiting and endless telephoning is tough. I must admit I enjoy
> this gatekeeping business the least and get the greatest thrill from
> doing the actual data collection. So in my more positive times, I know

that this difficulty is telling me that accessing sites is my biggest challenge, and perhaps the place where I have to put most of my strength, energy, and focus. (October 13, 1992)

NEGOTIATING ACCESS

While arranging access to multiple research sites proved cumbersome and at times overwhelming, gaining entrance to large white-collar corporate settings proved particularly daunting. My journal entries documented these complications. An entry dated April 26, 1992, reads thus:

> I'd like very much to get in there [a large insurance company]—a white-collar environment would be invaluable, particularly in contrast to Development and hopefully to a health care setting. (April 26, 1992)

And five months later, I wrote the following:

> The difficulty of gaining access to businesses has become more evident to me in the past few weeks. Without the support of a larger agency, negotiating entry to six separate sites is extremely difficult.[2] I make requests over and over again. Although I thought I had negotiated entry to the insurance company through MM, access now seems to be questionable at best. And even though positive during our initial meeting, DF of the Bank, hasn't answered or returned my phone calls since July. I'm beginning to wonder if both of these large companies are avoiding my data collection requests.
>
> Getting into small companies has been much easier. Development responded to my request almost immediately. The owner at Concordance invited me to visit the company and immediately arranged interviews. And even the personnel officer at Church Hall arranged an interview with her supervisor and with two nurse assistants on my first visit. Are these large companies avoiding me? Or are my contacts simply too busy to get back to me and do those extra things, making introductions or inviting me to an initial meeting? (September 29, 1992)

At the beginning of this research I thought about research sites in terms of the ideal. The following is from my notes of March 12, 1992:

> I've thought about an array of ideal work sites at which I can look. A union-mediated work site, one employing women in nontraditional work roles, one in which the welfare and work linkage was con-

structed within the employment training proposal, one where language differences are negotiated, one with a responsive employer.
This list seems to provide a range of work settings. (March 12, 1992)

But rather than choosing from a myriad of possible settings, I found
that the diaphanous, nearly nonexistent network between welfare
and work made negotiating access to work places arduous and
forced selection from the few available and accessible sites that fit
project criteria.

GETTING IN

Once approached, managers of three of the four companies in which
I eventually found myself quickly granted access. While Development, with forty-seven employees, and Concordance, with thirty-
five, were relatively small, all three workplaces had uncomplicated
management structures. My original contacts at Development and
Church Hall, for example, were both second in command. The
human resource director at Development and the director of personnel at Church Hall each passed my request to their directors, who
both consented quickly and without objection to my proposed research. Gaining access to Concordance, the smallest of the four sites,
was even swifter. A telephone call to the company's director resulted
in a followup meeting, immediate access to the employees, an introduction to the shop foreman, a tour of the shop floor, and a follow-up
appointment. Because of the size of the institution, negotiating
entry to Jackson Hospital's pharmacy department was the most
cumbersome of all four sites. Winning the support of my first contact, the director of the pharmacy's technician training program, and
that of her supervisor, one of the pharmacy's six assistant directors,
was swift. Yet despite their interest in the questions posed in this research, a formal review of my research protocol by the hospital's
Research on Human Subjects Committee delayed the process by a
month.

At Development, Concordance Steps, and Church Hall, I explained my research and obtained verbal consent from informants,
who were told the project was school-related research and concerned the role training programs played in their obtaining employment and in the kinds of jobs they had obtained. Jackson required
signed consent from all informants, and so a consent form was developed in conjunction with one of the pharmacy department's assistant directors. The form was reviewed jointly with and signed by

each informant before a first interview, and a copy of each signed form was stored in my files.

THE CHALLENGE OF DATA COLLECTION

In order to make reliable comparisons, I designed my data collection strategies to be consistent across sites. But dependent upon my informants and gatekeepers and restricted by site constraints, I found myself tailoring data collection to meet the unique realities and contingencies of each workplace. Many examples of the need for flexibility come to mind. I had envisioned videotaping formal reviews, conferences, and interviews, as well as facilitating focus groups of former welfare recipients, employers, and trainers across sites. But given time constraints, transportation demands, and issues of privacy, neither videotaping nor the formation of focus groups across sites was feasible. Over the course of the project I documented these changes, my reflections, questions, concerns, thematic assertions, and other pertinent information in a researcher journal.

I had also planned to spend my initial weeks at Development and Church Hall following men and women through daily work and social activities, meetings, and training sessions, and talking with them at the end of each work day about the day's events. But even though he did not directly employ former welfare recipients, Development's human resources director scheduled interviews for me with his own staff. Driven by those interviews, my initial gaze was on Development's training and human service component. After these initial interviews however, I redirected my focus to the departments in which the former welfare recipients were employed. In the end, I conducted formal and informal interviews and life histories focusing on employment, education, and prior cross-cultural experiences with a total of seventy-four individuals employed or in training at Development and observed activities in all departments of the company. Although eighteen men and women who had been hired at Development were my primary informants, this circle grew to include thirteen supervisors and administrators, fifty-one salaried and hourly employees, and ten training program participants. In addition to these interviews and observations, I also reviewed documents that included company memos, personnel policy manuals, public relations brochures, annual reports, organizational charts, project reports, company newsletters, position papers, training materials, schedules, and correspondence.

The personnel officer at Church Hall also arranged initial interviews, in this case with two former welfare recipients and their supervisor, the director of nursing. From that point on I was on my own, and over the next twelve months I interviewed 110 men and women, including eighty-one nurse assistants, twenty-six supervisors, and three administrators at Church Hall. Again, while five women, the only individuals employed at the Church Hall from the welfare rolls, were my primary informants at the geriatric facility, I also observed activities in various parts of the workplace, assisted in a range of workplace tasks, and reviewed company newsletters, public relations brochures, applications and personnel policy manuals, inservice and training materials, handouts, and workplace activity forms.

At Concordance, arranging interviews was far more straightforward. As was mentioned earlier, gaining access to the stair-building company took only a single phone call, and each informant there referred and introduced me to a next. Over my twelve months at the company I conducted formal and informal interviews with twenty-three men, including eight supervisors and fifteen woodworkers. I observed activities on the shop floor, and collected log and cutting order forms, diagrams and computer printouts of specifications, production reports, and memos that documented workplace activities. Negotiating entry and access to informants was uncomplicated at Concordance; however, conversing with and obtaining life histories from limited English speakers whose pasts were defined by turbulence and pain was a looming challenge. The company's director prepared me for these linguistic difficulties.

> Problems, trying to understand their English. We communicate through International sign language. Chan, his English's no better, but I'm understanding him better, when Chan's not there, it's difficult for me to communicate to the others. (Jay Hawks, owner, Concordance Steps)

As a former English as a Second Language (ESL) teacher, however, I have had a good deal of experience working with non-English speakers, and so was undeterred by the Cambodians' strongly accented language. But the challenge went beyond linguistic difference. Sociocultural distinctions associated with refugee experiences, including a prevalent acceptance of one's present circumstances often made interviews frustrating. Responses to questions about problems at work were difficult to elicit from four of the six Cambodian men, and the responses that were given tended to be more accepting and less critical than those of their American peers. For instance, Moeun Daun, a thirty-nine-year-old Cambodian man working in Concordance's straight stairs department, told me "It's fine, no problem," when we talked about his job and the company, even though he had been seriously injured at work during the previous year. Whether cultural or linguistic or both, this lack of explicitly verbalized critique from the Cambodians, at least in English, was fairly consistent both during interviews and across my observations at Concordance.

Arranging interviews at Jackson presented a different kind of logistical complexity, first because individuals were spread across nine pharmacy satellites and three buildings; and secondly, because the department requested that interviews be initiated by the technicians themselves, who were to be notified through interhospital correspondence. Although the method felt plodding as one technician told me about another, over eighteen months at the hospital I managed to conduct interviews with thirty-seven staff members, including fifteen pharmacy technicians, two technician trainees, eleven supervisory staff, and nine administrators, and to observe in pharmacy satellites, training sessions, and meetings. I also collected pharmacy newsletters, memos, minutes from monthly pharmacy technician meetings, and university class listings, descriptions, and schedules.

PARTICIPATION OBSERVATION

I took notes in the field, sometimes during observations or conversations, and other times as soon after an encounter as possible. I always carried a notebook, pen, tape recorder, a number of empty audio tapes, and a camera in a Thai cloth bag slung over my shoulder, yet my note taking varied depending on the encounter. Often feeling uncomfortable making extensive notes as an interaction unfolded, I resorted to what I later learned was what Sanjek (1990b, 95) called "scratch notes . . . sometimes produced in view of informants, while observing or talking with them, and sometimes out of sight." I found isolated spots in each workplace in which I felt more comfortable filling in these scratch notes. At Development I stood in a stairwell, used the bathroom, or if the day was warm and no other individuals were outside, sat in the agency's urban garden lulled by the sound of its waterfall-like fountain. At Church Hall I also made use of the stairwells, as well as the center's reception area, TV rooms, or in off-hours, the dining rooms. Notes were fleshed out later, after my observations, in the car while parked in the parking lot and at home at night on a computer.

These notes, my notebook, and my note taking occasionally inspired curiosity at the sites, as illustrated in the following notes taken during a visit to Church Hall:

> At the nursing desk in Wing Four, I copied the wing's schedule for the shift's nurse assistants. Standing, I used a corner of the C-shaped counter to rest my notebook, and took care to note each nurse assistant's name, her assigned rooms for the day, and the residents scheduled for showers or baths on a chart I'd sketched in my notebook.
>
> Although no one was behind the desk, nurse assistants moved in and out of residents' rooms and a new LPN, a young white woman, stood in the back hall by one of the unit's two medical carts. Jerry, a large, dark skinned African American woman who worked as one of the center's five restorative aides, came to the desk and seeing me, asked about my notes. I explained that I was copying the schedule and slid the notebook towards her. She paged through the notebook, asking, "Where's my name?" I responded that she surely appeared since I had observed her restorative classes, but that I didn't know where those notes were in my notebook. She shrugged and slid the notebook back to me. (April 30, 1993, field notes, Church Hall)

Observation as a data collection strategy can by its very nature have a confounding effect upon informants. The experience of the researcher watching and asking questions about everyday occurrences and commonsense judgments was often perplexing and at times even suspect to staff members. I had what I thought was a cordial relationship with Charles Smith, who was employed in Church Hall's housekeeping department. Yet he routinely referred to me as "the spy," and warned others, "Don't talk to her, she's a spy," whenever he saw me during my site visits. His admonishment to a nurse assistant of, "Don't tell her our secrets. She's writing an exposé. Taking our knowledge," reflected a concern about me and my partisanship, and perhaps also suggested something about his own relationship to the facility's administration. Despite my declarations of allegiance to the employees, Smith's accusations continued throughout my time at the geriatric center.

This bafflement at my role came from all levels. Bill Perkins, Development's director, checked my progress starting as early as my second visit to Development. "Have you learned anything yet?" he'd ask whenever he saw me in the hall or parking lot. Beginning around my fourth month of site visits at Church Hall, Nia Gates, the personnel officer and my original contact at the geriatric facility, regularly queried, "Are you still here?" whenever we talked. We had negotiated a time frame when we first met, yet I realized she didn't fully grasp the time involved in conducting ethnographic research. I had no concise response to offer, and her questions catalyzed my growing desire to shrink whenever I saw her shadow in the hall.

INTERVIEWS

Interview protocols were not predetermined, iron clad structures, as much as they were guides for what Sanjek (1990a, 246) called a "control shared" dialogue, in which informants, Henry, Ruth, Kay, and Tom, for instance, were encouraged to elaborate on particular topics of personal interest. The ordering of subjects was dependent upon their flow of talk. The best interviews stopped being interviews and became conversations, and in most cases individuals found at least one topic that aroused their interest. Many informants actually expressed pleasure in having an opportunity to talk about work with a willing listener.

So that I could obtain information on decision and meaning making, interview questions were often contextualized in workplace examples. I asked about an individual's perceptions of the workplace, professional goals, how decisions were made at work, opportunities for promotion, and feelings about training program preparation. I similarly queried colleagues about their preparation for work in lieu of participation in employment training. I asked midlevel supervisors to talk about good workers and the meanings they themselves attached to work. We talked about problems they experienced with the former welfare recipients in their employ and with their employees in general. I asked individuals involved in hiring decisions at each site about their criteria for making hiring-related decisions, about desirable and unattractive characteristics of potential employees, and about the specifics of hiring procedures. In interviews with company owners or directors, I focused on their perceptions of the company and its goals, the strengths and weaknesses of its labor force, its recruitment, retention, and promotion processes, and the roles, statuses, and performance of former welfare recipients within the company.

Many employees at both Development and Church Hall were either too busy with workplace responsibilities to take time for formal interviews or had so little control over their time at work that they could not or would not take time to be interviewed on site. In some instances we were able to schedule interviews after work. At other times, informal interviews, consisting of a combination of directed questioning and casual conversation, were conducted during work (Sanjek 1990a). Since employees' sense of their own status at work seemed precarious at Development, Church Hall, and Concordance, I did not tape record either formal or informal interviews at these three workplaces. Instead, I recorded a combination of shorthand notes and informant quotes in one of thirteen bound composition notebooks, later transcribed them into text format, and returned them to the informant for his or her review, modification, and feedback. Even without the use of a tape recorder, I made efforts to note exact wording as each individual delineated responsibilities, described experiences at work and in training, and told stories about life in and outside work. At Jackson Hospital, on the other hand, where jobs were more secure, I audio recorded all interviews. I also transcribed the conversations and, as at the other three sites, returned the transcripts to the informants for their review. In general, feedback on these interviews was minimal across workplaces. One technician at Jackson made corrections concerning pharmaceutical nomenclature, and one telephoned to confirm that his verbal space fillers, his "uhs" and "umms," would not be included in any quotes in a final report. At Concordance, one woodworker requested changes in the technical information he had provided. Only at Development did anyone voice concern that supervisors or colleagues would misinterpret their originally transcribed quotes. There, three hourly employees requested small but substantive changes in the transcripts.

As in the workplaces, I used a protocol to guide, rather than impose a strict order on interviews at training initiatives. I interviewed individuals participating in two of the training projects, Development's supported work and Jackson's pharmacy technician training. But the woodworking training and DPW's nurse assistant recruitment had been discontinued a year before my data collection began, and no trainees were available to be interviewed from either of these programs. Fortunately, I was able to observe nurse assistant certification training sessions facilitated on site at Church Hall, meet with individuals responsible for designing and facilitating the DPW and Church Hall training models, and review training curricula and materials with them.

Jackson Hospital's pharmacy technician training continued, but a significant change had occurred in the program. In 1989, seven years after this public/private collaboration began, the Private Industry Council terminated its funding of the union/hospital training collaboration. However, the hospital continued to offer the pharmacy technician training for individuals who paid the then $2,000 tuition themselves. I met with hospital employees had worked with the training effort during both funding situations, with staff employed since the training program had become self-paid, and with union employees who were involved in the JTPA funding phase. I also surveyed curriculum and teaching materials and reviewed JTPA related training files.

SUPPLEMENTAL DATA COLLECTION

Ethnographers typically enter the field with a research question or issue in hand, yet their work remains context dependent, and decisions concerning the direction of the researcher's gaze, as well as about numerous other data-related concerns, are often made in the field as life unfolds in context. For me, field research raised more questions. Questions catalyzed by data collection activities on the rapid flight of nurse assistants from Church Hall, for example, compelled me to conduct additional investigations into the health care field. I became curious about the work of nurse assistants, the workforce practices of nursing homes, and how Church Hall's salary structure compared with similar facilities, and so moved in several directions. To address these emerging concerns, I randomly selected twenty-two, or 37 percent of the sixty nursing homes in the city, and gathered information on their wage structures, hiring practices, certification training, and turnover of nurse assistants by telephone. Through phone calls and site visits, I also gathered information on three other nurse assistant training programs in the area, two of which were government funded. Since many of the nurse assistants who had been employed at Church Hall left to do agency work, I also conducted interviews with administrative staff and surveyed two hundred nurse assistants employed at a temporary agency that staffed nursing homes with nurse assistants and licensed practical nurses. In an effort to investigate and better imagine alternative work environments for nurse assistants, I also conducted formal and informal interviews with staff and trainees at a worker-owned home health care company, and observed thirteen hours of the company's training sessions for home health aides. I also wanted to assess the feasibility of nurse assistants continuing their education and understand more about the demands of LPN coursework. With those objectives in mind, I conducted interviews with representatives of the three LPN training programs conducted in and around the city.

In addition to these supplementary investigations, I also became interested in the fit between welfare-related training and work. To address my questions, I surveyed thirty-four area training programs that had consistently offered classes to individuals from the welfare rolls and compiled the responses into a framework of citywide job development efforts for welfare recipients.

Appendix B:
The People

THE UNEMPLOYED AND UNDEREMPLOYED

Development

Mohamed Abdul, 44-year-old African American maintenance man
Josefina Burges, 21-year-old Puerto Rican assembler, kits department
Enid Castro, 20-year-old Puerto Rican receptionist
Will Chandler, 27-year-old African American crew supervisor
Noreen Diaz, 41-year-old Puerto Rican assembler, kits department
Ruth Fallows, 36-year-old white assembler, kits department
Greg Hanson, 25-year-old African American driver
Donna Hastings, 46-year-old African American bookkeeper
Ronnie James, 58-year-old white maintenance man
Edith Jenkins 27-year-old African American assembler, kits department
Sam Jessup, 23-year-old African American crew supervisor
Andy Johnson, 35-year-old African American weatherization technician
Maria Lopez, 22-year-old Puerto Rican assembler, kits department
Tomas Lopez, 22-year-old Puerto Rican crew supervisor
Juan Martinez, 47-year-old Puerto Rican warehouse manager
Henry Thompson, 49-year-old white manager, kits department
Carla Whitaker, 24-year-old Puerto Rican assembler, kits department
Barbara Wilson, 25-year-old African American assembler, kits department

Church Hall

Lynn Brown, 25-year-old African American nurse assistant
Donna Dixson, 28-year-old white nurse assistant
Joan Ford, 30-year-old African American nurse assistant

Nil Harper, 23-year-old African American nurse assistant
Dina Haskell, 28-year-old African American nurse assistant

Concordance Steps

Sefan Ang, 40-year-old Cambodian woodworker in the straight stair department
Moeun Daun, 39-year-old Cambodian woodworker in the straight stair department
Chan Monivong, 42-year-old Cambodian foreman and CNC operator
Tang Preah, 39-year-old Cambodian woodworker in the straight stair department
Koung Sisowath, 30-year-old Cambodian woodworker in the rail department
Peang Sothearos, 38-year-old Cambodian woodworker in the straight stair department

The Pharmacies at Jackson Hospital

Namib Anwari, 38-year-old Afghani pharmacy technician, cardiac wing
Kay James, 33-year-old African American pharmacy technician, floater
Pauline Pierce, 30-year-old African American pharmacy technician, anesthesia program
Ahmed Roashan, 35-year-old Afghani pharmacy technician, obstetrics
Mary Russell, 31-year-old African American pharmacy technician, cardiac wing
Tom Russo, 33-year-old white pharmacy technician, psychiatric wing
Donna Watkins, 32-year-old African American pharmacy technician, obstetrics
Samantha Wright, 36-year-old African American pharmacy technician, psychiatric wing

TEACHERS, SUPERVISORS, AND COLLEAGUES

Development

ADMINISTRATIVE, COUNSELING, AND TEACHING STAFF

Helen Anderson, office manager, Archives
Karen Casey, computer lab coordinator
Joan Chance, homeless project manager

Ron Duncan, systems coordinator, Archives
Helena Gay, case manager
Nava Gopalan, job skills counselor
John Harris, job skills counselor
Joe Jenkins, human resources director
Dick Jones, manager, Archives
Catherine Peace, business consultant
Bill Perkins, director
Pat Prescott, Kits Department supervisor
Theresa Randle, case manager
Mike Small, comptroller
Ray Smith, Kits Department supervisor
Walt Smith, files manager, Archives
Ben Spencer, case manager
Mary Spencer, business skills trainer
James Taylor, human resources manager
Miriam Velez, former receptionist
Frank Young, job skills counselor

TRAINEES

Tyrone Brown
Tom Clark
Joan Coltrane
Blake Danner
Charles Henderson
Robert James
Richard Price
Mia Sanders

Church Hall

ADMINISTRATIVE AND PROFESSIONAL STAFF

Rose Banks, LPN
Liz Bishop, quality assurance
Maryann Clark, director of nursing
Ron Driver, director
Linda Donaldson, LPN
Nia Gates, personnel officer
Evita Gomez, nurse assistant trainer
Pam Griffin, LPN

Kathy Hicks, LPN
Ann Miller, LPN
Carol Nelson, physical therapist
Pat Sherwood, RN
Charles Smith, housekeeper
Brenda Turner, supply clerk
Debra Waterman, DPW trainer
Terry Whitman, RN

NURSE ASSISTANTS

Ophelia Adams
Helen Blackman
Tesha Brown
Alice Burton
Kathy Hahn
Phyllis Hamptom
Nancy Henderson
Carlita Henry
Gladys Hopkins
Cynthia Hudson
Sophia Hudson
Jerry James

Henrietta Jessup
Cari Jones
Linda Jones
Charlotte Kingston
Teresa Sanchez
Katie Simon
Tasha Simpson
Jane Turner
Allie West
Mary Winston
Barbara Young

Concordance Steps

TRAINERS AND STATE OFFICIALS

Bill Dougherty, VES training program director
Caren Kurtz, VES job developer
Alfred Russell, program manager, State Office for Refugee Affairs

SUPERVISORY STAFF

Tim Brown, computer programmer
Jake Hansen, supervisor of the rail department
Jay Hawks, owner
John Jacobson, draftsperson
Pete Somelski, shop foreman

SHOP FLOOR WORKERS

Albert Medina, woodworker in the rail department
Dave Somerton, woodworker in circular stairs
George Simpson, woodworker in the rail department

The Pharmacies at Jackson Hospital

SUPERVISORY STAFF

Khristin Carlson, assistant director
Bob Clay, clinical pharmacist

Jim Howell, training director, health care Local
James Kelly, former training director
Karen Miller, director of training
Sunny Morris, operations coordinator
Cindy Peterson, pharmacist
Dan Quick, manager, outpatient service
Teddy Stokes, clinical pharmacist
Donald Phillips, clinical pharmacist who conducted research on the pharmacy's manpower needs
Joe Smith, clinical pharmacist who conducted research on the pharmacy's manpower needs
Carol Sullivan, clinical pharmacist

PHARMACY TECHNICIANS

Missy Brown, home infusion service
Cathy Chambers, cardiac wing
Faith Hansen, chemo wing
Lisa Henry, chemo wing
Chas Hopewell, outpatient pharmacy
Johnny Michaels, home infusion service
Kim Sherman, split shift technician
Barb Silver, technician trainee

Appendix C:
State-Mandated Nurse Assistant
Certification Training (Forlizzi 1992)

NURSE ASSISTANT TRAINING COURSE CONTENT

At least 16 hours of training in the following areas before any patient contact:

- communication and interpersonal skills
- infection control
- safety/emergency procedures, including the Heimlich maneuver
- promoting residents' independence
- respecting residents' rights

And must also address the following areas:

- Basic nursing skills:
  - taking and recording vital signs
  - measuring and recording height and weight
  - caring for the residents' environment
  - recognizing abnormal changes in body functions and the importance of reporting such changes to a supervisor
  - caring for residents when death is imminent

- Personal care skills:
  - bathing
  - grooming, including mouth care
  - dressing
  - toileting

- assisting with eating and hydration
- proper feeding techniques
- skin care

- Mental health and social service needs:
  - modifying aide's behavior in response to resident's behavior
  - awareness of developmental tasks associated with aging
  - responding to residents' behavior
  - allowing the residents to make personal choices, providing and reinforcing other behavior consistent with the residents' dignity
  - using the residents' families as a source of emotional support

- Care of cognitively impaired residents:
  - techniques for addressing the unique needs and behaviors of individuals with dementia
  - communicating with cognitively impaired residents
  - understanding the behavior of cognitively impaired residents
  - appropriate responses to the behavior of cognitively impaired residents
  - methods of reducing the effects of cognitive impairment

- Basic restorative services:
  - training the residents in self-care according to the residents' abilities
  - use of assistive devices in transferring, ambulation, eating, and dressing
  - maintenance of range of motion
  - proper turning and positioning in bed and chair
  - bowel and bladder retraining
  - care and use of prosthetic and orthotic devices

- Residents' rights:
  - providing privacy and maintenance of confidentiality
  - promoting the residents' rights to make personal choices to accommodate their needs
  - giving assistance in resolving grievances and disputes
  - providing needed assistance to residents in getting to and participating in resident and family groups and other activities

- maintaining care and security of residents' personal possessions
- promoting the residents' rights to be free from abuse, mistreatment, and neglect, and the need to report any instances of such treatment to appropriate facility staff
- avoiding the need for restraints in accordance with current professional standards

Appendix D:
Church Hall's Clinical Performance Summary

Skill	*Date Practice*	*Satisfactory*	*Needs*
Admission			
Assessment of ADL			
Bed making			
occupied			
unoccupied			
Bedpan use			
Bladder training			
Bowel training			
Catheter care			
Communication			
Visually impaired			
Hearing impaired			
Discharge			
Exercise			
Passive Range of Motion			
Active Range of Motion Feeding			

Appendix E:
Pharmacy Committees at Jackson Hospital

Education Committee	looks at staff development and education programs in the department
Program Standards	writes and reviews department policies
Technician Drug Distribution	looks at, improves, and updates department
Information Systems Committee	procedures, information systems, drug distribution (all techs)
Pharmacy Practice Committee	looks at how pharmacy practice is changing and what the department can do
Robotics team	planning installation of robot
Committee on nursing and pharmacy	meets quarterly as a forum for communication between nursing and pharmacy
Technician Trainee Selection Committee	helps interview and select technician trainees

Task Forces

Improving communications

Improving job satisfaction

Looking at dress code issue

Quality Improvement

Looking at medicine transfers

Preventing medical errors

Notes

INTRODUCTION

1. Federal guidelines require states to "conduct a program, designed to serve all political subdivisions in the State (not necessarily in a uniform manner), that provides assistance to needy families with (or expecting) children and provides parents with job preparation, work, and support services to enable them to leave the program and become self sufficient" (HR 3734 1996).

2. Because the studies differ in terms of methodology and sample size, exact comparisons of income earned have been difficult to make across states.

3. The Pennsylvania Department of Welfare (1999) also found that wages of former welfare recipients who continued to work in the same job increased 3 to 5 percent each quarter.

4. The earned income tax credit has been positioned both as an antipoverty measure and a remedy for low-wage jobholders. Eligible individuals apply the credit directly to their federal income tax, and receive a refund when the credit is greater than taxes paid (U.S. Department of Labor 1997).

5. In an attempt to protect Henry, Ruth, and the other men and women mentioned in this book—welfare recipients, trainees, trainers, employees, and employers alike—they all have been given pseudonyms. Many of these individuals occupied low-wage, low-status jobs, and they often reminded me of their precariousness in the workplace. In order to avoid any risk of their losing their jobs, I therefore made all attempts to maintain their anonymity. In the same vein, the names of government officials, the four workplaces, and the city itself have also been changed or, at times, omitted.

6. A transitional housing project also under Development's auspices.

7. Jean Jackson's (1990, 3) writing is relevant here. "Given the sample's lack of systematic representatives, this essay should be seen in qualitative terms. The reasonably large sample size guards against bias in only the crudest fashion, since so many complex variables are present."

CHAPTER 1. DEVELOPMENT AND THE HARDEST TO SERVE

1. This early MDRC evaluation revealed four factors associated with early termination from supported work programs across the nation. The individuals who left early:

- had more sources of nonlabor income;
- were white;
- received welfare upon enrolment in a supported work project;
- lived in Oakland or Philadelphia.

Trainees who left early believed they could access better options outside the program. In the same vein, the supported work programs that targeted AFDC recipients evidenced the highest retention rates, perhaps because many women felt they had few workplace options outside the training.

2. According to organizational consultant Larry Hirschhorn (1984), Taylor's scientific management, the assembly-line work that is done by 10 percent of all industrial labor is characterized by its:

- standardization;
- continuity of production;
- constrained or rigid machinery;
- reduction of work to simple labor.

Work at Development did not fit this description. It was not standardized, production was not continuous, and the use of machines was at a minimum.

3. CETA, the Comprehensive Employment and Training Act of 1973, was one of a long list of attempts to streamline federally funded job training. CETA both consolidated training programs under one umbrella and made job training available to anyone who had been employed for more than one week.

CHAPTER 2. CHURCH HALL AND SINGLE MOTHERS ON WELFARE

1. PTC, or Private Training Corporation, was a for-profit proprietary school downtown that offered training for nurse assistants, data processors, and security guards.

2. The facility offered physical and occupational therapy, audiological services, and recreational therapy. Its activities department also coordinated a range of recreational services for residents including arts and crafts, games and socials, Happy Hours on Fridays, intergenerational programs in conjunction with area elementary schools, holiday celebrations, a restaurant night the last Wednesday of each month, and birthday parties.

3. According to a report by the state's Department of Public Welfare, the program had placed more than 122,000 former welfare recipients in jobs during its first three years of existence. The report continues that "this novel program does not merely find jobs for welfare recipients: It devises personalized training for clients and supports them with extended health care benefits, child care subsidies, transportation stipends, and help with paying for work clothes and tools" (Department of Public Welfare 1990, 3)

4. While Dina had been able to obtain her certification by participating in a welfare-funded training program, certification had been elusive for Joan and eighty of her fellow nurse assistants. Through the DPW/Church Hall collaboration, Joan was able to both re-enter the job market and become certified through the facility's in-house training.

5. OBRA also required that every nurse assistant be enrolled in a state-maintained nurse aide registry. To be enrolled, an aide must complete a state-approved nurse aide training program within two years of taking the state certification exam.

6. Hammond Hall was a geriatric facility owned by the same physician consortium that owned Church Hall. Three nurse assistants attending this certification training had been hired to work at Hammond Hall after the training.

7. The 1999 poverty guideline set by the Department of Health and Human Services for a family of four is $16,700 (Federal Register 1999). An hourly rate of $6.00 translates to $12,480 a year.

CHAPTER 3. CONCORDANCE STEPS AND SOUTHEAST ASIAN REFUGEES

1. According to an article published in a local newspaper, Concordance's market consisted of custom builders of new single-family homes that cost anywhere between $250,000 and $1 million (Binzen 1989).

2. According to Hopkins (1996), of those one million, 150,000 were from Cambodia. The largest numbers fled during 1980 to 1982.

3. Apple quotes from Michael Omi and Howard Winant's *Racial Formation in the United States* (1986) in his explanation of the political forces at play in the United States during the 1980s.

4. Defined as "disturbance of regular rhythm," Erickson and Shultz

(1982) include the *false start*, the *double take*, *startling expression*, *nervous gestures*, the *stammer*, and *arrhythmia* in this category.

5. Like many other small businesses, Concordance was embroiled in battles with OSHA, EEOC, and the EPA, skirmishes that consumed the director's time and energy and caused employees concern. One of several ongoing battles concerned Moeun's injury. According to OSHA regulations, the electric saw that Moeun had been using should have been covered with a saw guard. Concordance was fined $24,000 for the omission. Although the case was in appeal, it catalyzed employees' constant discussion and concern over the possibility of OSHA's closing down the company, their losing their jobs, and their varying courses of possible action.

CHAPTER 4. JACKSON HOSPITAL'S PHARMACIES AND THE CREAM OF THE UNEMPLOYED

1. The other nineteen pharmacy technicians had work experience in other hospital pharmacies, in the military, or were hired before the implementation of Jackson's pharmacy technician training and were subsequently trained on the job.

2. PICs dispersed funds for job training, customized job training, retraining, and dislocated worker training as part of Title II of the 1982 federal Job Training Partnership Act (JTPA)

3. According to Phillips and Smith (1984), success on the entrance examinations reflected a minimum of one year of high school algebra and 10th grade reading skills.

4. Sixty dollars a year was afforded to each full-time technician for association or membership dues, and two technicians attended the American Association of Pharmacy Technicians conference each year.

CHAPTER 5. ANALYZING THE CIRCLE

1. Wilson quotes "What Getting Ahead Means to Employer and Inner-City Workers," a paper presented by his colleague Kathryn Neckerman at the 1993 Chicago Urban Poverty and Family Life Conference.

CHAPTER 6. OTHER POSSIBILITIES

1. The findings of a multisite study, conducted the fourth quarter after participant enrolment on CET and three other programs targeting mi-

nority female single parents, found "large increases in employment and earnings" only at CET. One year after enrollment, a higher proportion of CET's participants worked in administrative support, clerical and production capacities, a higher percentage received fringe benefits, and a lower proportion worked in lower-level service jobs and as laborers (Gordon and Burghardt 1990).

2. Another strategy that has been offered as a solution for the problem of low-wage jobs involves training that pays a livable wage. The most highly touted of these efforts has been Step-Up, an employment training project with Chicago's Housing Authority. Step-Up used housing rehabilitation funds to train welfare mothers in construction skills. During the eighteen-month training, women received an average wage of $13.52 an hour to paint, lay tile, and hang doors in the city's housing projects. According to program operators, the initiative was an attempt to "give all of them [participating welfare recipients] a vision of how things could be" (Wilkerson 1994, D21). But while anecdotal evidence reveals participants who were proud of both their newly acquired skills and increased cash flow, Step-Up's strategy was short term at best. The jobs were not permanent. Sixteen percent of the trainees moved into temporary or lower paying jobs with the Housing Authority, and six percent were offered apprenticeship-related training with the carpentry union. However, there has been no assurance that the "vision of how things could be" has ever translated into how things are.

3. According to a report written by Amy Brown, Maria L. Buck, and Erik Skinner (1998) for the Manpower Demonstration Research Corporation (MDRC), "Tax credits have been mainly utilized by large firms in the retail and service sectors who learned of the eligibility of their workers after they were hired, and thus received the credit retroactively. In other words, the credit did not affect the firms' hiring decisions. Overall, utilization rates of tax credits have been low, accounting for less than half a percent of the private employment during their peak use in 1985. The low utilization rates have been attributed to regulatory burdens and lack of support and marketing by the administering agencies. One study suggests that tax credits may actually reduce a targeted individual's chance of being hired. In the study, welfare recipients were randomly assigned to one of three groups: one presented vouchers to potential employers for direct cash rebates; the second presented vouchers for tax credits; and the third had no vouchers. Both groups of job seekers with vouchers were significantly less likely to find employment than the job seekers without vouchers. One explanation for this result is that the voucher signaled to employers that the job seeker was a welfare recipient and thus attached a stigma that discouraged hiring."

APPENDICES

1. According to DPW's "Annual Report" of 1990–1991 (1992, 52), the Job Development Unit's (JDU) "primary goal is to place Public Assistance recipients with multiple problems into jobs. Job openings are developed through mass mailings to local employers. Those expressing an interest in JDU services are contacted by telephone or visited for an in-depth assessment of their employment needs. Employers with job openings submit their requirements to JDU. Job orders are prepared and transmitted to all 19-district offices. A computerized 'Client Tracking and Reporting System' assists caseworkers in obtaining a list of all suitably skilled clients who are then contacted and referred to the employer for a job interview. Interested employers are periodically contacted to determine if new job opportunities have arisen."

2. While I began this project with the intention of collecting data in six worksites, during the first year of the research process I scaled back to four in order to ease logistical demands.

3. The form was completed by the trainer during the nurse assistants' clinical training.

Glossary

AFDC: Aid to Families with Dependent Children, welfare nomenclature for welfare recipients with one or more dependent children under the age of eighteen, generally associated with single female heads of households. AFDC was replaced in 1996 by TANF.

BLOCK GRANT: A quantity of money given by the federal government directly to the states for provision of particular services. Although block grants are designated in terms of purpose, the states have some latitude in the way the money will be spent.

CETA: Comprehensive Employment and Training Act of 1973, a large scale subsidized-work program designed to decrease unemployment through Public Service Employment. The Job Training Partnership Act replaced CETA in 1982.

CHRONICALLY NEEDY: A General Assistance (GA) category for individuals who received cash assistance from the state on a permanent basis. Recipients were: age forty-five and older: under the age of eighteen or in school and expecting to graduate by the age of nineteen; distinguished by a physical or mental handicap that prevented their working; in treatment for substance abuse; or unemployed but had worked full time for forty-eight months of the previous eight years and run out of unemployment benefits. The category was abolished during this research.

CHURCH HALL: A long-term health care facility.

CONCORDANCE STEPS: A for-profit woodshop that built customized stairs.

CNC: The computerized, numerically controlled lathe, operated by Chan Monivong at Concordance Steps.

DEVELOPMENT: An inner-city supported work program.

DISLOCATED WORKERS: Individuals who are unemployed because of layoffs or company closings.

DPW: Department of Public Welfare.

ESL: English as a Second Language.

FAMILY SUPPORT ACT (FSA): Was passed in 1988 as an attempt to deter long-term dependence on AFDC. It required AFDC recipients'

273

participation in, instead of simply registering for, states' JOBS programs. FSA also extended that requirement to recipients whose youngest child was age three or older and oldest child was age six and older.

GA: General Assistance, a state-funded welfare program providing assistance to adults under the age of sixty-five years. Most recipients were individuals or couples with no children. In the state in which this research was conducted, General Assistance was divided into two categories, Chronically and Transitionally Needy.

JACKSON HOSPITAL: A large urban teaching hospital.

JOBS: Job Opportunities and Basic Skills Training Program, enacted by the Family Support Act of 1988. JOBS required state and local governments to implement a welfare employment program for AFDC recipients, involving a minimum proportion of eligible recipients, and targeting funds to individuals most likely to become long-term welfare recipients.

JTPA: Job Training Partnership Act of 1982, a Federal Act that provides funds for job training. Title IIA specifically targets youth and unskilled adults. Title IIB funds summer employment and training programs for disadvantaged youth, and Title IIC, year-round programs for youth. Title III assists dislocated workers.

MEANS TESTED: Programs that base eligibility for participation upon economic status.

MULTIPLE BARRIERS: Term for individuals who faced more than one impediment (e.g., substance abuse, being handicapped, homeless, ex-offenders, etc.) to obtaining successful employment.

PIC: Private Industry Council, originally established in 1978 by Title VII of the Comprehensive Employment and Training Act (CETA) as the structure for private sector involvement in training and employment efforts. Under JTPA, PICs were given the leadership role in planning and developing employment training in 1982, and dispersed and monitored JTPA moneys for job training.

PERSONAL RESPONSIBILITY AND WORK OPPORTUNITY RECONCILIATION ACT (PRWORA): The most recent welfare reform bill, passed in 1996, which replaced AFDC with block grants to states for Temporary Assistance for Needy Families (TANF), limited government assistance to five years, and modified provisions for the receipt of food stamps.

PERFORMANCE-BASED FUNDING: Funds disbursed to training program providers in a series of steps built around performance standards (usually a minimum percentage of individuals enrolled, completing training, and placed in jobs).

REFUGEE RESETTLEMENT PROGRAM: Federally funded program

for refugees, providing cash and/or medical benefits during an individual's first months in the United States. After this initial period, refugees were eligible for DPW benefits.

SDA: Service Delivery Area, a term used by government to designate a local area for fund dispersal and service allocation.

SPOC: Single Point of Contact, the state's program to coordinate services among the Office of Employment Security, the Private Industry Council, and the Department of Public Welfare for AFDC recipients who participate in the JOBS program. Implemented by local PICs, SPOC offered educational screening, classes, job training, job search, and extended medical and child care benefits.

TANF: Temporary Assistance for Needy Families, federal block grants to states that replaced AFDC and other programs under the Personal Responsibility and Work Opportunity Reconciliation Act (PRWORA) of 1996.

TAP: Targeted Assistance Program, a grant initiative developed through the State's Refugee Resettlement Program to fund employment programs in counties with high refugee populations.

TN: Transitionally Needy, the state's welfare nomenclature for one category of its General Assistance (GA) population. Defined as unemployed, ablebodied adults, aged eighteen to forty-five, who were eligible for cash assistance and full medical benefits for ninety days of each year. After the ninety days, TNs continued to be eligible for limited medical benefits. In 1994, the TN category was combined with that of Chronically Needy and benefits were scaled back from 90 days a year to two months every two years. In 1995 the category was completely abolished when state legislators eliminated all welfare-related cash assistance for single adults.

VESL: Vocational English as a Second Language

References

Abrahamson, M., E. H. Mizruchi, and C. A. Hornung. 1976. *Stratification and Mobility*. New York: Macmillan.

Adas, M. 1986. "From Foot Dragging to Flight: The Evasive History of Peasant Avoidance Protest in South and Southeast Asia." In *Everyday Forms of Peasant Resistance in South-East Asia* (Library of Peasant Studies, No 9), edited by J. C. Scott and B. J. TriaKerkvliet, Totowa, N. J.: Frank Cass & Co. Ltd.

Abt Associates. 1993. *The National JTPA Study: Title II-A Impacts on Earnings and Employment at 18 Months*. Research and Evaluation Report Series 93-C. Washington, D. C.: U.S. Department of Labor.

Anderson, E. 1994. "The Code of the Streets." *The Atlantic Monthly*, May.

Apple, M. W. 1993. *Official Knowledge: Democratic Education in a Conservative Age*. New York: Routledge.

Ashforth, B. E., and R. H. Humphrey 1997. "The Ubiquity and Potency of Labeling in Organizations." *Organization Science* 8:48.

Auletta, K. 1983. *The Underclass*. New York: First Vantage Books.

Bailey, T. R. 1987. *Immigrant and Native Workers: Contrasts and Competition*. Boulder, Colo.: Westview Press.

Ball, J. 1984. "Implementation of the Supported Work Program Model." In *The National Supported Work Demonstration*, edited by R. G. Hollister Jr., P. Kemper, and R. A. Maynard. Madison: University of Wisconsin Press.

Bane, M. J. 1997. "Welfare as We Might Know It." *The American Prospect* 30:47–53.

Bassie, Laurie J. 1994. "Stimulating Employment and Increasing Opportunity for the Current Work Force." *The Work Alternative*, Washington D. C.: The Urban Institute Press.

Becker, G. 1975. *Human Capital*. New York: National Bureau of Economic Research.

Binzen, P. 1989. "Back on Land, He's Building a Stairway to Success." *Philadelphia Inquirer*, 23 January.

Bluestone, B., and B. Harrison. 1982. *The Deindustrialization of America*. New York: Basic Books.

Bostwick, F. J. 1982. Job Order/Church Hall Nursing Home Nursing Assistants. Internal memo, Community Services Department of the Department of Public Welfare, 28 October.

Bourdieu, P. 1977. *Outline of a Theory of Practice*. New York: Cambridge University Press.

———— 1990. *The Logic of Practice*. Cambridge: Polity Press.

———— 1997. "The Forms of Capital." In *Education: Culture, Economy, and Society*, edited by A. H. Halsey et al. Oxford: Oxford University Press.

Brown, A., M. L. Buck, and E. Skinner. 1998. Business Partnerships: How to Involve Employers in Welfare Reform. (published and disseminated as part of MDRC's ReWORKing Welfare technical assistance project) New York: Manpower Demonstration Research Corporation.

Bureau of Employment Training Programs. 1993. Joint Job Initiative Results 1987–1993, Transitionally Needy. Pennsylvania: Department of Public Welfare, Commonwealth of Pennsylvania.

Bureau of National Affairs 1986. *The Changing Workplace: New Directions in Staffing and Rescheduling*. Washington D. C.: General Accounting Office.

Burkhardt, F. (ed.) 1981. *The Principles of Psychology*. Volume 1. Cambridge: Harvard University Press.

Cammisa, A. M. 1998. *From Rhetoric to Reform?: Welfare Policy in American Politics*, Boulder, Colo.: Westview Press.

Carnevale, A. P., L. J. Gainer, and A. S. Meltzer. 1988. *Workplace Basics: The Skills Employers Want*. Alexandria, Va.: The American Society for Training and Development.

Carnevale, A. P., L. J. Gainer, and J. Villet. 1990. *Training in America: The Organization and Strategic Role of Training*. San Francisco: Jossey-Bass Publishers.

Center for Occupational and Professional Assessment. 1989. *Nurse Aide (Assistant) Written-Oral Examination*. Princeton, N. J.: Educational Testing Service.

Clark, B. 1960. "The 'Cooling-Out' Function in Higher Education." *American Journal of Sociology* 65:576–96.

Clinton, W. 1998. Remarks by the President at Signing Ceremony for the Work Force Investment Act of 1998. The White House, Office of the Press Secretary, August 7. *http://www/whitehouse.gov/WH/New/html/19980807.html*.

The Commission on the Skills of the American Workforce. 1990. *America's Choice: High Skills or Low Wages!* Washington D. C.: National Center on Education and the Economy.

Couch, K. A. 1992. "New Evidence on the Long-term Effects of Employment Training Programs." *Journal of Labor Economics* 10:4.

County Assistance Office. 1992. Open Line to Welfare. In-house report, April.

Cross, K. P. 1981. *Adults as Learners*. San Francisco.: Jossey-Bass, Inc..

D'Andrade, R. G. 1991. "Schemas and Motivation." In *Human Motives and*

Cultural Models, edited by R. G. D'Andrade and C. Strauss. Cambridge: Cambridge University Press.

Danziger, S. H., and D. H. Weinberg. 1986. *Fighting Poverty: What Works and What Doesn't*. Cambridge: Harvard University Press.

Dean, M. M. 1999. "Activists Assess PA Welfare Reform: Low-Paying Entry-Level Jobs are Target of McProtest." *Philadelphia Daily News*, 2 December.

DeParle, J. 1997. "Getting Opal Caples to Work." *The New York Times Magazine*, 24 August.

————— 1998. "What Welfare-to-Work Really Means." *The New York Times Magazine*, 29 December.

————— 1999a. "Bold Effort Leaves Much Unchanged for the Poor." *The New York Times*, 30 December.

————— 1999b. "As Welfare Rolls Shrink, Load on Relatives Grows." *The New York Times*, 21 February.

Department of Public Welfare. 1990. A Steady Progression 1987–1990. Commonwealth of Pennsylvania.

————— 1992. Annual Report of 1990–1991. Commonwealth of Pennsylvania.

DeWolf, R. 1992. "PIC Schools that Didn't Make the Grade." *The Philadelphia Daily News*, 5 November.

Dixon, J. 1994. "Welfare Reform Hot with Candidates." *The Philadelphia Inquirer*, 28 September.

Dreyfus, H. L., and P. Rabinow. 1982. *Michel Foucault: Beyond Structuralism and Hermeneutics*. Chicago: University of Chicago Press.

Edin, K., and L. Lein. 1997. *Making Ends Meet: How Single Mothers Survive Welfare and Low-Wage Work*. New York: Russell Sage Foundation.

Ellwood, D. T. 1988. *Poor Support: Poverty in the American Family*. New York: Basic Books.

Erickson, F. 1987. "Transformation and School Success: The Politics and Culture of Educational Achievement." *Anthropology of Education Quarterly* 18:335–55.

Erickson, F. and J. Shultz. 1982. *The Counselor as Gatekeeper*. New York: Academic Press.

Esping-Anderson, Gosta. 1990. *The Three Worlds of Welfare Capitalism*. Princeton, N. J.: Princeton University Press.

Federal Register. 1999. 64:52, (March 18): 13428–30.

Fine, M. 1991. *Framing Drop-Outs: Notes on the Politics of an Urban Public High School*. Albany: State University of New York Press.

Firestone, W. A., and R. E. Herriott 1984. "Multisite Qualitative Policy Research." In *Ethnography in Educational Evaluation*, edited by D. Fetterman. Beverly Hills, Calif.: Sage Publications.

Forlizzi, L. 1992. Nurse Aide Training and Competency Evaluation:

Memo to Administrators of Long-Term Care Facilities and Nurse Aide Training Programs. Commonwealth of Pennsylvania, June 22.

Freire, P. 1970. *Pedagogy of the Oppressed*. New York: Herter and Herter.

Geertz, C. 1973. *The Interpretation of Cultures*. New York: Basic Books.

General Accounting Office. 1983. *Greater Emphasis on Early Employment and Better Monitoring Needed in Indochinese Refugee Resettlement Program. Report to Congress*. Washington, D. C.

———— 1992. *Integrating Human Services: Linking At-Risk Families with Services More Successful than System Reform Efforts*. Washington, D. C.

———— 1993. *Self Sufficiency: Opportunities and Disincentives on the road to Economic Independence*. Washington, D. C.

———— 1994a. *Multiple Employment Training Programs: Overlapping Programs Can Add Unnecessary Administrative Costs*. Washington, D. C.

———— 1994b. *Multiple Employment Training Programs: Conflicting Requirements Hamper Delivery of Services*. Washington, D. C.

———— 1994c. *Multiple Employment Training Programs: Most Federal Agencies Do Not Know If Their Programs Are Working Effectively*. Washington, D. C.

———— 1994d. *Multiple Employment Training Programs: Overlap Among Programs Raises Questions about Efficiency*. Washington, D. C.

———— 1994e. *Multiple Employment Training Programs: How Legislative Proposals Address Concerns*. Washington, D. C.

———— 1994f. *Multiple Employment Training Programs: Basic Program Data Often Missing*. Washington, D. C.

Gibbs, N. 1994. "The Vicious Cycle." *Time*, 20 June, pp. 25–33.

Gibson, M. 1988. Accommodation Without Assimilation: Sikh Immigrants in an American High School. Ithaca, N. Y.: Cornell University Press.

Giddens, A. 1984. *The Constitution of Safety*. Berkeley, Ca.: University of California Press.

Giroux, H. 1983. *Theory and Resistance in Education: A Pedagogy for the Opposition*. South Hadley, Mass.: Bergin & Garvey

Goffman, E. 1959. *The Presentation of Self in Everyday Life*. New York: Doubleday.

———— 1961. *Encounters: Two Studies in the Sociology of Interaction*. Indianapolis: The Bobbs-Merrill Company, Inc..

Gordon, A., and J. Burghardt. 1990. *Short-Term Economic Impacts*. New York: Rockefeller Foundation.

Gordon, L. 1994. *Pitied but Not Entitled: Single Mothers and the History of Welfare*. Cambridge: Harvard University Press.

Gray, K. C., and E. L. Herr. 1998. *Workforce Education: The Basics*. Needham Heights, Mass.: Allyn & Bacon.

Grinker, W. J. 1979. "Supported Work: An Employment Strategy for the Underclass." *USA Today* 107:39–41.

Gueron, J. M., and E. Pauly. 1991. *From Welfare to Work*. New York: Russell Sage Foundation.

Hand, L. 1989. "Cambodians Help Ease Labor Crunch." *Woodshop News*, September.

Hannerz, U. 1969. *Soulside*. New York: Columbia Press.

Harrington, M. 1962. *The Other America: Poverty in the U.S.* Kingsport, Tenn.: Macmillan.

Harris, K. M. 1997. *Teen Mothers and the Revolving Welfare Door*. Philadelphia: Temple University Press.

Herr, T., R. Halpern, and A. Conrad. 1991. *Changing What Counts: Re-Thinking the Journey out of Welfare*. Evanston, Ill: Center for Urban Affairs and Policy Research.

Hirschhorn, L. 1984. *Beyond Mechanization: Work and Technology in a Post-Industrial Age*. Cambridge, Mass.: The MIT Press.

Holcomb, P. A., L. Pavetti, C. Ratcliffe, and S. Riedinger. 1998. *Building an Employment Focused Welfare System: Work First and Other Work-Oriented Strategies in Five States*. Washington, D. C.: The Urban Institute.

Hollister, R. G. Jr. 1984. "The Design and Implementation of the Supported Work Evaluation." In *The National Supported Work Demonstration*, edited by R. G. Hollister Jr., P. Kemper, and R. A. Maynard. Madison: The University of Wisconsin Press.

hooks, b. 1990. *Yearning: race, gender, and cultural politics*. Boston: South End Press.

Hopkins, C. 1996. *Braving a New World: Cambodian/Khmer Refugees in an American City*. Westport, Conn.: Bergin and Garvey.

Hudson Institute. 1988. *Opportunity 2000*. Indianapolis: U.S. Department of Labor.

Hymes, D. 1972. Introduction to *Functions of Language in the Classroom*, edited by C. B. Cazden, V. P. John, and D. Hymes. New York: Teachers College Press.

Jackson, J. E. 1990. "I Am a Fieldnote: Fieldnotes as a Symbol of Professional Identity." In *Fieldnotes: The Making of Anthropology*, edited by R. Sanjek, 3–33. Ithaca, N. Y.: Cornell University Press.

Jenkins, R. 1992. *Pierre Bourdieu*. London: Routledge.

Johnson-Pawlson, J., and M. E. Goodwin. 1990. *How to be a Nurse Assistant: Career Training in Long Term Care*. Washington, D. C.: American Health Care Association.

Kahler, D. W. 1982. *Literacy at Work: Linking Literacy to Business Management Skills*. Washington, D. C.: Creative Associates, Inc.

Katz, M. B. 1989. *The Undeserving Poor*. New York: Pantheon Books.

Kemper, P., D. A. Long, C. Thornton, R. Hollister, V. Leach, C. Whitebread, and D. Zimmerman. 1980. "The Supported Work Evaluation:

Final Cost Benefit Analysis." In *Youth Knowledge Development Reports, Youth Work Experience, Enhanced Work Projects—The Supported Work Approach for Youth*. New York: Manpower Demonstration Research Corporation.

Kingfisher, C. Pelissier. 1996. *Women in the American Welfare Trap*. Philadelphia: University of Pennsylvania Press.

Kutner, M. A., R. Z. Sherman, L. Webb, and C. J. Fisher. 1991. *A Review of the National Workplace Literacy Program*. Washington, D. C.: Pelavin Associates, Inc.

LaLonde, R. J. 1986. "Evaluating the Econometric Evaluations of Training Programs with Experimental Data." *American Economic Review* 76:4.

Lave, J. 1993. "The Practice of Learning." In *Understanding Practice: Perspectives on Activity and Context*, edited by S. Chaiklin and J. Lave. Cambridge: Cambridge University Press.

Liebow, E. 1967. *Tally's Corner: A Study of Negro Streetcorner Men*. Boston: Little, Brown and Company.

Lopez, S. 1994. *Third and Indiana*. New York: Viking Press.

Lurie, I., and J. L. Hagen 1993. *Implementing Jobs: The Initial Design and Structure of Local Programs*. Albany: The Nelson A. Rockefeller Institute of Government.

MacDonald, J. 1990. *Annual Report*. 1 January–31 December 1980. Development Corporation.

Marsick, V. J. 1990. "Action Learning and Reflection in the Workplace." In *Fostering Critical Reflection in Adulthood* , edited by J. Mezirow and Associates. San Francisco: Jossey-Bass Publishers.

Mason, S. R. 1986. *Training Southeast Asian Women for Employment: Public Policies and Community Programs 1975–1985*. Minneapolis: Southeast Asian Refugee Studies Project.

Maynard, R. A. 1984. "The Impacts of Supported Work on Youth." In *The National Supported Work Demonstration*, edited by R. G. Hollister Jr., P. Kemper, and R. A. Maynard. Madison: The University of Wisconsin Press.

——— 1995. "Preparing Recipients for Work." *Public Welfare* 53:21–26.

Mehan, H. (ed.) 1996. *Constructing School Success: The Consequences of Untracking Low-Achieving Students*. New York: Cambridge University Press.

Meredith, R. 1999. "Testing Welfare Applicants for Drugs." *The New York Times*, 30 May.

Mikulecky, L. 1993. "Workplace Literacy Programs: Organization and Incentives." In *What Makes Workers Learn: The Role of Incentives in Workplace Education and Training*, edited by D. Hirsch and D. A. Wagner. Philadelphia: Organization for Economic Co-operation and Development and Center for Educational Research and Development.

Mongaeu, S. (ed.) 1991. *Directory of Nursing Homes 1991–1992*. 5th edition. Phoenix: Oryx Press.

Nasar, S., and K. B. Mitchell. 1999. "Booming Job Market Draws Young Black Men into Fold." *The New York Times*, 23 May.

Oakes, J. 1986. *Keeping Track: How Schools Structure Inequality*. New Haven, Conn.: Yale University Press.

Ogbu, J. 1974. *The Next Generation: An Ethnography of Education in an Urban Neighborhood*. New York: Academic Press.

———— 1987. "Variability in Minority Responses to Schooling: Non immigrants vs. Immigrants." In *Interpretive Ethnography of Education at Home and Abroad* , edited by G. and L. Spindler. Hillside, N. J.: Lawrence Erlbaum Associates.

Omni, M., and H. Winant. 1986. *Racial Formation in the United States*. New York: Routledge.

"One Million Quit Welfare, Clinton Says." 1997. *The New York Times*, 6 July.

Ortner, S. 1984. "Theory in Anthropology since the Sixties." *Comparative Study of Society and History:*[vol?] 126–65.

Osterman, P. 1980. *Getting Started, the Youth Labor Market*. Cambridge, Mass.: MIT Press.

———— 1989. "New Directions for Job Training." In *Job Training for Women: The Promise and Limits of Public Policies*, edited by S. L. Harlan and R. J. Steinberg. Philadelphia: Temple University Press.

Passell, P. 1998. "Benefits Dwindle along with Wages for the Unskilled." *The New York Times*, 14 June.

Pennsylvania Association of County Affiliated Homes. 1992. PACAH Annual Survey.

Pennsylvania Department of Welfare. 1999. *Welfare Reform after Two Years*. Washington, D. C.: The Office of Income Maintenance.

Phillips, D., J. M., and J. E. Smith. 1984. "Six-month hospital-pharmacy-based technician training program." *American Journal of Hospital Pharmacy* 41:2614–17.

Polakow, V. 1993. *Lives on the Edge: Single Mothers and their Children in the Other America*. Chicago: University of Chicago Press.

Private Industry Council. 1992. Mission Statement.

Puchner, L. 1993. "Incentives for Adult Learning in Developing Countries: Lessons and Comparisons." In *What Makes Workers Learn: The Role of Incentives in Workplace Education and Training*, edited by D. Hirsch and D. A. Wagner. Philadelphia: Organization for Economic Co-operation and Development and Center for Educational Research and Development.

Rankin, R. A., and D. Hess. 1994. "President Outlines His Plan to Change Welfare System." *The Philadelphia Inquirer*, 15 June.

284   References

Reich, R. 1991a. "The REAL Economy." *The Atlantic* 267:2.

————. 1991b. *The Work of Nations: Preparing Ourselves for 21st Century Capitalism.* New York: Alfred A Knopf.

Reichert, D., and J. Tweedie. 1999. Programs and Services Funded with TANF and MOE. Paper developed for National Conference of State Legislatures.

Roberts, B., and J. Padden. 1998. *Welfare to Wages: Strategies to Assist the Private Sector to Employ Welfare Recipients.* Vol. 1 Flint, Mich.: Charles Stewart Mott Foundation.

Roseberry, W. 1989. *Anthropologies and Histories: Essays in Culture, History, and Political Economy.* New Brunswick, N. J.: Rutgers University Press.

Rubenson, K., and H. G. Schutze. 1993. "Learning at and through the Workplace: A Review of Participation and Adult Learning Theory." In *What Makes Workers Learn: The Role of Incentives in Workplace Education and Training,* edited by D. Hirsch and D. A. Wagner. Philadelphia: Organization for Economic Cooperation and Development and Center for Educational Research and Development.

Ryan, P. 1993. "Adult Learning and Work: Finance, Incentives, and Certification." In *What Makes Workers Learn: The Role of Incentives in Workplace Education and Training,* edited by D. Hirsch and D. A. Wagner. Philadelphia: Organization for Economic Co-operation and Development and Center for Educational Research and Development.

Sacks, H. 1972. "Notes on Police Assessment of Moral Character." In *Studies in Social Interaction,* edited by D. Sudnow. New York: The Free Press.

Sanjak, R. 1990a. "The Secret Life of Fieldnotes." In *Fieldnotes: The Makings of Anthropology,* edited by R. Sanjak. Ithaca, N. Y.: Cornell University Press.

———— 1990b. "Vocabulary for Fieldnotes." In *Fieldnotes: The Makings of Anthropology,* edited by R. Sanjak. Ithaca, N. Y.: Cornell University Press.

Schein, V. E. 1995. *Working From the Margins: Voices of Mothers in Poverty.* Ithaca, N. Y.: Cornell University Press.

Schwarz, J. E., and T. J. Volgy. 1992. *The Forgotten Americans.* New York: W.W. Norton & Company.

Scott, J. 1986. "Everyday Forms of Peasant Resistance." In *Everyday Forms of Peasant Resistant in Southeast Asia* (Library of Peasant Studies, No. 9), edited by J. C. Scott and B. J. TriaKerkvliet. Totowa, N. J.: Frank Cass & Co. Ltd.

Seitchik, A., J. Zornitsky, and C. Edmonds 1990. *Employer Strategies for a Changing Labor Force: A Primer on Innovative Programs and Policies.* Washington, D. C.: National Commission for Employment Policy.

Sewell, D. O. 1971. *Training the Poor: A Benefit-Cost Analysis of Manpower Programs in the U.S. Antipoverty Program*. Kingston, Ontario: Industrial Relations Center.

Sidel, R. 1996. *Keeping Women and Children Last: America's War on the Poor*. New York: Penguin Books.

Siegel, R. 1999. "Whitman Says Welfare Rolls Have Been Cut in Half." *The Philadelphia Inquirer*, 15 December.

Sipress, A. 1992. "Cardinal, Mayor Ask for Peace." *The Philadelphia Inquirer*, 21 July.

Skidmore, F. 1984. "The Impacts of Supported Work on Former Drug Addicts." In *The National Supported Work Demonstration* , edited by R. G. Hollister Jr., P. Kemper, and R. A. Maynard. Madison: University of Wisconsin Press.

Skocpol, T. 1991. "Targeting within Universalism: Politically Viable Policies to Combat Poverty in the United States." In *The Urban Underclass*, edited by Christopher Jencks and Paul E. Peterson. Washington, D. C.: Brookings Institute.

Smith, T. J., and C. Trist. 1988. *Training and Educating the Work Force in the Nineties: The Rationale for Public-Private Collaboration*. Columbus, Ohio: ERIC Clearinghouse on Adult, Career, and Vocational Education.

Spears, G. 1994. "Clinton Welfare Plan Short on Funding." *The Philadelphia Inquirer*, 13 June.

Stark, K. 1994. "Private Industry Council Job Training Draws Fire." *The Philadelphia Inquirer*, 26 May.

Sticht, T. G., W. B. Armstrong, D. T. Hicky, and J. S. Caylor. 1987. *Cast-off Youth: Policy and Training Methods from the Military Experience*. New York: Praeger.

Stromquist, N. 1993. "Adult Learning under Conditions of Hardship: Evidence from Developing and Developed Countries." In *What Makes Workers Learn: The Role of Incentives in Workplace Education and Training* , edited by Daniel Wagner. Philadelphia: Organization for Economic Cooperation and Development and Center for Educational Research and Development.

Thurow, L. 1970. *Investment in Human Capital*. Belmont, Calif.: Wadsworth Publishing Company.

——— 1975. *Generating Inequality*. New York: Basic Books Inc.

TriaKerkvliet, B. J. 1986. "Everyday Resistance to Injustice in a Philippine Village." In *Everyday Forms of Peasant Resistance in Southeast Asia* (Library of Peasant Studies, No. 9), edited by J. C. Scott and B. J. TriaKerkvliet. Totowa, N. J.: Frank Case and Company Ltd.

Turner, V. 1974. *Dramas, Fields, and Metaphors: Symbolic Action in Society*. Ithaca, N. Y.: Cornell University Press.

Tweedie, J., D. Reichert, and M. O'Connor. 1999. Tracking Recipients after They Leave Welfare. Report to National Conference of State Legislatures.

U.S. Department of Labor 1989. *Work-Based Learning: Training America's Workers.* 780-A-1. Washington, D. C.: U.S. Department of Labor, Employment, and Training Administration.

———— 1992. *Learning a Living: A Blueprint for High Performance, A SCANS Report for America 2000.* 0745. Washington, D. C.: Secretary's Commission on Achieving Necessary Skills.

———— 1997. The New Work Opportunity and Welfare-To-Work Tax Credits: A Summary of Major Changes in the Law.

Varenne, H., R. McDermott, S. Goldman, M. Naddio, and R. Rizzo-Tolk. 1998. *Successful Failure: The School America Builds.* Boulder, Colo.: Westview Press.

Vocational Employment Services. 1987. Preparing Refugees for Skilled Employment: Methods and materials for coordinated instruction in vocational skills, English as a Second Language, mathematics, work orientation, and independent job-search. Philadelphia: Department of Public Welfare.

Warner, W. L., and P. S. Lunt. 1941. *The Social Life of a Modern Community.* New Haven, Conn.: Yale University Press.

Weis, L. 1990. *Working Class without Work.* New York: Routledge.

Welfare to Work Partnership. 1998. Facts and Stats. In-house fact sheet.

West, J. 1945. *Plainville, USA.* New York: Columbia University Press.

Wilkerson, I. 1994. "Taste of Middle-Class Pay for Welfare Mothers." *The New York Times*, 10 February.

Willis, P. 1977. *Learning to Labor*, New York: Columbia University Press.

Wilson, W. J. 1987. *The Truly Disadvantaged.* Chicago: The University of Chicago Press.

———— 1996. *When Work Disappears: The World of the New Urban Poor.* New York: Alfred A. Knopf.

Wiseman, M. 1999. In Midst of Reform: Wisconsin in 1997. ANF Discussion Paper 99-03.

Zucchino, D. 1997. *Myth of the Welfare Queen.* New York: Scribner.

Zwerling, S. 1976. *The Crisis of the Community College: Second Best.* New York: McGraw-Hill Books.

Index

ability: perception of, 11, 148, 151, 175, 182
absences: from training, 176; from work, 42, 78; leaves of absences from work, 40
academic assistance: 230, 240; credentials, 64; experience 125, 158, 190, 197, 198; academically focused, 221; and occupational preparation, 227; potential, 157, 203; ranking, 176; scholarship, xiv; success and nonimmigrant minorities, 194; skills, xvi, 199; skills requirement, 119, 150
accelerated job placement. *See* job placement
access: to funding, 104; to off-site work experience, 37; to research sites, 246–48, 250; to resources and opportunities, 53, 151–52; to training, 7, 156, 225
accommodation in the workplace, 108, 137–41, 205, 210
acculturation of nonimmigrant minorities, 194
Adas, Michael, 54, 67, 105, 111
adult education: as a responsive, inclusive system, 17, 228–29, 234; as separate from welfare-related training, 227
advancement: in-house, 102; advancement strategy for low-wage workers, 228; opportunities for advancement, 139, 165, 208, 211, 217; self-advancement and immigrants, 135; in the workplace, 240
agency: constrained, xiv; of men and

women, 13; of the poor, 235; and resistance, 16; and social structure, 56, 183–84, 211
agent: responsible, 192; socially inferior, 150; typification of, 204
Aid to Families with Dependent Children (AFDC): changes in, 2, 3, 274, 275; definition of, 273; and the Family Support Act, 73, 185, 203, 273; funding for training, 153; and General Assistance, 21; ineligibility for funding, 223; and JOBS, 274, 275; and JTPA, 202; and leaving welfare, 5; mothers on, 23, 193; recipients of, 73, 192, 245
Alcoholics Anonymous (AA), 35
American Management Association, 233
America's Choice: High Skills or Low Wages (Commission on the Skills of the American Workforce), 217
Anderson, Elijah, 188
anthropology, 13, 237; anthropological linguistics, 117
antipoverty strategy, 70, 241
Apple, Michael, 77, 114
apprenticeship, x, 227
arrests. *See* criminal activity
Ashforth, Blake E., 198
assembly-line work, 38–39, 170; assembly-line worker, 161, 163
assessment, 149, 151, 155, 184, and the cream of the unemployed, 196–98; of identity; and potential, 205; and Project Match, 224

287

assimilation: into the dominant group, 194; into the workplace, 66, 175, 205, 210

associate's degree, 226

at risk: as target population, 24; youth and adults, 243

attributes: ascribed, 204; status attributes, 151–52; unofficial and emergent attributes, 157

Auletta, Kenneth, 23, 191

automotive service industry, 186

Bane, Mary Jo, 3

banking method of teaching, 81–86

barriers: educational, 28; identifying, 32–35, 76; language, 42, 130–31; multiple, 25, 185, 190, 198, 274; overcoming, 30, 199; structural, 36, 220; to work, 201–2

basic education classes, ix–x, 200, 240

basic skills: academic, ix, xi, 225; nursing skills, 262–63; office skills, 47; screening for, 150

benefits package: at Church Hall, 86, 95–96, 98, 101; at Concordance, 117, 119, 134–35, 140–41, 218; and DPW, 79; at Development, 39–41, 43–44, 48, 207–8, 220; discrepant, 7, 11, 181–82, 197, 205; fringe benefits, 239–41, 244; good benefits, 231–32; health care and welfare reform, 2; at Jackson Hospital, 164–65, 174, 177; manager's decisions about, 218; and the Refugee Resettlement Program, 274–75; and SPOC, 275; and TN, 275

bilingual education, 227

bilingualism, 46

Bluestone, Barry, 65

bonuses: attendance at Church Hall, 96, 110; attendance at Development, 40–43; Christmas, 63; creativity bonus, 62

Bourdieu, Pierre, xiii, xiv, 39, 45, 148, 150, 214

Braving a New World (Hopkins), 122

bread and butter issues, 59–60

Brown, Les, 35

Bureau of National Affairs, 244

Burghardt, John, 225

Calvin, John, xii

Cambodia, 112–13, 118, 135, 137–38, 140

Cambodian language, 127, 129, 131, 138

Cammisa, Anne Marie, 222

capital: cultural, 45, 123, 150–54, 199, 220–21; cultural and social, 146, 159, 197, 209; economic, 150; human, 12, 16, 181, 201; as a melding of variables, 48, 137; screening for cultural capital, xvi; social, xiii, 39, 44–46, 148–49; and social worth, xii

career: advancement, 139, 165, 199, 208; change, 146, 186; connections to career ladders, 5, 66, 219–21, 223, 226; counseling, 229–31; exploration, 227; options, 102, 185; path, 111, 141, 173, 224

care givers, 70–71, 183, 185

care team meetings, 92–94, 110

Carl D. Perkins Vocational and Applied Technology Education Act, 231

Carnevale, Anthony, 233

Center for Employment Training (CET), The, 224–26, 240, 270–71n. 1

certificate of reliability, 153

certification: by the American Society of Hospital Pharmacists, 172, 174, 181; and general training, 108, 208, 220; nurse assistant certification, 82–86, 98–99, 185; and supported work, 38, 67

Clark, Burton, 62

Clinton, Bill, 2–4, 189, 214, 216, 234

Clinton, Hillary, 102

Chamber of Commerce, and job training, 243

child care: and the Family Support Act, 73, 98; and the Perkins Act, 231; public child care, 203, 234; and SPOC, 275; and working mothers, 74; worker training, 118, 224

Chinese chess, 129, 136, 138

Christmas Carol, A (Dickens), xii

Chronically Needy, 22, 273

citizen mother, 203–4

class: and culture 13; deviant class, 187; class difference, 66; differentiation, 199, 210, 243; dominant class, 150; hierarchy, 1; class position, xiv; and cultural production, xv; class struggle, 59

CNC, 273; CNC operator, 126, 137

cold calling, 80, 111

college: attendance, 144, 152–53, 154, 171, 173, 190; and the Health Care Local, 147; plans to attend, 136, 139; tech prep programs with, 226–27

co-membership, 151, 199

Commission on the Skills of the American Workforce, 217–18

committee: management by, 166–68, 170, 216 ; at Jackson Hospital, 166–68, 266; participation on, 177, 218

communication: difficulties in the workplace, 111, 130–31, 142, 166; culturally different communication styles, 159; training in communication skills, 120, 262

community based organizations, 200

community college: and employment training, 29, 200; as continuing education, 104, 141, 165, 219, 231; cooling out, 62; as lifelong education, 229

community development, 213

community of work practice, xv–xvi

commute. *See* transportation

competency-based training, 224–26, 240

Comprehensive Employment Training Act (CETA), 200, 273, 268n. 3; funding for displaced homemakers, 45; and the Job Training Partnership Act, 200; and the Private Industry Council, 274; funding for pharmacy technician training, 146; and work, 213–15

computer: assisted learning, 29–31; use in the pharmacy, 160–61, 163, 165, 171–72; programming, 126, 136–37; welfare-funded training, 71, 118, 183

cooling out, 62–63, 175, 216–18

cost-benefit analyses of employment training programs, 239–42

creaming the unemployed, xvi, 29, 147, 196–98, 203

criminal activity, 23, 150, 190–91, 239–41; criminally suspect, xii

cross-cultural relationships, 81

culture: of American common sense, xvi; and appropriate practice, 159; and class, 13; and perceptions of difference, 98, 116–17, 129–31, 137, 142; and identity, 114, 126; and language, 61; mainstream, 114, 194; na-tional, xii, 217; of poverty, xiii–xiv, 12, 193; and professional choice, 73; of social workers, 187; workplace culture, 67, 161, 168, 210, 242

cultural: belief and practice, 16, 159, 243; constructions of the poor, 75, 182; deficiency, 24, 110,187; deprivation, 28, 193; frame of reference, 194; framing, xv, 204; group membership, 94; knowledge and meanings, 242; manifestations of worth, 168, 181; norms, 118; presentation styles, 151; production and reproduction, xii, xv, 183

cycle of identity and expectations, 198, 211

deficiency: model of, 68; personal, 28, 32, 202, 220

demand-side model of job training, 214–15

DeParle, Jason, 5, 212

Department of Education, 227, 230

Department of Labor, funding dispersal, 200, 224; and SCANS, 225; and the School to Work Opportunities Act, 227; performance standards, 201; projections, 118, 245

Department of Public Welfare: and Church Hall collaboration, 105, 193, 220, 254; and employers, 233; Employment Training Program, 71; financial support, 113; job developers, 81; orientation to work, 75–81, 86–87, 193, 198, 214; and the Refugee Resettlement Program, 274–75; and single mothers, 73–75; Single Point of Contact (SPOC), 275

Department of Public Welfare case worker: as gatekeeper, 185; as matchmaker, 70, 98; and training referrals, 7, 21, 29, 44, 46, 72, 85, 116; and well-intentioned paternalism, 187

Department of Public Welfare Job Development Unit, 117, 190, 246, 272n. 1; trainer, 73

deserving and undeserving poor, xii–xvii, 11, 78, 188–89, 204

Dickens, Charles, xii

difference: disarmed, 159, 176–77; language of, 189; as a melding of characteristics, 39; socially

difference *(continued)*
  constructed, 189, 205; and social
  meaning, 129–31, 135, 137, 142
Directory of Nursing Homes, 107
disadvantaged: and Department of
  Labor statistics, 245; and job training, 213, 230, 239; and JTPA, 153–54,
  200–201, 274; label of, 16; and the
  Targeted Jobs Tax Credit, 233; and
  the Transitionally Needy, 21; truly
  disadvantaged groups, 229
disappearance of work, 191
discrimination: and immigrants,
  135–36, 195; and job placement, 158;
  sexual discrimination, 49–50; in the
  workplace, 32, 53–54
dislocated workers, 273, and
  Department of Labor statistics, 245;
  and JTPA, 200–201, 274; and PIC,
  243; training for, 227, 230, 239
displaced homemakers: and CETA, 45;
  and JTPA, 202; and the
  Transitionally Needy, 25–26
Domination and the Arts of Resistance
  (Scott), xv
dropouts. *See* high school dropouts
drug abuse: at Church Hall, 97–98; at
  Concordance Steps, 122, 196; at
  Development, 54–55, 62, 65–66
Drug abusers, recovering: as
  Chronically Needy, 273; and coping
  mechanisms, 35; and the deserving
  poor, xii; at Development, 57, 142,
  190–91; as the hardest to serve,
  25–27, 29; and multiple barriers, 274;
  and supported work, 23, 38; as
  Transitionally Needy, 12, 22, 201–2
drug testing, and welfare reform, 4
dysphoria, 207

earned income tax credits. See
  Targeted Jobs Tax Credit
earnings: and education, 197; pre- and
  post-program, 232, 237–41; and welfare reform, 5–6
economic development, 9, 11–12, 24,
  222–23
economic forecasts and job training,
  118–19, 244–45
economic restructuring, 216
educational accounts, 4, 229

Educational Opportunity Centers,
  230–31
Educational Testing Service (ETS), 82
Ellwood, David, 189
employment: irregular, 214; public-
  service, 23, 200, 273
employment rates: at CET, 240; and
  the economic boom, 212; and job
  training, 213; and performance standards, 201
*Encounters: Two Studies in the Sociology
  of Interaction* (Goffman), 174
English as a Second Language, 190;
  classes 6, 140, 149; and the Refugee
  Assistance Act, 115–17; vocational
  English as a Second Language,
  120
English: class, 71, 164–65, 173; improving language skills, 225, limited
  English and the hardest to serve, 22,
  25–28, 55; limited English and JTPA,
  202; limited English and Khmer
  refugees, 122, 129–31, 136, 138–40,
  250; limited English and TN, 202;
  nonstandard, x, 159; problems, 61
entry-level: employment training, 123;
  employees, xvi; job, xiv; and PIC,
  219; and Project Match, 223; and
  welfare reform, 5
Equal Employment Opportunity
  Commission (EEOC), 49–50, 53
Erickson, Frederick, 133, 151, 157, 208
Esping-Anderson, Gosta, 199
ethnography, xvi, 13–16, 237, 242–43,
  251–53
evaluations, econometric, 237–42
ex-offenders: as hardest to serve, 22, 25;
  and JTPA, 201–2; and supported
  work, 23; and TN, 202
expectations of work, 23, 51–57; and
  capabilities, 41–42, 175; cyclical relationship, 183, 210–11, 217–18; meeting, 157, 210; as a refugee, 135–37;
  scaled down, 141–42; in school to
  work initiatives, 227; in the social
  world, 224

family, extended, 8, 29, 74, 104, 182,
  235
Family Support Act: funding for AFDC
  recipients, 73–74, 185; and JOBS,

174, 213; and the Private Industry Council, 202–3

federal job-training money: and block grants, 3, 273; and the Family Support Act, 73; and JTPA, 153–54, 202–3; matching money, 3; and PIC, 243; and refugee assistance 115–17, 123; and the School to Work Opportunities Act, 227; and Temporary Assistance for Needy Families (TANF), 275

federal refugee assistance. *See* Refugee Assistance Act

fictive kin relationship, 54–55, 60, 99

field, xiii–xv

Fine, Michelle, xii, 109

Firestone, William A., 243

folk models of schooling, 194

food-service sector, 246; training in, 71, 183, 203, 224

food stamps: and Oregon's Jobs Plus, 2; and PRWORA, 274; and the Transitionally Needy, 21

Foucault, Michel, 209

Framing Dropouts (Fine), xii, 109

Freire, Paulo, 81

From Foot Dragging to Flight (Adas), 111

From Rhetoric to Reform? Welfare Policy in American Politics (Cammisa), 222

Gainer, Lela, 233

gatekeepers, 78, 82, 185, 249; choices made by, 182; and co-membership, 151

gatekeeping, xvi, 246; and interviews, 152

GED: classes, 61, 64; earning, 46, 48, 223, 225; as requirement, 76; taking the GED test 37

Geertz, Clifford, 242

General Accounting Office (GAO), 115, 230, 239

General Assistance (GA), 21–22, 116, 274; recipients, 233. *See also* Chronically Needy, Transitionally Needy

general training, 108

geographic mismatch, 70

Giddens, Anthony, 184, 204

Giuliani, Rudolph, 4

glass ceiling, xv, xvii

Goffman, Erving, 151, 174, 206–8

Gordon, Anne, 225

Gordon, Linda, 182, 187, 192

Governor's Achievement Award, 37–38

Gray, Kenneth, 227

Greater Emphasis on Early Employment and Better Monitoring Needed in Indochinese Refugee Resettlement Program (General Accounting Office), 115

growth opportunities. *See* professional development

habitus, xiii–xv

Hagen, Jan, 73, 203

handicapped, physically, 120, 202; as multiple barriers, 274; and the Targeted Jobs Tax Credit, 233

Hannerz, Ulf, 188

hardcore unemployed, 8–9, 153, 176, 190, 205,

hardest to serve: defined by, 22–27, 114, 201–2; funding streams, 153; image of, 186–87; and training, 51, 192–93

Harrington, Michael, 193

Harrison, Benjamin, 65

healthcare benefits. *See* benefits package

Health Care Local Training and Upgrade Fund, 147–50, 171; organizing efforts, 101–2; trainers as gatekeepers, 185

Herr, Edwin, 227

Herriott, Robert E., 243

high performance workplaces, 215–18, 231, 233

high school diploma: as a certificate of docility, xiii; as criteria, 150, 158; jobs and, 55, 64

high school dropout: and Department of Labor statistics, 245; gender, 27; as hardest to serve, 25–26, 46–48, 202; perceptions of, 187, 199; and self-confidence, 43, 109; and supported work, 23; training for, ix–xi; training at Development, 23, 210

home health care temporary agency. *See* temporary employment

homelessness: and difference, 158, 189; as characteristic of multiple barriers, 25–26, 201–2, 274; and support, 74

hooks, bell: *Homeplace*, 87
Hopkins, Mary Carol, 122
hospitality industry, 113, 138–39
hotel services. *See* hospitality industry
housing: rehabilitation funds and em-
　　ployment training, 271n. 2; subsi-
　　dized, 80, 213, 239, temporary, 74;
　　transitional, 24, 267n. 6
How to Be a Nurse Assistant (Johnson-
　　Pawlson and Goodwin), 82
human action. *See* agency
Humphrey, Ronald H., 198
Hymes, Del, 129, 131

immigrant, and deserving poor, xiii, xvi;
　　literature on, 135–40; identity,
　　194–96; as single mothers, 192; as
　　target clientele, 239
Improving Poor People (Katz), xiii
incentives: employer, 233; learner,
　　215
individual Training Accounts. *See* edu-
　　cational accounts
information centers, 234
injury, in the workplace, 134–35,
　　139–41, 270n. 5
in-service workshops: at Church Hall,
　　91; at Jackson's pharmacies, 165
interactional dissonance. *See* resistance
International Sign Language. *See*
　　English, limited English and Khmer
　　refugees
Interpretation of Culture, The (Geertz),
　　242

Jackson, Jean, 267n. 7
job abandonment, 105–11
job development, 213–16, 239, 256; and
　　DPW, 73, 213; and VES, 118–20
job ladder. *See* career
job markets, local, 118–22, 245
Job Opportunities and Basic Skills
　　Training Program (JOBS), 73–74, 79,
　　213, 269n. 3; evaluation of, 73; and
　　Family Support Act, 273–74; and
　　SPOC, 275; and Step-Up, 231
job placement: accelerated, 123; at
　　Development, 37; and DPW, 79; and
　　Jackson Hospital, 148, 158; and
　　JTPA, 200; as manifestation of labor
　　market status, 239; and welfare re-
　　form, 2

job placement rates, 213, 232; and PIC,
　　244–46
job readiness: classes, 15; program, 21,
　　27, 29
job retention: at Development, 23,
　　63–67; and DPW, 79; as official indi-
　　cator of success, 232; and PIC, 244
jobs: and career ladders, 219–20; entry-
　　level, low-wage, xiv–xvi, 5, 111, 232;
　　and Project Match, 223, 226; and
　　welfare reform, 5, 234–35, 267n. 3.
　　See also minimum wage jobs
job search: at Development, 219; and
　　JTPA, 200; and SPOC, 275; at VES,
　　120; and welfare reforms, 4
job training: and adult education, 229;
　　competency based, 224–26; and the
　　Family Support Act, 202–4; govern-
　　ment funded, 146, 185, 234, 237–44;
　　and JTPA, 145, 184, 200–202, 274;
　　on-the-job training, ix, 147, 200, 227,
　　233–34; and PIC, 274; and refugees,
　　185; retraining, 228; and SPOC, 185,
　　275; supply and demand side,
　　213–15; for TNs, 22, 185; and unem-
　　ployment, 213. *See also* federal job-
　　training money
Job Training Partnership Act (JTPA),
　　274; and the cream of the
　　unemployed, xvi, 147, 196–98, 203;
　　and employment, 213, 232; history,
　　200–203; income guidelines, 150;
　　participants, 157–58, 171, 202; and
　　PIC, 274, 270n. 2; Title IIA, 184,
　　200; Title IIB, 200; Title IIC, 201;
　　Title III, 201; tuition support,
　　145–47, 153–55, 184, 196, 255
Job Training Reform Amendments of
　　1992, 201
Johnson, Lyndon, 237

Katz, Michael, xii, xiii, 11, 188, 189
Keeping Women and Children Last (Sidel),
　　1, 187, 222, 240
Kensington Welfare Rights Union, 235
Khao-I-Dang refugee camp, 112–13
Khmer Rouge, 112–13, 137–38
Kingfisher, Catherine Pelissier, 103
kinship network. *See* family, extended
knowledge: academically sanctioned,
　　159, 182, 225; and cultural capital, 45,
　　76; local, 81, 92–94, 98–101, 110–11,

168, 177; official, 77, 86, 98, 111, 118, of the workplace, 22, 36, 76, 193

labor demand, pharmacy technicians, 147–48
labor market: access to, 206; bottom of, xiv–xvi; and cultural capital, 123; demand, 215; disconnected from, 208; and employment training, 244; local, 118–19, 122, 195, 215, 245; policies, 227; a return to, 184; secondary, 115; slack labor market, 195; self-sufficiency in, 241; survey, 147; tightening, 215
labor queue, 198, 205, 220, 239
laborer jobs, 113, 195, 219
language: and cultural capital, 151–53, 199; as difference, 129, 176, 210, 248, 250; as dissent, 58–59; and education, 28; problem of, 42, 61, 69, 98, 130–31; of stairs, 120, 127, 141, 198
Lave, Jean, xv
legal offenses. *See* criminal activity
legitimate peripheral participation, xv
Lewis, Oscar, xiii
Licensed Practical Nurse (LPN): at Church Hall, 72, 75, 193; license, 99; managerial training for, 81, 109–10; as target of resistance, 100–101, 105–6, 110; as supervisor, 79, 82, 97–99; training toward, 102–4, 110, 147, 220, 255; in the workplace hierarchy, 91–95, 97–105
Liebow, Elliot, 209
life-cycle employability, 239
life-long education, 229–30
Life Skills training, 31–37, 241
liminality, 41
linguistic difference. *See* language as difference
literacy: assessment, 22, 26, 202; basic, 225; education, 73, 227, 229; low level of, 122, 159; workplace literacy programs, 215
livable wage: the cry for, 216; from employment training to jobs with, 117–18, 221, 271n. 2; as equitable treatment, 134, 182; the inability to access, 12, 207; justification for, 44, 109
Lives on the Edge (Polakow), 203
loan payments, to college, 104; to proprietary schools, 70–71, 85, 103–4, 220
low-wage choice, 217–18
Lunt, Paul, 188
Lurie, Irene, 73, 203

mainstream culture, 114, economic, 12, 32, 181, 222, 235; models of achievement and success, 103; moving welfare recipients into the, 222, 228–29, 237; outside the, 16, 135; society, 189; workforce, 12, 191
mainstreamers, 188
management: an advocate in, 63; assimilation into, 66–67; by committee, 166–68, 175, 216; and framing, xii–xiii, xvi, 42; and meetings, 50–51, 101; priorities, 110; and profit, 91, 110; as target of resistance, 57–60, 207–10; responsible strategies, 233; structures, 248; style, 126–31, 203–5, 216–18; views, x–xi, 28, 109, 128, 199
management training of LPNs. *See* LPN training
management/union collaboration. *See* unions
Manpower Development Research Corporation (MDRC), 23, 38, 268n. 1
manpower programs, targeted, 229
manual labor, 178
manufacturing sector: experience in, 190; the loss of, 9, 191, 195, 208, 223
market share, 86
Marx, Karl, xii
Mason, Sarah R., 117
materials management, 161–62
maternity leave, unavailability of, 49, 203
McCurdy, Dave, 2
medical school, 144, 173
meetings, in the workplace, 50, 101, 165, 170. *See also* care team meetings; committee, management by
mentoring, 46–47, 130–31, 156, 168–71, 198
merit raises, and committee participation, 167
minimum wage jobs: and education, 103; and job training, 37, 238; survival in, 219; and welfare reform, 5

minorities: immigrant, 135–40, 194;
nonimmigrant, xvi, 42, 194; and the
union, 119; racial minority workers,
xi; minority youth, 25–26
mistakes: in the workplace, 112, 121,
156, 266; handling, 126, 131–33; and
trainees, 169
mobility, job: and education and training, 11–12, 199; in the food service
sector, 246; impeded, 220–21; incremental, 229; internal, 102; social, 14,
141, 222; and welfare reform, 5
Moynihan, Daniel Patrick, xiii
*Multiple Employment Training Programs:
Overlap Among Programs Raises
Questions about Efficiency*, 230

narratives, as programmatic evaluation,
237, 242
National Conference of State
Legislators (NCSL), 5
New Directions for Employment Training
(Osterman), 244
New Jersey "Work First," 4
New York City welfare reform, 4
New York Times, 5, 212, 220
nonprofit organizations, and
Educational Opportunity Centers,
230–31; and training, 7, 120; and
work experience, 37
numeracy skills, 159
nurse assistant certification: and DPW,
98, 220, 269n. 4; as hiring criteria, 76;
and job abandonment, 108, 208; and
proprietary schools, 70; and respect,
99; and wages, 95. *See also* Omnibus
Budget Reconciliation Act of 1987
nurse assistant certification training: at
Church Hall, 75, 81–87, 254–55, clinical instruction, 120; as general training, 108; PIC funded programs, 107,
185, 203; state-mandated training,
262–64. *See also* proprietary school

objective mechanisms, 150–51
Ogbu, John, xiii, 135, 137, 140, 194
Omnibus Budget Reconciliation Act of
1987 (OBRA), 81–82, 269n. 5
on-the-job training. *See* job training
open entrance/open exit training,
224–25
opposition. *See* resistance

Oregon's Job Plus, 2
orientation to the workplace: as banking, 85; at the Center for
Employment Training, 225; at
Church Hall, 91; and the DPW, 70,
75–79, 87, 193, 198; at Development,
32–36; at VES, 120
Ortner, Sherry, 16, 206
Osterman, Paul, 244
Other America, The (Harrington), 193
overtime, 88, 128, 134; to augment
salaries, 96–97, 104

parents, working, 176
payroll set asides, employer, 234
PELL grants, 104
pension plan, 8, 40, 109, 220
Pennsylvania Association of County
Affiliated Homes, 107
performance-based: contracting, 203;
funding, 122, 245, 274
performance evaluation, 167, 218
performance standards, 217, 240, 274;
and JTPA, 201; and PIC, 238, 245;
and SCANS, 226; and TAP, 117
personal front, 151
Personal Responsibility and Work
Opportunity Reconciliation Act
(PRWORA), 3–6, 212–13, 274
pharmacy school, 152, 165, 178, 186,
221
pharmacy technician: float, 145; race,
176; responsibilities, 143–44, 159–64,
168–70, 172, 174; in retail, 149,
154–55, 165
pharmacy technician training, 143;
clerkship phase, 156, 169–70; criteria, 149–53; didactic phase, 155–56;
and JTPA, 145–46, 153–55, 200–203;
and professionalization, 162–63,
170–75, 177
Philadelphia Daily News, 235
pink-collar jobs, 203
placement assistance: contracted services, 2; by DPW Job Development
Unit, 74; by in-house job developers,
121–22, 148, 158; and the Work
Force Investment Act, 229
Plainville USA (West), 188
Polakow, Valerie, 187, 203, 204, 218
post-secondary education. *See*
Educational Opportunity Centers;

tech prep programs; School to Work Opportunites Act

poverty, discourse, 187, 189; poverty line, 6, 8, 95, 269n. 7

Private Industry Council (PIC), 274; and employers, 233; and entry-level jobs, 219; and the Family Support Act, 202–4; follow-up, 238; funding employment training, 107, 118, 184, 200, 243–45; gatekeeping, 185; mission, 241; partnering with Jackson hospital, 145, 148, 254; performance-based funding, 122; and SPOC, 275. *See also* Job Training Partnership Act

professional: front-line, 218; identity, 170, 178, 210; jobs, 143, 159, 162–63, 172–74; organization dues, 170, 270n. 4; quasi-professional, 198

Progressive Era reform, 187, 222; reformers, 192

Project Match, 223–24, 226

proprietary school: loans to, 85,103–4, 220; nurse assistant certification programs, 70, 94, 111, 268n. 1; and PIC, 200

public sector, and CETA, 200; and employment training, 214

Public Service Employment, and CETA, 200, 273

punctuality, 32, 152

Putnam, Hilary, xiii

quality control, 132

radon training, 37

Reagan administration: and employment training, 115; and JTPA, 200

Reagan, Ronald, 2, 24

Refugee Assistance Act of 1975, 115

Refugee Cash Assistance, 115–16

Refugee Resettlement Program, 274–75; and Targeted Assistance Program, 117, 275

Registered Nurse (RN): as Church Hall staff, 72, 75; and nurse aide training, 79, 82; as target of resistance, 100, 105–6; salary, 95; in the workplace hierarchy, 91–94, 110

Registered Nurse training, 103–4, 147

Reich, Robert, 216, 229

reproduction: cultural, xii; cycle of production and, 16, 184; and objective

mechanisms, 150; social, xiii–xiv, 11, 13

resistance: as affirmation of self, 66–67; as cooling out, 62–63; as disrespect, 100, 110; everyday, 54, 58, 68; formal, 235–36; as job abandonment, 110–11; as language, 58–59, 139–40; to low-status positions, 53; as petty theft, 59; theory, 208–9; as work slow down, 57–58

retail sector, 5, 26, 118

Rockefeller Foundation, The, 240

role, distancing, 206–8, 216–17; embracement, 170–75, 178

Sacks, Harvey, 151, 152

Sanjek, Roger, 15, 251, 253

School College and Ability Test (SCAT), 150–51

School to Work Opportunities Act (PL 103–239), 227

Schwarz, John E., 240

Scott, James, xv, 59–60

secondary labor market, 115

Secretary's Commission Achieving Necessary Skills (SCANS), 225–26

security guard training, 10, 37, 118, 203

selective voluntary program, 201

self-sufficiency, economic, 199, 222, 232, 241–42; and TAP, 117

Service Delivery Area, 275; and job-training funds, 200–201

service sector, 5, 195; and Department of Labor projections, 118–19; and economic shifts, 223

Shultz, Jeffrey, 133, 151

Sidel, Ruth, 1, 187, 192, 222, 240

silencing, 50, 111

single adults, and job training, 213; and Transitionally Needy, 7, 12, 21, 185, 191–92, 275

single female heads of households, 1, 104, 203–4, 239–40; and AFDC, 273; as mothers, 3, 70–75, 87, 187, 192

situated activity systems, 206–7

situated learning experiences, 214

Small Business Centers, 234

Smith, Thomas, 200, 214

social identities: and change, 243; constructed, 74, 114, 153, 182, 209–10; discarded, 108; and fit, 139, 142, 148, 175; and funding, 153; imposed, 27,

social identities *(continued)*
67–68, 136–37, 194–95; multiple,
196; negotiation of, 123, 206–7; prerogatives and obligations of, 204–5;
and socially approved tasks, 185-87
social meaning, 129, 131, 177
social positions, 204–5
Social Security Act of 1935, 3
socially approved tasks, 185
starting salaries: at Church Hall, 95,
107; at Concordance, 123, 134; at
Development, 41; at Jackson,
164–65, 177
State Office for Refugee Affairs,
115–16, 123
Step Up, 231
stratification: sorting and, 204; studies,
188–89; system of, 199
Stromquist, Nelly, 211
structural: change, 191, 195;
constraints, 35–36; 183–84, 220, 223;
forces, 192; improvements 102; opportunity, 222; properties, 184
structuration theory, 184
substance abuse: counseling, 6, 190;
counselor, 66; recovery, xii, 13, 54,
57, 142. *See also* drug abuse
supply-side stance: issues, 242; model
of job development, 213–14
supported work: as compensation, 6,
75; description of, 36–38; deviations
from, 44–47; history, 22–24, 239,
268n. 1; presuppositions, 29, 193;
rationale, 68

Targeted Assistance Program (TAP)
grant, 117, 275
Targeted Jobs Tax Credit (TJTC), 6,
233, 267n. 4, 271n. 3
Tawney, Richard H., xii
Taylorism, 39, 268n. 2
tech prep programs, 226–27, 231
Temporary Assistance for Needy Families (TANF), 275; and AFDC, 3, 273
temporary employment, 55, 203, 208;
agencies, 26, 190, 246; health care
agencies, 79, 111, 174, 220, 255; and
welfare reform, 2, 5
Thompson, Tommy G., 2, 4
Three Worlds of Welfare Capitalism, The,
(Esping–Anderson), 199

Thurow, Lester, 86, 108, 197
*Training in America: The Organization
and Strategic Role of Training*
(Carnevale, Gainer, and Villet), 233
Transitionally Needy (TN): beliefs
about, 27–29, 186–87; description,
21–22, 24–27, 201–2, 275; employment statistics, 212; employment
training program, 37–38; funding for,
185; and General Assistance, 274; as
underclass, 190–93
transportation: costs, 107–8; government subsidized, 79, 171, 231; to
work, 75
TriaKerkvliet, Benedict J., 54, 58
Trist, Carolyn, 200, 214
Truly Disadvantaged, The, (Wilson), 228
tuition, assistance: as company benefits, 102, 164–65, 173, 216, 220–21;
from JTPA, 145, 171; for the lower
and middle class, 227; loan repayment, 70–71, 103–4; reimbursement,
40–41; and Step Up, 231
Turner, Victor, 41

uncomfortable moments, 133, 269–70n.
4
Underclass, The, (Auletta), 23, 191
underclass: disadvantaged, 228–30; as
discourse, 189, 190–93; habitus of,
xiv; as as undeserving, xvi
Undeserving Poor, The, (Katz), 188
unions: and the construction industry,
119; organizing efforts, xvi, 59,
101–2; screening responsibilities,
151; sponsored training, 145–49,
254–55; tuition support from,
153–55, 171; union-management
collaboration, 215
universal programs, 228–29
Urban Poverty and Family Life Study
(UPFLS), 194–95

Villet, Janice, 233
Vocational English as a Second
Language (VESL), 116, 120, 275
vocational skills training, 6, 223–25; and
the Perkins Act, 231; in tech prep
programs, 226–27
Volgy, Thomas J., 240
Vygotsky, Leonid, 46

Warner, W. Lloyd, 188
War on Poverty, 237
Weber, Max, xii
Weis, Lois, 209
welfare categories: and the Center for
  Employment Training, 225; categorical delineations, 11, 181–82, 201;
  categorical funding, 153, 185; categorical identities, 185–90, 198,
  204–5, 211; and Project Match, 224
welfare queen, 2
welfare reform: and the Family Support
  Act, 203; impact of, 13, 17, 221, 241;
  and PRWORA, 1–7, 212–13, 274;
  strategies, 222, 228; and
  unsubsidized employment; and
  work, 216, 231, 234–35
Wenger, Etienne, xv
West, James, 188
When Work Disappears (Wilson), 214
Whitman, Christine, 4
Willis, Paul, 209

Wilson, William Julius, 17, 190, 191
Wisconsin Works (W-2), 2–5
Wolfe, Tom, 149
Women in the American Welfare Trap
  (Kingfisher), 103
woodworking: training, 116–21, 131,
  139, 141–42, 198, 254; training costs,
  123
Workforce Investment Act, 229–31
working poor, xv, 221, 228, 236
workloads, overwhelming, 91–95, 99
work slowdowns, 57–58, 66, 68, 208
World of Work, 23, 32; classes, 6

youth: employment training programs
  for, 230, 239; and JTPA, 184,
  200–201, 232, 274; and supported
  work, 23, 25–26; and Targeted Jobs
  Tax Credit, 233

zero tolerance policies, 106
zone of proximal development, 46–47